D1564308

INDIVIDUALS AND THEIR RIGHTS

INDIVIDUALS AND THEIR RIGHTS

TIBOR R. MACHAN

Open **✳** Court
La Salle, Illinois

OPEN COURT and the above logo are registered in the U.S. Patent and Trademark Office.

© 1989 by Open Court Publishing Company

First printing 1989

Printed and bound in the United States of America.

Library of Congress Cataloging-in-Publication Data

Machan, Tibor R.
    Individuals and their rights / Tibor R. Machan.
        p. cm.
    Bibliography: p.
    Includes index.
    ISBN 0-8126-9089-3. — ISBN 0-8126-9090-7 (pbk.)
    1. Human rights. 2. Natural law. 3. Individualism.
4. Libertarianism. I. Title.
JC571.M225 1989
323'.01 — dc20   89-8689
                                                                      CIP

Yes, say what you will — the Communists were more intelligent. They had a grandiose program, a plan for a brand new world in which everyone would find his place. The Communists' opponents had no great dream; all they had was a few moral principles, stale and lifeless, to patch up the tattered trousers of the established order. So, of course, grandiose enthusiasm won out over the cautious compromisers and lost no time turning their dream into reality: the creation of an idyll of justice for all.

— Milan Kundera,
The Book of Laughter and Forgetting

FOR JIM AND VICKY

CONTENTS

PREFACE

One concern above all motivates this book. The values that undergird the distinctive American political tradition — a conception of political and legal justice that upholds each individual's basic right to life, liberty, and property — haven't been acknowledged as pressing and formidable enough to withstand criticism and widespread denigration. I will call this distinctive political outlook libertarianism. In this book I want to identify the justification for its moral superiority. I will argue that we ought, from a moral standpoint, to support, establish, and maintain this kind of a polity.

In a way this book is a response to Thomas Nagel's criticism of Robert Nozick's, *Anarchy, State, and Utopia* (1974), a criticism often endorsed by others, to wit, that libertarianism lacks moral foundations.

The term 'libertarianism' is itself controversial. Some who favor the free society and its economic system of free-market capitalism dislike the term because 'libertarians' include many strains of defenders of liberty, including individualist anarchists. Yet 'libertarian' is the term by which a free society, with a distinctively moral (rather than economic) justification, has come to be known in academic philosophical and ordinary political circles and for brevity's sake I will make use of it throughout this work. 'Libertarianism' refers to a system of politics that implies free-market capitalism, political and civil liberties, and room for ample pluralism in cultural, artistic, educational, and religious approaches to human life. (Interestingly, the system doesn't *require* economic competition!)

There are different defenses of libertarianism, some purely economic, some praxeological, some utilitarian, and yet others intuitionist. I want to show the moral foundations of this political idea in the tradition of ethical naturalism. I hope to satisfy both consequentialist and deontological concerns vis-à-vis the character of a good or just human community.

In particular, I argue that human individuals have basic rights because of what they are. And what they are, combined with what their world is, implies also how they ought to live. Both the ethics and the politics of human living will be discussed from within a naturalist (or as some call it 'essentialist') meta-ethical perspective. I will argue that persons have basic rights to life, liberty, and property. I will show that these rights rest on the ethics of classical egoism. And I will argue that the libertarian political economy requires a government that is legally authorized to protect the requisite basic and derivative rights but is not authorized ever to violate or abridge these rights.

In the course of arguing for the free society I will have as one of my major tasks the clarification of the concept 'liberty' as it functions in political discourse. I will argue that the liberty human beings ought to prize and seek protection for in communities rests on a theory of negative rights. The explanation of basic rights and that of individual liberty will turn out to be mutually interdependent. For example, it is not a right to liberty in the sense of the opportunity for or power of action in general, that matters. Instead, it is the right to liberty in the sense of persons respecting each other's moral sovereignty, including its concrete implication, namely, the right to private property. That is the quintessential public good, while opportunity for or power of action concerns a more general problem — not uniquely related to human community life — namely, human life itself.

The term 'capitalism' for the free society may be misleading since it suggests that the primary purpose of that system is economic. No doubt, prosperity is vital to a morally good human life, but it isn't its major objective. Human happiness is. And such happiness is by no means attained by being merely prosperous. That is one reason a utilitarian approach to political economy, one that deals largely with beneficial consequences, is insufficient. Rather the mode of life, namely, *chosen* conduct of the agent that attains his or her happiness, is a vital element of the human happiness that a good human community ought to facilitate for all.

It was mostly critics of the classical liberal political ethos who labelled the free system 'capitalist'. Classical liberalism, in turn, has been associated with the philosophical schools of empiricism and mechanistic materialism, effectively rejecting or recasting the moral nature of human life. It will not then serve my purpose to label what I aim to defend with either of these terms.

The task of giving a reasonably thorough, detailed, and philosophically comprehensive moral defense of the libertarian system has not previously been achieved, despite the longstanding admiration for some of its features among most economists and a few philosophers. The moral defense of the system has not been developed, at least not in the terms demanded of such systems, namely, those that can meet the standards of philosophic argumentation surrounding matters of political economy. Robert Nozick did not give a moral argument for the system; F. A. Hayek, Milton Friedman, and other prominent free market advocates largely eschew the moral issues; Ayn Rand dealt with the issues only suggestively. An exception is Loren Lomasky who, in his *Persons, Rights and the Moral Community* (Oxford, 1987), gave a beautiful and powerful expositon of some of libertarianism's major virtues. However, he dealt with the topic in quite a different way, one I am persuaded at this time cannot accomplish our task with sufficient thoroughness. Moreover, Lomasky gives too much to advocates of the welfare state by conceding that some measure of state welfare is appropriate. In my view this undermines the integrity of free constitutional law and government.

Can libertarianism largely escape the difficulties which have been uncovered in defenses of freedom from within utilitarian, contractarian, and neo-Hobbesian frameworks? It seems to me that what is necessary for this purpose is a moral defense of individualism and its political implications that rests on a naturalist philosophy.

A central task here will be the establishment of a certain kind of moral individualism, different from the individualism familiar to most people. This itself will require some preliminary work in metaphysics, epistemology, and meta-ethics. Fortunately some of the groundwork for meeting this challenge has already been laid and I make use of it, gratefully, in this book.

In what follows I plan briefly to identify and then utilize what may be called a contextualist-naturalist approach in metaphysics, epistemology, and in the determination of the theoretical adequacy of relevant philosophical theses. One ought not to seek *formal* comprehensiveness, completeness, and integrity beyond what can reasonably be presented for inspection by those who embark upon theorizing in the various fields of relevance to one's task.

While preliminary to the substance of my project, these features of what I plan to do here play a key role. They are meant to lay the groundwork for demonstrating the present view's superiority to the many views with which it competes and help to show that the resulting framework can handle certain cases and objections that have been thought to pose insurmountable obstacles to its success. They could also help indicate why the present view does not disparage objectives its competitors would raise to primary status. Indeed, with an understanding of the futility of utopian politics — an understanding that political idealisms of all varieties breed cynicism and despair, as well as concrete human misery — libertarianism could be embraced by many who may very likely but mistakenly regard it as threatening to their values.

Despite the ambitiousness of these promises, this work cannot deal with all the relevant problems. Just in order to proceed in one special area of philosophy, one must economize and cannot focus on the rest with full attention. (That alone may account for some of the popularity of Rawls's 'independence of moral theory' thesis.) The systematic approach I recommend and defend needs much support from the work of like-minded scholars. Still, my arguments go as far as have those of any contemporary natural-rights philosopher. The direction of further development should be clearly evident once I have finished with my argument for natural-rights individualism.

In choosing a style for this book I had to decide between charging ahead, not heeding actual or possible criticisms except to present what one takes to be a good argument, and looking often at criticisms that can steer one toward treating important problems a theory must confront. It is simpler to read a work with the former style. But when one's views are out of the mainstream on a variety of philosophical fronts, such a technique is a luxury. Moreover, in my effort to bring this work to publication, I have received numerous criticisms and learned that I cannot afford to ignore many challenges to the various steps in my theoretical argument. I have tried to do justice to most of these criticisms. (For those interested in a more streamlined treatment, I am preparing my *The Moral Case for the Free Market Economy* for publication in English — it is now in print in Swedish, as *Frihetens Filosofi*.)

So I have chosen the somewhat cumbersome approach of keeping in mind the various critics of foundationalism, meta-ethical naturalism, ethical cognitivism, egoism, political individualism, and capitalism. I want to be sure that when I address the difficulties surrounding my subject, I deal with criticisms actually presented, and not merely imagined. This style will get me into some trouble but I am aware of that. (I could have chosen the other approach — I write newspaper columns, magazine articles, and essays in which there is no room for casting extensive glances over one's shoulder to fend off the critics!) In this work my first priority has to be thoroughness, within limits. If a comprehensive treatment places these ideas in circulation, smoother treatments may serve them better subsequently.

I wish to thank a few individuals for commenting on initial versions of my work. Thomas Morawetz, Bill Puka, Antony Flew, Renford Bambrough, James Sterba, and Gilbert Harman have all given me some helpful comments, as have some anonymous reviewers. All along I have discussed these matters extensively with Douglas Rasmussen (who, along with David Gordon and David Ramsay Steele, also made detailed suggestions for revising the structure of the work), with Douglas J. Den Uyl, and occasionally with J. Roger Lee, James Chesher, Jack Wheeler, Randy Dipert, Nicholas Capaldi, Jeffrey Wallin, Leland Yeager, Cliff Perry, John Hospers, John O. Nelson, Eric Mack and David L. Norton, all of whom patiently contended with me while I tried out on them many of the arguments presented in these pages.

I have published less developed versions of some of the views advanced herein and have benefited from comments and criticisms these published works have generated. Of course, I take full responsibility for what finally emerged.

I want also to thank the John M. Olin Foundation for its continued support of this and related work.

Many of the thoughts I develop in this work have had partial airing in various forums. I wish to thank the publishers of *The American Philosophical Quarterly*, *The New Scholasticism*, *The Occasional Review*, *The Review of Metaphysics*, *The Journal of Applied Philosophy*, *Policy Review*, *The Journal of Value Inquiry*, *The American Journal of Jurisprudence*, *The Monist*, and *Tulane Studies in Philosophy*, as well as the volumes *The Main Debate* and *Ideology and American Experience* for permission to use segments of my work previously published.

INTRODUCTION

In recent years some outstanding efforts have been made to develop a case for the individualist or libertarian political framework. Some of these works have gained prominence, some have acquired a loyal following, and others have gone the way of so many good books, remaining largely unread.

For various reasons, however, those who are most active in thinking about political principles have focussed mainly on a particular line of defense. They have mostly examined approaches within the classical liberal tradition. Here one begins with the idea — a supposed observation, an analytic truth, or a heuristic assumption — that human beings seek to satisfy their desires, that they aim for objectives. From this idea one proceeds to find out what is a just social and political order by inferring what moves these desire-satisfying, objective-pursuing human beings would make in social circumstances or what is implicit in their goal-seeking.

This approach has not only found favor with many but also managed to elicit some very harsh criticism. Some critics have actually repeated a serious charge levelled over a century ago by Karl Marx, in his essay 'On the Jewish Question', namely, that 'political emancipation is not human emancipation' and that the freedom of the capitalist, individualist or libertarian system amounts merely to treating "man . . . as an isolated monad and withdrawn into himself." They have echoed Marx's point that "the right of man to freedom is not based on the union of man with man, but on the separation of man from man. It is the right to this separation, the rights of the limited individual who is limited to himself."

Other critics have repeated another of Marx's observations, pertaining to one of capitalism's most vital features. This is that "the right of man to property is the right to enjoy his possessions and dispose of the same arbitrarily, without regard for other men, independently from society, the right of selfishness. It is the former individual freedom together with its latter application that forms the basis of civil society. It leads man to see in other men not the realization but the limitation of his own freedom. Above all it proclaims the right of man 'to enjoy and dispose at will of his goods, his revenues and fruits of his work and industry'."[1]

Such complaints against the individualist tradition are still quite telling. Many who would never dream of embracing Marxism accept their force. Thus several of the reviewers of Robert Nozick's *Anarchy, State, and Utopia* advance the idea that its thesis is but an expression of limited class interest.[2] Rebutting the Marxist line of criticism does not by any means show the soundness of the libertarian, individualist perspective. Yet, it is important as one of the initial steps toward establishing at least the plausibility of the capitalist system. When a viewpoint is taken to be a mere rationalization or apology, no philosophical attention is paid to it at all—it is treated as a psychological disposition.

Under Marx's influence, but with the support of many non-Marxist views, American-style individualism has been dubbed an ideology by many social commentators. Some only mean by this that individualism, when expressed in simplistic terms, does not deserve to be called a serious social philosophy. But others really think the doctrine merely serves to rationalize the status quo—especially when there is little evidence that a society actually embodies individualist principles and policies, as is the case in our time.

For Marxists, a system of laws based largely on the 'rights of man'—such as the right to private property—had a limited function in human history, viz., to facilitate production and technological development. Once this function had been achieved, these principles would be abolished by a new phase, and eventually by the last phase of human history, communism:

> Communism is for us not a state of affairs which is to be established, an ideal to which reality will have to adjust itself. We call communism the real movement which abolishes the present state of things. The conditions of this movement result from the premises now in existence.[3]

Marx implied that his is a 'God's eye' perspective on humanity, which he saw as a growing 'organic body'.[4] He spoke of early Western civilization as a stage of childhood when he wrote that "the Greeks were normal children".[5] His method of analysis supposedly entitled him to pinpoint the stages of humanity's development from its beginning through to its full emancipation. And thus for him capitalism was humanity's adolescence. As in adolescence, so in capitalism, we experience intense joys and sorrows, tragic benefits and costs, all quite unavoidably but only temporarily, with better times to come.

This is not the place to refute Marx's theory. But it will be useful to allude to some of its major problems so that we can appraise his claim that individualism as a theory of society is an ideology that should be rejected.

First, Marxism conceives of human beings collectively, as if humanity, not you and I, were the individual person with purposes, intentions, ideas, health and illness, values, and so on. Marx discounts the importance of individuality and measures all values by reference to an idea of collective human essence. As he says, "The human essence is the true collectivity of man."[6] The foundation of this essence is material production, *ergo*, the labor conception of value and the messianic rôle of the working class.

But human nature appears to be incoherent unless we give a central place within it to individuality. Human beings are unique in being self-motivated and thus self-differentiating. The Marxist edifice rests on a misunderstanding of human nature, inspired largely by Hegel's dialectical and teleological metaphysics. The error of seeing individuals as merely parts of the larger whole of humanity's 'organic body' ultimately infects not only Marxian historical analysis — which is its most influential part — but also the practicability of socialism and communism, which supposes the further development of human nature so that the principles of universal love and non-egoism will eventually become reality.

Second, Marxian characterizations of capitalism and its social-philosophical foundation, individualism, are unfounded. If humanity does not undergo the developmental process of a biological organism, as Marx suggests, then his understanding of human history on the model of that process is unsupported. In turn, the various arguments about how human society should be organized, the right way for people to live together, cannot be dismissed as mere ideology. Rather, these are serious contenders for the answer to the perennial question of how we should live in one another's company, the central political question from time immemorial. The belief that in tribal societies human beings were at their stage of infancy, whereas in capitalist times they are in their adolescence, is an appealing, progressivist notion, but it turns out to be an unwarranted extrapolation. Human nature is far more stable than this view would have it. One need not deny the possibility of some changes in human nature to accept far greater stability over time than is implied in the Marxian analysis. The key question is what human nature is and how we must accommodate it, not at what stage of humanity's growth-period or maturation we happen to be, as Marx and many of his followers suppose. They do deny that the basic nature of human beings lacks stability through time.

And here emerges a crucial difficulty of attempts to show the moral superiority of individualist, libertarian, or capitalist political economy, including some modified forms of it such as the welfare state. Intellectual assent to capitalism has largely rested on a crucial feature of Thomas Hobbes's philosophy. This is that each person acts so as to satisfy his desires or, as Hobbes himself put it, "the proper object of every man's will, is some good to himself"[7] (where "good" is understood purely subjectively). It has given intellectual ammunition to critics of every stripe—from communists to Christians and Moslems, as well as to fascists. Each finds capitalism ignoble, crass, morally callous, and inconsiderate.

The charge that capitalism demeans human nature has always seemed to me forced and ultimately unfair. While a system may have originated from within a certain philosophical framework, so that its tenets became known mainly in the terms of that position, it does not follow that it fully and exclusively depends for its soundness on that framework. In short, individualism need not be Hobbesian or neo-Hobbesian, nor has it always been so defended.

Outside the neo-Marxist—or near-Marxist—criticisms there have been others, both religious and secular. The value-free neo-classical economic approach has been questioned by many, often in the pages of various prominent journals of ethics and public policy. One such criticism notes, this time in connection with the neo-classical libertarian critique of rent control, that "A more complex ethical analysis might question the two assumptions [underlying the economic approach] and find the normative conclusions barring rent control not so obvious. Might the level of efficiency losses be outweighed by other gains? Might some right of tenants 'trump' the utility analysis?"[8] And the same kind of response can be made to all the economic approaches which tend to lead to the normative conclusions of laissez-faire capitalism, for example, analyses of welfare, government regulation, and redistribution of wealth by the state.

Critics do not like to focus on moral arguments for the capitalist political-economic system, but that is the only way their arguments can be met. Eventually, perhaps, they will admit that they must contend with an alternative moral view.

Accordingly, my own approach will not rest on economic analysis at all. I will invoke little more than commonsense economics in my discussion, except where it is crucial to indicate that economic reasoning has produced insights contrary to common expectation. I plan to argue the case for laissez-faire primarily on moral grounds.

I will argue that a sound meta-ethics of naturalism supports the classical egoist ethics, which in turn is the foundation for a theory of natural rights that spells out universal, equal, negative human rights to life, liberty, and property. The classical egoist holds that the primary ethical task for each person is the fullest development of himself or herself as a living human being *and* as the individual that he or she is. This view ties values to life and moral values to human life. The valuation of human life for every individual amounts, in turn, to the valuation of the particular human life over which the person has direct responsibility, namely, oneself. Since a person's pursuit of values — and first of all his or her life as a human being — is a matter of choice, this pursuit is a moral task which, ultimately, amounts to the fulfillment of the (initially) chosen responsibility to enhance oneself to the fullest, as dictated by human nature and one's own individual identity.

I will show that such an egoistic view can support the position that people's moral nature and, therefore, requirement for (negative) freedom (within which to exercise their moral agency) may be forcibly secured in society, even when those whose rights are thus secured do not explicitly agree to that practice. In short, from my moral responsibility to seek my happiness in life, and my choice to do this in a social context, it follows that I am obliged to respect others' rights.

Thus the position I develop is both orthodox and radical. John Locke's defense of the rights to life, liberty, and property has generally been seen as the beginning of the task I myself have set out to accomplish. I plan, however, to put matters somewhat differently, not denying for a moment that some of the Lockean points are vital to understanding why a libertarian society is just and good. Yet Locke's philosophy seems to leave no room for genuine moral choice by individual human beings — indeed, he seems to have accepted, in some of his works, psychological hedonism and even physicalism. These ideas do not seem to me to lend support to any political economy that stresses the moral nature of human life.

Given the context of contemporary philosophical scholarship and political consciousness, my arguments are meant to improve the case for the free society in the tradition of classical liberalism and Lockean natural-rights political thought. For I argue that human nature exists, a point widely doubted now by philosophers. I also argue that by 'human nature' we must mean a reasonably distinct group of living beings with the capacity to engage in rational thought as a matter of choice, who rely for the successful conduct of their lives on doing this well. And I argue, furthermore, that a just society is one in which all individuals are able to fulfill the possibilities which arise from being the rational living beings they are, with their particular needs, desires, capabilities, and circumstances. In short, a just human community is one that first and foremost protects the individual's right to life and liberty — the sovereignty of human individuals to act without *aggressive* intrusion from other human beings.

It is the overall qualitative, including moral, superiority of this kind of free society that should be demonstrated in the course of a philosophical treatment of its worth, rather than its economic productivity or even simply its capacity to accommodate human diversity and the desire for progress. Nor is it sufficient to show that the free society's principles, when implemented, lead to social consequences that correspond to some of our preferences or moral intuitions, as argued by Nozick. It may be important, of course, to know that methods such as those Nozick and John Rawls employ can support a libertarian political alternative, but it is by no means sufficient. To uphold the superiority of such a system requires showing, for example, why the intuitions favoring a free society should be honored before and in preference to competing intuitions. This can be done by way of a theory of natural rights which answers the question: 'How should human beings, as such, live in each other's company?' or 'What is the best system of political principles?'

Communities extending beyond familiar or tribal bonds require the best possible answer to this perennial question. The more personal, spontaneous, practice-based principles that can guide social life in more or less intimate human communities will not be sufficient to provide a framework for peaceful and civilized life in communities where strangers need to know how to interact. Political philosophy has aimed since Socrates to reduce the confusion and the arbitrariness of the standards of such large human community life. This is the objective of a theory of natural rights — not the rationalization of special class interests or the enhancement of society's material productivity, nor again, providing solutions for all moral problems persons face. Natural-rights theory holds that we must live with one another, at the minimum, by respecting everyone's fundamental moral nature or personhood. This is accomplished by identifying, protecting, and preserving, without compromise — given the context of our concern, namely, social life — certain basic rights, namely those to life, liberty, and property. Based on the consideration of human nature, such a theory defends the contention that when considering adult persons who are not crucially incapacitated, none may attack another's life, none may dictate another's actions, and none may obtain another's belongings, without proper authorization, a process which itself may not violate these prohibitions or rights.

Other theories bearing on politics give different answers. As we aim to come to terms with our existence in communities — learning what we should tolerate, what we should reject, what we should resist, what we should promote in the myriad political alternatives of our lives — we need to compare the various proposals, select the best, and try to shape our institutions in a way that will reasonably accommodate our conclusions. Yet it is sometimes maintained that no such good answers are even possible, none at least that give us a coherent approach to our problems in the political sphere.

It is true enough that no answer can be implemented all at once, nor may any one person learn all facets of the general approach we are to take — as is true in any other discipline of learning. Improvements can only be made within the context of the traditions and practices that have gone before. And when an effort is made to restructure the institutions of a human community, it is likely that some sacrifices will be extracted in the process, with some values at least temporarily given up. Yet just because any system must be eased into place, it does not follow that it should not be discussed as a system, in terms of how it would function at its fullest possible realization, and whether it would be better than alternatives. It is not idealistic to first conceive of what would be best, within reason, and then try to implement it.

There are philosophers, such as John Rawls, who think that to answer the kinds of questions I am addressing we need not first dwell on numerous philosophical topics — for example, "the theory of meaning, epistemology, and the philosophy of mind". Instead of seeking to build on truths that have "methodological priority," Rawls urges that "the question as to the existence of objective truth . . . depends [for an answer] on the kind of and extent of the agreement that would obtain among rational persons who have achieved or sufficiently approached, wide reflective equilibrium." For Rawls — and following his lead, for many other political philosophers in our time — "a central part of moral philosophy is . . . moral theory [and] it consists in the comparative study of moral conceptions, which is, in large part, independent" of the rest of philosophy.[9]

If this is to be a guide to proper thinking in the field in which I am to enter my reflections, I cannot follow suit. There are too many areas of moral and political theory that call to mind problems of the philosophy of mind, epistemology, and even metaphysics. What Rawls asks for cannot be satisfied. For example, as one develops a conception of human rights, would the violation of such rights have to involve the intentions of the aggressor? Even such a relatively nontechnical issue brings into play the problems of *mens rea* — the mental element in crime — that invites work in the philosophy of mind.

Concepts that figure in moral and political theory depend for their meaningfulness or validity in part on the way they are related to concepts in a more basic system of principles and facts than those of the moral or political principles themselves. In natural-rights theory this point is explicitly recognized. And that itself makes the position more demanding. Samuel Scheffler notes, for example:

> Given the metaphysical associations of the tradition, [natural rights] philosophers must explain what they mean by assigning rights to people. They must, further, say something about the sources of these rights, and they must deal with a variety of epistemic questions.[10]

The questions of political life and theory require going beyond what many in the twentieth century regard as the scope of the field. This may mean that no one book can handle them all. But that is another issue — it does not imply that the tasks can be avoided.

The approach that Rawls recommends seems also to have encouraged some recklessness, as when a number of political discussions begin with not much more than the announcement that 'our considered moral judgments' lead us to this or that conclusion or require doing justice to this or that moral idea, and then proceed simply to derive various policy implications and test them back against these and related considered moral judgments, that is, intuitions. But that the considered moral judgments may themselves lack any solid base, that they may indeed be prejudices that happen to be well entrenched — akin more to sentiments than to moral awareness — seems not to be troubling too many people. Indeed, while in the early twentieth century meta-ethics had been the end of most moral philosophy, in its second half one encountered little meta-ethics, at least in the context of dealing with normative ethics and public policy.

One result, it seems to me, is another problematical issue of contemporary normative philosophy. It poses a problem with even getting started on constructive work. Can one hope to produce a consistent set of principles of conduct, virtues, moral ideals, or a code of ethics and law in the first place?

In recent philosophical reflections, especially in the United States and Western societies, an attitude about ethics and politics has emerged that stresses the ultimate inherent conflict within any set of human values and principles of conduct. Samuel Scheffler offers one version of this position when he says that "in political theory as in life there is cause for heartache as well as hope."[11] Sidney Hook put the point differently:

> Whether we take as our supreme value knowledge or truth or beauty or love or friendship, there are some situations in which their pursuit may have to be morally condemned.[12]

More recently John Gray reiterates this sentiment. He tells us that "the consideration — that the various components of human flourishing may often be in intractable conflict with one another — seems to me to be decisive against any prospect of reviving natural law ethics" and that "It is, in general, a problem for all natural rights theories whether they specify only one basic natural right — to liberty, to property or whatever — and, if so, how they account for other important moral claims."[13] He concludes that "Recent attempts to specify a set of composible or nonconflictable rights succeed only at the formal level: they fail to give those rights any adequate content."[14] Stuart Hampshire makes the same point:

> . . . That ends of action should be stated in a conjunctive form, and should permit conflicts that cannot always be settled by one overriding

criterion, which is sufficiently definite to count as a criterion, is not in itself an unintelligible suggestion. To admit an irreducible plurality of ends is to admit a limit to practical reasoning, and to admit that some substantial decisions are not to be explained, and not to be justified as the right decisions, by any rational calculation. This is a possibility that cannot be conceptually excluded, even if it makes satisfying theoretical reconstruction of the different uses of "good," as a target-setting term, impossible.[15]

This seems to me to flow from a profoundly anti-metaphysical, piecemeal approach to philosophizing that has reigned for much of the twentieth century (but with foundations laid much earlier). My work should indicate why I regard that approach as quite unsuitable for reaching reasonable answers within normative moral and political thought. The pessimism is, I think, unwarranted, provided certain philosophical notions can be substantiated. As a start, let me indicate a brief reply to the challenge of those we might call 'perplexionists', from David L. Norton. It should at least open the door to considering an argument for the alternative that Hampshire, Hook, Gray and many others dismiss.

> I think it is not an exaggeration to say that ninety percent of the extant writings of Socrates, Plato, and Aristotle are devoted directly or indirectly to the problem of interpersonal and intrapersonal conflict, in terms on the one hand of analysis, and on the other of proposed resolution. What do they offer? It would not be mistaken to say that the beginning and the end of it is the metaphysical principle of the inherent "congeniality" of the varieties of goodness or human excellence. But to dismiss this as unwarranted and counterproductive apriorism, as is routinely done today, is to ignore what goes on *between* the beginning and the end. What the metaphysical principles of congeniality of excellences is is a functional presupposition. It attests that among actual human excellences as they appear in the world, harmony subsists *in potentia*. This is not to say that harmony is already achieved, nor is it to hold that it will be the inevitable outcome of processes that work independently of human initiative, by some metaphysical "invisible hand."[16]

Whether this same point can be made about natural rights, we will explore subsequently. Famous alleged moral dilemmas—such as the trolley careening down one of San Francisco's hills toward five people, a trolley that could be diverted, but only at the sacrifice of another person standing elsewhere — add fuel to perplexionism. Yet, in the end I will argue either (a) that insofar as these cases are realistic possibilities — wherein the context provides no materials by which a rational solution may be reached — they are very rare and tragic, or (b) that they are unrealistic hypotheticals that an ethical theory need not handle.

In addition to perplexionist views advanced by those in the Anglo-American analytic philosophical community, the prominence of existentialism in the mid-twentieth century was also symptomatic of this belief in the ultimate absurdity or inherently paradoxical nature of human existence, involving the inherently conflicting nature of moral judgments. Reality's absurdity has its most direct relevance to normative concerns and the general problem of guiding human conduct, since it is supposed to stem from the fact of human freedom. From our capacity to choose what we will do — to choose perhaps even what we will be — we derive the confounding circumstance of not having any consistent, coherent guidance in life, no standard that does not in the end leave us confounded rather than intellectually satisfied.

If norms of personal or public conduct can ultimately conflict — if there is no hope for a consistent set of right decisions as to what we should and should not do — then there is no prospect for establishing the truth of any moral and political theory or system. Some theory might be deemed adequate, workable, preferable, suitable, satisfactory, or whatnot. But not *true*. And indeed, this is just the approach that seems to appear in much of contemporary ethical and political thought.

A sound theory clearly requires internal consistency among the various principles that may form the hierarchy of its code of personal or public conduct. Is the challenge of the pragmatist, the ordinary-language philosopher, the existentialist, and other anti-foundationalists capable of being met? Must we give up the prospect of identifying the truth within the normative domain?

If we must, I think we will have to reconcile ourselves, intellectually as well as practically, to the irresolvability of some of the major conflicts of human life. In such a case no rational complaint could be entertained concerning the persistence of such conflicts as Palestinians versus Jews, Irish Protestants versus Irish Catholics, various ethnic and religious groups in India, the quarrels between domestic groups such as industrial-growth versus environmental-quality advocates, prudential versus generous actions, compassion versus integrity.

We should not deceive ourselves about this. If there really are no foundations by reference to which we should develop our normative theories, our ethics, and politics, then moral criticism, in the end, is arbitrary—at best related to some group's purposes but not based on anything binding on us all. Everyone's story will have to be seen as equally plausible, tenable, tolerable—including everyone's story as to how well our stories are told, how well we argue—for the philosophical enterprise does not escape moral relativism and perplexionism. (The Feyerabendian intellectual sword cuts in all directions.) We will have to discipline ourselves to accept this or find the grounds for why we should not. Granted, finding foundations is no guarantee that we will reach solutions in each case. But it is a necessary step toward the prospect of good solutions.

Throughout this work I will be countering the pessimist outlook on these issues, while attempting not to fall prey to utopian idealism on the other side. In the process I will be developing and utilizing an account of reality and knowledge (as well as truth) which may well meet the challenges of the pessimists.

At this point I wish only to assert, with no argument, that the metaphysical framework I draw upon combines monistic and pluralistic elements. Thus, while the requirement of consistency as a universal feature of everything, including the facts of ethics and politics, is undeniable, the manifestation of that consistency will be nonreductionistic. This implies that within different domains of reality the character of the ontological domain will determine what in particular can and cannot occur. For instance, at the level of human existence, it is possible that free choices can be made. So while human life is part of an integrated system of existence, its *type* of existence gives rise to factors that make rational ethics and politics possible, without in the slightest cancelling out the reality of human freedom of choice.

As to the problem associated with knowledge in the context of normative inquiries, I will defend an account of knowing reality that parallels the metaphysical position mentioned above. While some universal features of human knowledge are evident, some elements of knowledge admittedly arise in the light of the character of what is known. Since different ontological domains are in evidence, knowledge about facts within these different domains will not admit of full reduction to knowledge of facts within others.

It should also be noted at this point that despite the need for logical integrity, I am not going to aspire to the impossible goal of completeness of the present theory. Any theory concerning substantive matters must admit of the possibility of eventual up-dating, modification, recasting of some terms, and so on. Because no theorist or group of theorists is omniscient, none can have checked every possible and possibly possible (conceivable) turn of relevant events to check the theory being discussed. The evaluation of a substantive theory must, then, be comparative — as must be the determination of a definition, once all the accessible facts have been taken into account and placed in a coherent order.

Rights Theory at a Glance

What are Rights?

Answering our question requires knowing something about what must be done to get the answer. It also requires some discussion of whether there may not even be more than one answer.

First, then, I will be arguing that the concept 'rights' can be given a definition that is sound, even true, although by 'true' I do not mean some final, unalterable, timeless statement that corresponds to some final, unalterable, timeless fact. Truth is a property of judgments or statements and since a great many judgments or statements are context-bound, a great many truths are tied to specific contexts. The truth of a definition of rights, for example, is bound to the context of social morality, politics, and law. It is also bound to the context of human reality within a world in which not all that one wishes for is available just by wishing it. 'Rights talk' is talk within the context of human existence in the familiar universe.

Rights are clearly not physical objects or even physical relations, although there are certain uses of the concept, in economic theory, which come close to suggesting that to have a property right is to be empowered to act in certain ways toward a physical object. But this is the nature of a legal right, not of a basic, natural right, which is a moral concept, not a descriptive one.

Nor is the concept 'rights' merely a legal notion, although there can be legal rights. These, however, are derivative, not basic, even in the normative sense, since law is something that is established by human decision. For instance, one's legal right to vote is a right established by legislators. There are conceptions of rights that are different, namely, those that people talk about when they urge their law-makers to create legal rights. Civil or women's or gay or just plain human rights-advocates want law-makers to establish legal rights based on rights they believe already exist in some sense, apart from the legal system. The notion that rights other than legal rights

exist is already familiar in our experiences with ordinary human affairs.

When considered generally, rights seem to be *social conditions
that ought to be maintained*, moral principles pertaining to aspects of
social life. As Joseph Raz notes, " 'x has a right' if and only if x can
have rights, and other things being equal, an aspect of x's well-being
(his interest) is a sufficient reason to holding some other person(s) to
be under a duty."[1] For instance, one's right to use a swimming pool
requires that one be free to choose between using and not using the
pool and others are under a duty to leave one free to make that
choice. The right-holder may not be prevented from using the pool,
even if it might be wrong for him to use it. Exercising one's rights
may, on a particular occasion, be wrong. But that is a different issue.
A right binds us to refrain from preventing others from acting in certain ways (they have a right to act) — using the pool, speaking their
minds, voting for their political candidate, and even wasting their
lives. In this sense a right is always relational — it pertains to the
moral responsibilities that arise among humans (and perhaps other
moral agents). Just because rights do not exist apart from a context of
persons living in one another's community, nothing diminishes the
objectivity of those rights — just as, but in a different context, a scientific principle may hold only conditionally, yet objectively, for example *if* sun reaches skin pigment, certain results will obtain. (It is to
caricature natural rights to construe them as obtaining somehow in
nature, independently of a social context of human life. The same
holds for a virtue such as generosity, while it need not for courage.)

The distinction between negative and positive rights, often discussed, does not affect the above characterization. Suppose George
has a negative right to ride a bicycle around his neighbor-
hood. The right is negative in that it requires nothing of other people,
save that they must not interfere with George's riding his bike. But
say that George has a positive right to be provided with medical help
when ill. The right is positive in that it requires others to do
something — provide medical care or the money to obtain it. Yet
when George has either of these rights, others must refrain from
preventing his exercise of it. It is this sense of the concept 'rights' that
is meant here. Further complications will be discussed later.

Initial Observations on Natural Rights

As with other moral concepts, so with rights, the question can arise how they can be validated. How can they be shown to be binding? If they are conventional, presumbly they exist as a matter of social agreement, tradition, temporary convenience, historical happenstance. If they are natural, they exist because of the nature of their possessor. Thus the right to copy some software if one is a member of a computer club would usually be conventional, institutional, special. It would not be natural. The club itself came about through agreement or convention. It is not inherent in human nature. So the right is conventional.

The right to life, however, is often held to be natural. That is to say, just in virtue of one's being human and living with other human beings, one is said to have the right to live. This right is conceived as a principle of social life requiring that no one prevent one from living (or even, in its positive aspect, that others make one's living possible). Whether negative or positive, the right to life is a clear case of a prospective natural right. The idea is that, given human nature, the principle is true. This leaves us many questions, including whether human nature can be identified.

SOME HISTORICAL QUESTIONS ABOUT RIGHTS

Some hold that 'rights' is an idea which had been around from ancient times, although it attained prominence only after Thomas Hobbes's characterization of it. It is said that there is some evidence of talk about rights in Aristotle, notably in his debate with the sophist Lycophron.[2] And William of Ockham made reference to natural rights as "the power to conform to right reason, without an agreement or pact."[3] Others deny this and hold that "there is no expression in any ancient or medieval language correctly translated by our expression 'a right' until near the close of the middle ages: the concept lacks any means of expression in Hebrew, Greek, Latin or Arabic, classical or medieval, before about 1400, let alone in Old English, or in Japanese even as late as the mid-nineteenth century."[4]

I will not be concerned with this dispute as a problem in the history of ideas. However, my argument implicitly tends to side with those who maintain that the concept of rights, including natural rights, is explicitly or implicitly present in major discussions of political problems from the earliest times. This is because I argue that from the time human beings emerged, they had the rights they now have, however clearly or unclearly this was recognized. And it seems reasonable that if there are such rights — if these moral-political principles are true in human social life — most generations of moral and political thinkers would have noticed this and given some appropriate testimony to that effect. In some ever so inconsequential and inarticulate form, perhaps, the issue of how in general one's fellow members in a human community ought to comport themselves toward one another has occupied the minds of human beings for as long as we have records of their political thought. And within all the thinking, and some of the writing, evidence is available that some limits exist to the variety of ways in which one may treat others, limits which spell out some spheres of personal authority. The fact that these limits were not universalized is due to the selective perception many thinkers had of human nature, to say nothing of who exactly *is* a human being proper, not to any absence of concern with the limits themselves.

Actually, of course, this is just a side issue. What is far more important is whether natural, individual human rights exist; whether there are principles of morality and politics based on human nature which require that others refrain from preventing individual human beings from engaging in certain activities, from conducting themselves in certain ways. The issue of whether this had been formally recognized in earlier times is only incidental to my inquiry.

No doubt the crucial challenge to this tradition is the Kantian type of objection to the very possibility of a confirmed, validated conceptual framework. As expressed by Stuart Hampshire:

> It seems that we can set no theoretical limit to the number of ways in which reality could be divided into recurrent elements for the purposes of thought and action; for there is no sense in 'could' or 'could not' as they are used here, unless we have first given the rules or principles that would exclude certain methods of differentiation as impossible. But to give such rules or principles for singling out and differentiating elements in reality is precisely to explain the structure of a possible or actual language. In order to show that elements of reality could only be distinguished for the purposes of language in one familiar way, we would have to show that nothing else would count as 'distinguishing elements in reality for the purposes of language' . . . Even less can we suppose that there must be some independently identifiable ground in reality, independent of the conditions of reference to reality.[5]

This challenge assumes that (a) the rules of language come from language itself, not from a source outside imposing standards on language, so that it can serve to discuss reality successfully; that (b) one must take on the burden of proving that "nothing else would count as 'distinguishing elements in reality for the purposes of language' "; and that (c) an "independently identifiable ground in reality" refers to a ground that is known independently of the conditions of reference to reality – that is, independent of human consciousness. The last is an impossible task: without the faculty of awareness of something one cannot be aware of it. The Kantian view that the nature of the faculty of awareness is an obstacle to its very task is self-defeating and thus unsound. It assumes (b), that is, it assumes that to show that something is the actual ground of reality one must prove that no other ground is possible. That assumption, in turn, rests on the dubious (Cartesian) claim (d), that to know that something is the case, one must prove first that one could not be wrong about the matter, that is, that one's consciousness is infallible, incorrigible, perfect. The entire project involves accomplishing what by its characterization is a task suitable only to a god.

Regarding (a), the rules of language are not invented out of thin air; rather they are gradually developed on the basis of the success we have in expressing ourselves about the world, a success that we are able to judge by reference to meeting our life-needs consistently and with relative constancy, just as we judge the success of other tools.

To view these rules as Hampshire does treats language as a mere game. But games are optional activities in human life, whereas language is a basic tool, not a game. Its rules or principles are not like those of chess or Trivial Pursuit – it is not enough for them to be consistent. (And why must they be that at least?) The rules of language are like those of photosynthesis, except that the last are not breachable, whereas the former, since they apply to conscious agents – not to inanimate matter – can be breached by those to whom they apply.[6] We should, *pace* Hampshire, regard the rules or principles of language the way Aristotle did: "It won't be possible for the same thing to be and not to be [not] just [as] a matter of the word – but where it's a matter of the thing."[7] Of course, by calling language a convention Hampshire and other contemporary philosophers do not mean that any individual could simply opt for another form of it. But then the designation 'conventional' is misleading. A convention, such as men opening car doors for women, could be abandoned at will by some community or culture. Perhaps by 'conventional' these philosophers mean that no Platonic, *timeless* forms of language pre-exist for us to identify and adopt. But that is better expressed by the term 'contextual'.

This also points up the fact that the strength of the Kantian and neo-Kantian critiques comes from their acceptance of what it takes to know something. The Platonic/Cartesian legacy infects them completely when knowledge is understood as a kind of timeless, changeless mutual-entailment relation. Thus Keith Lehrer explains that it is with the "conditions necessary and sufficient for man to have knowledge" that a philosopher concerns himself.[8] And "necessary and sufficient" means in this context logically, timelessly necessary and sufficient, precisely in view of the kind of objections that are advanced in order to test the candidates — e.g., in Gettier-type counterexamples where mere conceivable scenarios serve to defeat a definition of 'knowledge'. I suggest that we admit contextual aspects of knowledge into the meaning of "necessary and sufficient". The discussions surrounding attempts to define knowledge suggest that this is not how most philosophers treat the conditions.

So Lehrer's approach to analyzing knowledge introduces a bias. If knowledge must meet some logically necessary and sufficient conditions, no such requirement of knowlege will succeed since this is a fantastic requirement. The nature of any natural phenomenon, such as knowledge, simply cannot be required to live up to this 'ideal', one only attainable by an omniscient mind.

As to (b), again the model of knowledge Hampshire invokes is the same as Lehrer's, drawn from Descartes, for whom "to know that p" means "to be unalterably, forever certain, beyond a shadow of conceivable doubt about p."[9] This led to Hume's *reductio ad absurdum* radical empiricism and to Kant's impressive efforts to recast 'knowledge' in his famous Copernican revolution. If to know something one must be consciously related to it in the fashion envisioned by Descartes, then, of course, Kant is right and we cannot know things in themselves, and metaphysical knowledge, especially, is impossible. Only if to know 'p' requires also having proven that it is impossible that '−p', does the Kantian or neo-Kantian skeptical result follow. This is fantastic to expect, even of knowledge.[10]

Now, concerning (c), to doubt our ability to know reality or the ground in reality because the conditions of referring to reality may be obstacles to knowing it, is a grand confusion. Why may what enables us to know reality also amount to such an obstacle?

Here (d) enters with the now-familiar view that, presumably, nothing counts as knowing which does not logically guarantee against the absence of any possible obstacles to knowing reality. But this is just another rendition of the earlier absurd requirement made upon knowledge, namely: to know that 'p' means having proven ' – p' logically impossible. But knowing something is not knowing, also, that it is impossible that the denial of this be true. (This reminds one of the idea that the defendant ought to demonstrate that he is not guilty, rather than the prosecution that he is!)

The above should suggest how one can respond to the Kantian and neo-Kantian objections to metaphysics. It does not yet tell us what the content of a sound metaphysics is, although that is suggested from the reference to Aristotle. We received from him the best argument showing us the first principles of being – what being is *qua* being. And if one does not impose on oneself the requirement of meeting a fantastic Platonic/Cartesian model of knowledge in offering one's answer, then it seems clear enough that the Aristotelian view of the basic principles of reality makes very good sense: they are the principles of the Law of Identity, Law of Non-Contradiction, and Law of the Excluded Middle, understood in a substantive rather than purely formal sense. (That means, also, that the purely mathematical objections to the Law of the Excluded Middle do not serve to deny Aristotle's basic metaphysical position. I will support these points further in Chapter 4.)

A 'language' or system of concepts that rests on the three principles we learned from Aristotle – and is confirmed repeatedly, by implication, in all thought and action – and also on the processes of sensory perception, would appear to be adequate to account for what grounds our conceptual structure within which we can produce correct statements of the nature of various things, including man. For the time being, then, we can consider some other general problems of natural-rights theory. Later, in Chapter 4, when we develop more fully the case for the individualist natural-rights position, we will consider some other difficulties with this crucial problem, namely, whether a conceptual system and the definitions developed within it can be shown to be sound, that is, the best such system available for understanding reality.

INDIVIDUALISM, THE SELF, AND NATURAL RIGHTS

It is individuals who are supposed to have rights. These rights are significant, however, only if they are natural, grounded in something other than convention, 'contract', or interest. The reason is that by 'natural' is suggested a base that may reasonably be taken to refer to what all individuals of the kind that would be candidates for rights-possession may be said to be. This common aspect of the rights-holding individuals promises that the rights be stable and capable of being used for understanding and guiding social and political policy and law.

Yet a conflict seems to lurk here. Some argue that 'the individual' is itself a recently invented idea, not common to every age. If individuals are of recent invention, then they could not have had rights in earlier times because then they did not exist, not at least as individuals, who are the possesors of rights.

Let us suppose that it was the family that existed — or had a kind of ontological priority of existence — before the invention of individuals. This would mean that, in the relevant sense, individual human beings did not exist. That is, the crucial moral and political entity was not George or Harry or Sue or Socrates or Pericles but the family to which these persons belonged — or, rather, of which they were parts. Thus it makes sense that these parts of families had no rights since they could not make independent choices that might have been thwarted, whereby their moral nature could have been suppressed. Clearly, such yet-uninvented individuals had been thwarted in their choices in all sorts of ways, but none of this might have been regarded as objectionable.

The crucial issue is whether this was a mistake of omission or simply a correct approach to a different world. If individuals had always existed but were not recognized as such, this mistake or omission could well have been morally objectionable, just as slavery, though widely accepted, had been. Even if we deny the moral objectionability of this omission, it may nevertheless be defensible that the omission was a mistake, albeit perhaps an understandable one, due to, say, the inadequate development of our conceptual system. The recent 'invention' is, under such a description, a discovery, not an invention.

Still another puzzle remains. Individualism has tended to rest on philosophical ideas which reject the very notion of the 'nature of X' and thus human nature. Individualism would seem to be correct only if there is no human nature *as a feature of the world*, but only an artifact or invention, that is, if human nature — the classification of people by this concept — had only nominal status. Thus we have a dilemma: the individual exists and has always existed, in which case there is no human nature and natural rights; or the individual has been invented and there is a human nature, but no individuals have natural rights since no individuals exist to have such rights.

The dilemma has a solution. Individualism has had a philosophical base which is inadequate. It might have been given a different, more adequate philosophical base. Such a base does make room for human nature as well as for human individuals as a crucial feature of human nature, and from that base the idea of natural individual human rights makes sense. This is what I plan to argue, at any rate. For now I wish only to make clear what I am aiming for, with just a few hints as to how I plan to reach that aim.

For some the idea of individual natural rights has to be a contradiction in terms. But if I am right and we can make clear sense of human individuality — the idea that a person can be a unique being who nevertheless shares a nature with other such unique beings — then no contradiction should arise. To make out the position, it is necessary to enter the murky terrain of metaphysics. Here I give a hint how I will do this.

The problem of reconciling individuality and human nature arises because of the pervasiveness of reductionism instead of pluralism. We could accept the existence of a variety of beings that are to be classified as irreducibly part of some natural kind. The causal powers of these different beings could make sense of beings — for example, human beings — that could cause some of their own actions. Such beings, while members of a species, nevertheless acquire significant — not simply numerical — individuality in the course of choosing their behavior. As numerical individuals they already possess different properties from other individuals. But this is so with dogs and cats and even flowers. The individuality of a human being involves more than just being different from other individuals. It also involves that person's having made qualitatively different choices in his or her life. This would, I think, also solve the intractable problem that existentialists faced when they felt that to secure human existence — as creative consciousness — they had to deny human essence, a specific nature for human beings.

MODERNISM AND MORALITY

Does metaphysical pluralism offer hope? In other words, is it likely to be correct?

From initial appearance it would seem to be the only sensible idea. We have so many different kinds and types of beings — animals, humans, rocks, plants, and so forth, as well as melodies, noises, numbers, distances, weights, structures, arrangements, compositions, patterns, figures, objections, and the rest. Is it really credible that all of these different kinds and types of beings simply turn out to be one kind or two? Not really. Indeed, reductionist metaphysics tends to advance promissory notes, not conclusions of arguments. At best reductionism is a competing metaphysical hypothesis. It is fair to suggest that the reductionist stance is in retreat because of the loss of its philosophical base, namely, empiricism, materialism, and positivism. This has led to a broadening of options for explaining ethics and normative politics.

Although there have always been moral skeptics — those who deny that morality exists or is a meaningful area of concern — the subject simply won't go away. B. F. Skinner to the contrary notwithstanding, we have not left behind our human dignity.

What makes something a moral issue? When one distinguishes something as a moral concern, one has in mind conduct that is regarded as fundamentally right or wrong and within the power of individuals to engage in or not. To put it differently, morality or ethics involves self-directed (human) conduct that is open for evaluation or assessment as either right or wrong. This is narrower than value theory because the focus is those values that can be pursued as a matter of choice. It covers everything from private behavior to public and international policy. All these invite questions about whether one is acting rightly or wrongly.

So what is the problem? Why would one pit morality and normative politics (including the theory of natural rights) against knowledge and science in the first place? Given a conception of knowledge which requires that any claim to know something must be scientifically demonstrable, it appears that morality is impossible. Questions about what one ought to do, what policy one ought to support, appear to be meaningless, somewhat as astrological questions appear to astronomers, because an answer with moral content, which refers to what should or should not be done, is not provable by reference to observable facts of nature. This view of science restricts meaningfulness and knowability to what is capable of being made evident to observation or the sensory organs.

Following the dictates of positivism and its legacy, science would appear to preclude morality. Furthermore, as Skinner says, "A scientific analysis shifts both the responsibility and the achievement to the environment."[11] The reason is that morality rests on the reality of human self-determination or free will.

Skinner saw the connection between morality and free choice more clearly than many philosophers who keep talking of morality even though they do not accept free will. Human freedom of choice—not just the capacity to behave selectively but to determine one's conduct—is presupposed for human dignity. This covers any doctrine of political justice that places demands on persons to choose to adhere to right conduct—including the doctrine of human natural rights in the Lockean tradition, one that rests on human beings having a free and independent moral nature.

John Gray adds that "There seems little room for Aristotelian and Lockean ideas of final causes or natural ends in a modern scientific world view which has expelled teleology from itself, where it has not given the evidences of purposes in nature a mechanistic explanation."[12] While merely excluding teleology from science does not establish the uselessness of the concept, when we consider that incompatibility with science often renders a concept intellectually and philosophically suspect, the result is practically the same.

Science seems to conflict with morality because, as science is generally understood, it requires a view of reality that connects all events, including all actions, to prior (efficient) causes. On such a view, as Gray says, there is no room for any causality that is connected, not to past events, but rather to ends formulated about the future, which is the way we tend to view purposive human conduct. Such a view appears to eliminate self-determination as a possible event. If people's behavior is always caused by some prior event or preceding set of variables, then to speak of their own, self-directed conduct is confused. Rather, just as Skinner and other physicalists—including many members of the social-sciences community—claim, human beings engage in behavior which is always caused by factors in their prior history. As Gray concludes, "the conception of natural law [i.e., a moral system that rests on the idea that human beings ought, as a matter of what accords with their nature, to act in certain ways] needed to support a theory of natural rights is incompatible with modern empiricism."[13] And modern empiricism and the scientistic viewpoint are intimately related. This is why, when empiricism is seen as precluding some viewpoint, that viewpoint is also taken to be incompatible with science.

Another reason science appears to reject morality is that evolutionary biology seems to preclude any stable set of moral standards, not to mention any stable ground on which to rest moral claims. If Darwin or some version of his view is right, what we have are not facts pertaining to the good human life and right or wrong conduct, but various built-in processes that govern our behavior in line with the principles of natural selection. Conduct that enhances the reproductive performance of individuals within a population is favored by natural selection, conduct that hinders it is disfavored, and all there could be to morality would be, at best, a variety of behavioral strategies, but certainly no principles that may be known as we know principles of chemistry or physics. Here, too, a kind of genetic determinism of the human species appears to rule out morality understood as a system of objective standards by which we ought to abide.

Moral worries of the kind the older philosophical tradition took seriously seem to persist, despite this kind of skepticism. The notion that we are ourselves to blame for our conduct, rather than some prior causative event, is built into our laws as well as our everyday moral reflections and concerns. To deny the legitimacy of that notion comes close to denying that any firm reality exists outside of the mind that is perceiving it. Although it may be necessary to contend with such radical skepticism, such skepticism itself cannot provide the final answer because it denies the very possibility of *any* kind of answer. A similar problem confronts those who deny the very possibility of purpose and free choice. Such a one is, after all, criticizing others and often blames them for bad reasoning, in short, of some bad conduct (even if limited to philosophical argumentation).

Yet the skeptic's influence is considerable. Many of us insist on explaining immoral conduct by reference to causes that stand apart from the individual agent, so that the conduct no longer seems immoral as such but, instead, 'undesirable', 'lamentable', 'defective', 'destructive', or 'incorrect'. We blame not ourselves but account for misconduct by reference to our childhood traumas, chromosomes, the psychological pressures we experience, and the like. This may be no different from earlier times when we blamed such conduct on mysterious forces — the gods are responsible. Still, in our time it is science that has become the source of liberation from moral responsibility. It is, of course, a certain conception of science, one that is not universally embraced, yet one that is influential enough.

Within the positivist tradition science was seen as most clearly exemplified in classical mechanistic physics. It was a reductionist physics at that. Although positivists were no longer captive to Newtonianism, their philosophy of science and epistemology remained loyal to the influences of its achievements on philosophy. The mechanistic principles provided a premiss that was carried over into other disciplines besides physics, e.g., by materialists. Within this view the world could be accounted for completely by reference to certain ultimate laws and we could learn about these laws by adhering strictly to the principle of empirical verification. Indeed, while philosophy itself has abandoned the faith of the positivists, many of its branches, including ethics and politics, still feel the impact of the positivist criticism of the possibility of knowledge concerning their subject matter.

If the Newtonian legacy, however, is limited, and materialistic reductionism is not a full-blown metaphysics that can be defended, then we can also rethink the question of whether science and morality might co-exist. If not everything in nature must be matter-in-motion, then it is possible that there are different types of entities. Physics, chemistry, biology, botany, zoology, sociology, psychology, politics, ethics, and so forth could all have their own realms and their subjects might conform to different laws. In turn, it is possible that human life does not conform exactly to the life of birds, rats, or other non-human life forms, even if in part it resembles those. At some level human life may be drastically different from the rest. And there would be nothing unscientific about this.

Good science does not tolerate merely *imposing* a certain picture on reality. Rather it demands that we accommodate *discoveries*. The discovery that human life makes room for morality cannot be ruled out. As Roger Sperry notes, "in dealing with value questions the inner mental processes of the brain should regularly be forced to check and double-check with outside reality. This is the fundamental law underlying the scientific method—a point that seems simple but is sometimes overlooked in statements on the essence of science."[14] And there seems to be good reason to suppose, now, that science itself supports a value-laden conception of human life, rather than the value-free approach so long favored by positivist social science and philosophy. As Sperry maintains, "the advances of the last half-century in our understanding of the neural mechanism of mind and conscious awareness clear the way for a rational approach in the realm of values."[15]

FREEDOM AND THE HUMAN BRAIN

Dr. Sperry, a neurophysicist who is also a Nobel laureate in medicine, has argued that the human brain is so structured that human self-consciousness and, thus, self-direction are possible. He begins by defending mentalism as a better explanatory scheme than reductionism:

> There exists within the cranium a whole world of diverse causal forces, as in no other cubic half-foot of universe that we know. At the lowermost levels in this system, we have local aggregates of some sixty or more types of subnuclear particles interacting with great energy, all within the neutrons and protons of their respective atomic nuclei . . . .[16]

Furthermore,

> . . . the flow and the timing of impulse traffic through any brain cell, or even a nucleus of cells in the brain, are governed largely by the overall encompassing properties of the whole cerebral circuit system, within which the given cells and fibers are incorporated, and also by the relationship of this circuit system to other circuit systems . . . [and] if one keeps climbing upward in the chain of command within the brain, one finds at the very top those overall organizational forces and dynamic properties of the large patterns of cerebral excitation that are correlated with mental states or psychic activity . . . . To try to explain the pain pattern or any other mental qualities only in terms of the spatiotemporal arrangement of nerve impulses, without reference to the mental properties and the mental qualities themselves, would be as formidable as trying to describe any of the endless variety of complex molecular reactions known to biochemistry wholly in terms of the properties of electrons, protons, and neutrons and their subnuclear particles, plus (and this, of course, is critical) their spatiotemporal relationships.[17]

Sperry goes on to defend the view that in terms of this hierarchical conception of the human organism, which is arranged so that the conscious faculty is the organizing principle, a conception of self-deterministic free will arises that is not only compatible but clearly supported by science. Sperry explains that "the kind of determinism proposed is not that of the atomic, molecular, or cellular level, but rather the kind that prevails at the level of cerebral mentation, involving the interplay of ideas, reasoning processes, judgments, emotion, insight, and so forth." As Sperry develops the point,

> The proposed brain model provides in large measure the mental forces and abilities to determine one's own actions. It provides a high degree of freedom from outside forces as well as mastery over the inner molecular and atomic forces of the body. In other words, it provides plenty of free will as long as we think of free will as self-determination. A person does indeed determine with his own mind what he is going to do and often from among a large series of alternative possibilities.[18]

Self-determinism may not be the standard conception of free will in philosophical discussions but that is no liability — one would hope that any contribution to this discussion would produce something different in crucial respects from previous, shaky ideas. The free-will issue has in fact been somewhat problematic in recent philosophy since many philosophers do find it difficult to believe that people have free will in a world that seems to be governed by laws. Yet dismissing the issue would be difficult as well, since virtually all talk about how institutions, organizations, officials, spouses, department heads, and any human beings ought to act appears to be problematic if they cannot choose what to do.

Self-determinism is a compatibilist conception of free will, squaring it with universal causality without assuming that all kinds of causality must be of the efficient-cause variety. Once it is appreciated that the kind of causal interaction in which an entity is involved depends on the nature of that entity, then if human nature involves the capacity to initiate conscious processes, this initiation process can be regarded as a kind of cause. That is why self-determinism accurately describes the nature of human freedom of will.

So one of the types of causes in reality is self-causation, a power that had originally been ascribed only to God! With the enormously complex structure and composition of the human organism, human beings appear to have the power to initiate their own conduct. This confirms a commonsense idea about us, one at the center of moral individualism, the doctrine that we are all individually responsible to choose to do what is right.

There are other reasons to suppose that we are free or self-governed in crucial respects. Determinism seems incoherent, when fully scrutinized. First, if correct, we could not *know* that it were correct. That is because if we were fully determined in what we did, we would also be determined in what we thought, so we wouldn't be free and independent in the relevant respects to test our premises, check our arguments, and reconsider interpretations. The conclusions we reached then would simply be those we had to reach, which would be true of our intellectual opponents also. Any further determination of who was right would suffer from the same defect. Philosophical as well as scientific objectivity would be outside our power. We could not establish that others were wrong—they would have just been caused to think differently from us. But this puts the determinist's position on equal terms with its opposite which surely would not satisfy the determinist.[19] While one might suggest that one of the determinants of our behavior may just be the perception of truth, nevertheless we would simply have to perceive as we did, so we could never take the independent, objective (unforced) stance to make sure we were indeed under the sway of truth rather than something else. The point has, of course, been resisted by philosophers who endorse universal efficient causal determinism, but there is no way to escape the argument that the independence required in dispassionate search for truth is precluded by a deterministic account of reaching it.

Determinism also suffers the embarrassment of obliging its defender to imply that it is false in the very process of defending it. This is because the defender of determinism believes that his opponent should change his mind, which implies that his opponent is free to do this. If ought implies can, which is difficult to deny except for very special cases, then to argue that someone ought to change his mind is to assume that he is free to do so or refuse to do so.[20]

One might argue that 'ought implies can' is merely a principle of ethics and cannot be employed in the above line of analysis, but that is an *ad hoc* notion. If the point is valid vis-à-vis 'ought' judgments in ethics, because they are 'ought' judgments and not because of the particular moral edicts involved, then anywhere there are 'ought' judgments the principle holds as well. Consider a purely technical 'ought' judgment, such as 'If our goal is to obtain the most efficient fuel consumption in this machine, we ought to use leaded gasoline.' The 'ought' here implies 'can' just as much as in the moral judgment, 'You ought to live prudently.' If you ought to believe *x* while you do not, then you must be free either to change your mind or not to change it. It must be up to you whether you do the one or the other.

If it would merely be desirable that you change, that would be another matter—being tall may be desirable but it cannot be accomplished at will. But one can be expected to change one's mind at will, not solely by the 'force' of the argument. If the force of the argument sufficed, there would be no room for the concept of stubbornness!

There is also the data from self-examination: one sometimes knows about oneself that one did or failed to do something when one was perfectly free to do it and ought to have done it. For example, we sometimes observe that we didn't think! We cry out, 'Dammit, I didn't think.' (It also seems that our power of reason is just where our freedom of choice is located. This is what we inadvertently testify to at such times.) This introspective evidence could be viewed as scientifically acceptable, much as we regard the introspective evidence needed for medical examinations testing visual and auditory functions.

When we combine the data from science concerning the capacity of the human mind for self-direction, and the conclusions of philosophical reasoning concerning the flaws of the kind of determinism that excludes self-determination, we find that the doctrine of free will lacks little that we need for an adequate theory concerning the nature of some entity in the universe. If we add to this the notion that the hypothesis that human beings can choose freely helps explain a great deal of what occurs in human life and distinguishes such life from the rest of the animal world, we do not seem to be in any danger of running afoul of science.

None of this need rob the world of order and rationality, as feared by those who hold that science and free choice are mutually exclusive. There are those who hold that we can grant the reality of freedom of choice but precisely because of this we must give up the idea of any objective standard of moral values. Existentialists, who opt for freedom, believe that our freedom is exactly what puts us at sea where morality is concerned. For anything that has an indeterminate nature, it must be impossible to locate an objective standard of good and right. Existentialists also propose that the freedom we possess is an enigma, something that sits ill with an otherwise deterministic universe. But as we have seen, this is not the most sensible conclusion to be drawn from what we know of these matters. Both reason and freedom may be an integral aspect of reality, manifest in human life.

Neither is all this in conflict with the generally accepted facts of evolutionary biology. There is nothing in evolutionary theory which precludes the development of a species such that its members possess freedom of the will. It could be argued that of the various species resembling humans, the sorts that manage to survive best are those which have been most 'adaptable' to their environment — including the capacity to rearrange it — in just the way that a being with "volitional consciousness" (to use a phrase from Ayn Rand) would be capable of. Free choice presents one with a great variety of options; obviously human beings can take advantage of, and create, virtually boundless options in the task of forging a successful life.

Morality, in turn, could be the general principles that members of the species must themselves discover and follow in order to do well at life. That this kind of morality does not possess the fantastic characteristics of the categorical imperative — true in all possible worlds, for all possible rational agents, regardless of their circumstances — might be a disappointment. It is not such, however, in terms of realistic expectations about the nature of human morality.

Neither positivist scientism, nor the scientism of evolutionary biology — which fails to consider the possibility that certain products of evolution may objectively require morality — cancels out the moral viewpoint, namely, the one that sees human beings as free to choose their conduct and capable of identifying principles that both monitor and modify that conduct in the interests of living, successfully, a specifically *human* life.

VALUES IN A WORLD OF FACTS

Let me now consider briefly how all this gives rise to the moral perspective on human life, one that is both genuinely value-oriented and fully compatible with what science seems to require.

Values may be regarded as a different type of fact, nothing more. This is hard to conceive in the familiar framework. Most of us think of facts as concrete, something we can check out by observation. This was an idea circulated for us by those philosophers who advocated the simple view of science. But by now we know well enough that facts range from the simple to the very complicated. Some facts, say in quantum mechanics or astrophysics, are far from observable but highly inferential.

Once it is accepted that many facts must be inferred — particularly those not readily accessible to our forms of sensory awareness, and thus not on the surface of reality — it becomes easier to understand how values could be facts. The following sketch of a theory may then explain how values are indeed a certain kind of complex fact.

When life emerged in nature, something quite distinctive joined the furniture of reality. One thing we can grant about life is that it can perish — indeed, we know of no example of it that is not perishable. Other beings in nature — molecules, atoms, electrons, rocks, sounds, light, and so forth — possess their own characteristics that make them what they are. And in each case there may be numerous varieties — of atoms, molecules, structures or configurations within which they obtain, etc. When life enters the picture, this is the addition of a new variety. And values came into existence with the emergence of life.[21]

Since life can perish, and since to the living perishing is cessation of being, what contributes to perishing logically comes to be regarded as bad or a disvalue, from the viewpoint of the existing being. As Popper puts it,

> I think that values enter the world with life; and if there is life without consciousness (as I think there may well be, even in animals and man, for there appears to be such a thing as dreamless sleep) then, I suggest, there will also be objective values, even without consciousness.[22]

What this passage suggests is what has been argued here, namely, that the conceptual base for the very idea of value or goodness consists in the phenomenon of life. We have here a fact-based concept of value or goodness. Our experience of the existence of life and our logical organization of this experience along with the rest that we are aware of seems to make the best sense of the concept of 'value' or 'disvalue' or 'harm'. And from this experience-based concept it follows that to contribute to the likelihood of cessation is a disvalue, to contribute to continuation is a value. Good and bad, then, are features of living being. They are objective, relational features or aspects of living.

So with the emergence of life values also came to exist. Lives, of course, are not all the same kind. Neither are the standards of value — or of goodness — by which various kinds of lives are lived in the best way. The precise nature of the values are dependent on the kind of life in question. Biologists and botanists deal, in fact, with values. Ecologists are through and through concerned with values. And, of course, the same is true about values relating to individual human life. Surely all this undercuts the judgment John Gray and others make about the obsolescence of the teleological outlook.[23]

Whenever the life in question is extremely complex and individualized, the values involved will match this complexity and individuality. Can this individualist strain of the present position be defended? We shall attend to that task later, in Chapter 2, when we discuss classical individualism. Suffice it to say for now that we may find the Aristotelian metaphysics fully compatible with individualism if we are convinced, along with Emerson Buchanan, that "in identifying *ousia* (Being) with τὸ τί ἦν εἶναι ['what it is for each thing to exist'], Aristotle is asserting that the fundamental reality on which everything else depends is the existence of the individual."[24] It seems to me that the puzzles about cultural relativism, the apparent subjectivity of value judgments, historical relativism, and changes of values based on technological advances, can be explained by reference to the fundamental individuation of human life we witness around us. If we consider that even some slight variation in circumstance can alter the way a fundamental ethical principle should be applied, we can gain some glimpse of both the appeal and possible refutation of relativism. But, at some risk, the story (like most stories) can be better told without sliding into unnecessary complication.

As I suggested earlier, the mere reality of values is not yet sufficient as a basis for ethics or morality. That reality does, though, secure a ground for standards of judging good and bad (not yet 'moral' good and bad). The rest requires the addition of free choice. Only if the standards of good and bad can be freely adhered to or evaded does the framework for ethical or moral standards of right and wrong emerge. And if, as I argued briefly earlier, it makes sense to attribute to human beings free choice, then with respect to their own living they can be free to adhere to or to evade standards of good conduct.

It seems, then, that what has always been necessary for a rational conceptualization of moral values is a different idea of the kind of causality that may be found in reality.[25] This causality might be dubbed 'self-determination' or 'self-causation', despite the paradoxical sound of these terms. The idea is that due to its particular nature, the human being is free to motivate its own behavior, to govern its conduct. And because human life is open to evaluation — it can be a

good or a bad human life—individuals can have personal responsibility for conducting themselves well or badly. They can be morally
good or evil.

This is not the place to begin spelling out a doctrine of ethical
values. One vital feature of such a doctrine needs to be explained,
however. This will be of interest because it has served as a source of
considerable controversy for those seeking for ethical standards.

INDIVIDUALISM VERSUS COLLECTIVISM

When we consider ethical values that are to guide human conduct
(especially in social and political contexts), we can begin by considering whether a conception of human nature might help in identifying
them. It is reasonable to suppose that evaluating what people do is
dependent on knowing what they are. In most cases of evaluating
something, we need first of all to know what the thing is—a peach
tree is a good one of its kind if it fulfills the requirements that we expect from peach trees. And that depends on what the nature of a
peach tree is. The same seems to hold for both natural objects and
artifacts—for deer, bears, crows, or for knives, cups, or computer
mainframes. Whether this approach is ultimately sound in connection with ethics is not at issue here. All I am focusing on is whether it
is reasonable to expect it to yield standards of evaluation. And at first
blush there seems to be good reason for such expectation.

For many who in recent periods of history have attempted to
develop such a (naturalist) approach to standards of ethics, what
seemed to be most sensible was a collectivist idea. Marx immediately
comes to mind. If one believes, as he did for much of his career, that
"the human essence is the true collectivity of man,"[26] one will conceive of human values accordingly. One will usually be a socialist. So
called 'humanists', the most scientifically-minded of those who still
deign to embark on moral judgment and criticism, have either followed Marx or have embraced other types of collectivism.[27]

In contrast, if we conceive of human nature as individualists do,
believing that the human essence is the true individuality of man,
then a different system of political values will emerge. Of course,
whichever conception one invokes will influence other areas of
values as well, but for now let us focus on politics.

Why would it be more appropriate to conceive of the human
'essence' as the individuality of man? Mainly because what

distinguishes human beings from other living beings is the form of consciousness which they possess. And this form of consciousness—namely rational, conceptual consciousness—implies the capacity for original thought, for initiation of intellectual activity, for creativity, for volition. The human individual alone is capable of initiating original ideas—groups can only form the forum and fertilization for this. The mind of a human being is the mind of an individual. It does not operate alone, without props, without society, of course. I am not talking about a solipsistic mind. It does, however, perform creative acts, for which the individual brain is a necessary prerequisite. As John Hospers observes, "It is individual human beings who are born, live, enjoy, suffer, and die . . . . groups as such do not live, love or suffer . . . ."[28]

MORAL AND POLITICAL VALUES

At this point moral and political values arise. The creative mind is different from the largely passive minds of other living beings. Animals may 'think' a bit, but they do this only if prompted to do so, usually by eager researchers. The distinctive consciousness of human beings also raises the unique possibility that we can act (morally) wrongly, something not possible for animals. So our values may be neglected by us. And we can go on to cover up this neglect—we can cheat, lie, act cowardly, unjustly, imprudently, cruelly, dishonorably. All these are possibilities unique to human life, stemming from our creative role in governing our existence.

When we consider that much of human life is spent among others, the life-sustaining, life-enhancing, life-developing forms of activity available to us will mostly concern social moral principles. Our laws may be conceived of as our attempts to come to some sound agreement about our different, sometimes even mutually obstructive conceptions of how to live in one anothers' company. Not just any attempts will do, however, which is why morality must be a guide to public and economic policy.

We have here then the somewhat unusual though not wholly original suggestion that science and values are not in conflict, and that given the distinctive nature of human life, morality and politics involve principles which will enhance rather than defeat our lives. Thus values, including moral values, are a special sort of facts. If this is a sound approach, we can be sure that moral values are just as crucial to a successful treatment of our tasks in life as are other disciplines requiring understanding and competence. The fact that in the field of morals there is likely to be far more disagreement than in the rest does not prove that the field is inherently ambiguous, mysterious or bogus. All it suggests is that when it comes to tough personal choices, people will do a lot of hopping and skipping to evade reality. And this is another fact that seems to make better sense within the present framework.

The intellectual terrain is now open to explore natural rights, that is, principles of human conduct within communities, arising from an understanding of human nature. The next step that will take us closer to natural rights involves discussing ethics: standards of conduct for human beings in general, within or apart from their social or community existence. What I call 'classical egoism' provides this standard. Once we have examined this view, we can then turn to the question of natural rights. I argue that classical egoism fills the gap left by Nozick in the moral foundations of libertarianism.

FROM CLASSICAL EGOISM TO NATURAL RIGHTS

[In] ancient moral philosophy the duties of human life were treated of
as subservient to the happiness and perfection of human life. But when
moral, as well as natural philosophy, came to be taught only as subservient to theology, the duties of human life were treated of as chiefly
subservient to the happiness of a life to come. In the ancient philosophy
the perfection of virtue was represented as necessarily productive to the
person who possessed it, of the most perfect happiness in this life. In the
modern philosophy it was frequently represented as almost always in-
consistent with any degree of happiness in this life, and heaven was to
be earned by penance and mortification, not by the liberal, generous,
and spirited conduct of a man. By far the most important of all the different branches of philosophy became in this manner by far the most
corrupted.

— Adam Smith, *The Wealth of Nations*

EGOIST ETHICS TO LIBERTARIAN POLITICS

It is often noted that the natural-rights doctrine of John Locke and
later the similarly individualistic political economy of Adam Smith
rest on a type of egoistic or individualistic philosophy of human life.
Both Locke and Smith defend a political system founded on the basic
rights to life, liberty, and property of every person. Locke's argument
rests on a view of human nature as initially free and equal, from the
moral viewpoint, as well as on the idea that each seeking his own
wellbeing is proper to all. Smith's general line of reasoning, put differently, invokes our natural inclination to serve our own wellbeing.

Since Locke and Smith, many have taken it as a defect that
natural rights and the capitalist economy characteristically linked
with it, depend on a kind of egoism. Once again, Karl Marx is
perhaps the best known among these. He disparagingly remarks, for
example, that "The right of man to property is the right to enjoy his
possessions and dispose of the same arbitrarily, without regard for

other men, independently from society, the right of selfishness."[1]

Still, there remain defenders of capitalism who, in arguing mainly for its economic superiority, continue to invoke some form of egoism, usually of a psychological sort, which holds that persons are innately motivated to pursue their pleasure or to strive to satisfy their desires (maximize their utilities). Milton Friedman, for example, says that

> . . . every individual serves his own private interest . . . . The great Saints of history have served their 'private interest' just as the most money grubbing miser has served his interest. The *private interest* is whatever it is that drives an individual.[2]

While this view is a bit obscure—it leaves the concept "private interest" vacuous—it does remind us of the commonly-held idea that everyone is really pursuing his or her selfish interest, that no one can avoid doing this, which is the legacy of Hobbes's psychological egoism.

A different contemporary defense of the system of natural individual negative rights to life, liberty, and property, however, relies directly on an ethical egoism. Rand has argued that we ought all to pursue our rational self-interest, as a matter of a primary moral responsibility, from which every other moral principle and judgment gains its justification.[3]

Natural-rights theory, which largely undergirds the idea of a just political and legal system within the Western liberal tradition, requires some type of egoism. Which type, if any, is actually promising is in dispute. What is undisputed is that a form of individualism is fundamental to at least one prominent idea of a just community.

I will argue here that one version of egoism is indeed both realistic and morally satisfying, thus combining what practical political thinkers and those concerned with upholding human ideals have demanded of a sound ethical foundation for a human community. This ethical egoism is unusual and unfamiliar since it has a classical pedigree (drawing on, but not in full accord with, Aristotle's philosophy, including his ethics). At least it is not familiar in the sense of being widely promulgated by theorists and moralists. It may, however, be popular in the sense that many acting human beings may recognize in it what they believe to be reasonable and what they may well be acting on, if not from conviction then at least from common sense. It will be useful to examine the case for what may be called a classical ethical egoism or individualism.

First, here is a brief sketch of the argument: We as human individuals are responsible for *doing well at living our lives*. This, when understood, implies a system of moral and political principles. It implies, morally, that each person should aspire to live rationally as a human individual and, politically, that regarding their chosen conduct, everyone must be left free from, and should seek protection against, intrusions by others. Each person, in short, must be left with a rightful, defensible sphere of authority to make his or her own way in life — for example, play it safe or take risks, develop or falter, stay apart from others or join with them when this is mutually agreeable. All this rests on a conception of ethics as a firmly-based yet contextual system of guidelines required by human beings because they lack automatic, built-in (instinctual) prompters for how to carry on with their lives successfully. In what follows it will also be argued that the human self ought to be understood along not Hobbesian but Aristotelian lines. Then the egoism that emerges will prove to be the best and indeed most noble ethical system on which to ground a sound politics.

Some defend the capitalist political-economic system on utilitarian or pragmatic grounds or, somewhat more promisingly, on the basis of the requirements of morality itself, never mind what moral system is correct. This last approach saves us the trouble of having to commit ourselves to some particular moral system. And indeed this approach draws its appeal from being able to do just that, namely, to avoid specific ethical commitment. In a community that aims to make room for innumerable forms of human life, different purposes and aspirations, life-styles, religions, ideologies, and priorities, it seems to be almost incongruous to consider the idea of a common ethical framework. But if one leaves politics morally groundless, politics will reflect this in its amoralism, in lacking legitimacy and, in particular, the moral grounds for both its intellectual and international defense against competing doctrines and systems. And, as Quentin Skinner notes in his Harvard Lecture 'The Paradoxes of Political Liberty', "We are very poor guardians of our own liberties." He referred to a "minimalist view of civic obligation" and objected to the "dangerous privatization" of certain values of Western civilization.[4] And it is not only the liberal social order that requires moral grounding. Human life is such that we require some general confidence in the righteousness of our way of life. We need, in short, to know that the way we live is right, reasonably true to the standards by which human beings ought to conduct themselves. The reason for this is that human beings, unlike other living things, lack the automatic guidelines of instincts. Human beings must choose on some basis, and they need to have confidence in the basis that guides them, lest they find that when someone challenges their goals, purposes, or previous choices, they collapse under the pressure. A being guided by ideas cannot long continue without some assurance that those ideas are sound, especially not if it wishes to have a considerable degree of autonomy in its decision-making processes. In short, a more or less democratic society, in which everyone is responsible for the system, requires widespread moral confidence in that system — the sense that the system itself is a good one.

Why would a free society, especially, seem to need a reconsideration of its moral foundation? First, under some conceptions of morality no negative rights or liberty rights could emerge at all. For example, altruism, utilitarianism, consequentialism, and conventionalism disallow basic negative or liberty rights. They do not admit them in the sense in which we are interested in rights, namely as politically inalienable, fundamental. Focussing as these value-systems do on valued results (either of direct action or of agreements), they tend to omit from consideration freedom of choice, individual or personal responsibility for good conduct.[5] Such moralities ultimately amount to theories of value or of the good. They fail, in the main, to distinguish between the good and the morally good.

Other, more deontological ethics stress natural duties, thus making freedom rights or negative rights wholly subordinate to some logically or conceptually prior principles, the fulfillment of which may involve violation of negative rights. Here is where John Rawls's intuitionist contractarian morality is unsatisfactory as a defense of human liberty. Even James Buchanan's rendition, which seems to support negative human liberty, begs some crucial questions.[6] (We will see later, in connection with an argument of Gilbert Harman's, how this undercuts the free system.) Considerations of basic principles ultimately control politics and law. Stress cases — for instance, a proposal to institute selective rent control, which violates property rights, in times of soaring rents — may tempt a utilitarian or intuitionist to abridge or even violate individual negative rights.

It is my view that classical egoism is a sound system of morality, regardless of whether or not it supports negative natural rights. Ethics is conceptually prior to politics, as is metaphysics to epistemology. While I am doubtful that any argument could persuade me to deny the vital importance of negative liberty in human social life, if classical egoism were in some way to require its abandonment, then perhaps the libertarian political stance would have to be given up first. Ethics, in short, is prior to politics, since the question 'How should I conduct myself?' is prior to the question 'How should *we* conduct ourselves in one another's society?' In my view, however, the self-development of every person as a rational being is not possible in a society in which some have authority to regiment the lives of others.

Egoism is, then, important both because it is a sound system and because it handles hard cases in law and politics. In cases in which courts have decided whether one has a right to one's life and should strive to sustain it, within reason, the courts have often sided with the ethical-egoistic line of reasoning. In general, hard cases are the kind in which judges or legislatures need to invoke moral considerations. Especially when rights appear to conflict, moral considerations must be invoked to guide the law. While such considerations need not promise geometrically precise resolutions, it is reasonable to expect that what emerges from disciplined ethical reflection will be of ultimately greater consequence than what is derived from law or politics alone. (The Nuremberg trials are a good illustration of this point.)

Some believe that conflicts at this level can be dealt with by way of intuition or by reference to general utility, or the public interests. Yet even to learn what these concepts mean and whether they are decisive, some value theory is necessary, despite the fact that in practical politics the *grounds* for evaluative judgments are rarely touched on. There is little confidence in the source of evaluative judgments, even though it is continually necessary to make them. We are preached at interminably about 'the public interest', 'the common good', 'the general welfare', 'the decent society', 'the great society', and so on — all phrases that go begging for some clear understanding. The bottom line seems to be, as John Rawls affirmed, that we must push forward in ethics even if we have no general theory that backs up our proceedings.[7] Intuitionism accommodates our rudderlessness.

The appeal of intuitionism lies in the quite correct commonsense view that on any particular occasion there is really little chance for anyone to consult a comprehensive general theory. Yet it would hardly do to claim that there is no need for physics, since when we build bridges, homes, or ballistic missiles, we don't at every moment stop to check whether what we do accords with some written-out law of nature. The need for general guidelines in conduct does not refer to a need for some constantly-available book of rules, but for a sound educational grounding, a sound upbringing, and a sound background which may all need consulting when problems arise in certain areas that we aren't prepared to deal with via our well-honed and sophisticated automatic system of ideas. Tacit knowledge only *seems* mysterious because it is not constantly being entertained in any self-conscious, deliberate fashion.

Finally, some have argued that an egoistically-based natural-rights system is really utilitarian at heart.[8] The meager truth in this claim is that classical egoism contains consequentialist or teleological features. Acceptable principles of social life must be seen to be beneficial, must produce good results in one's life. But the framework is very different here from the sort that utilitarians rely on, because of the centrality of the element of moral choice or agency in this teleological approach to ethics and politics.

A BIRD'S-EYE VIEW
OF CLASSICAL EGOISM

Ethical egoism is often used in elementary ethics textbooks as illustration of an unsuccessful, even bogus, ethical doctrine. The reason, in my view, is that the idea of the human self that is involved in the standard versions of the theory is abhorrent: a purely desire-satisfying, crass 'individualist' who has no principles and cares only for achieving whimsical, idiosyncratic private goals. When we speak of the standard versions of ethical egoism the only difference between the 'economic man' of neo-classical economics and the ethical view is that the latter seems to admit that human beings can choose to be egoistic. The 'economic man' approach was already quoted from Milton Friedman. An even more pointed statement comes from another economist of great eminence, George Stigler:

> Man is eternally a utility-maximizer — in his home, in his office (be it public or private), in his church, in his scientific work — in short, everywhere.[9]

This is not the form of egoism capitalism has to rest upon, even if it is slightly modified to allow for the agent's choice whether or not to practice it.

In place of the Hobbesian idea of the 'atomistic', isolated human self, the classical conception of the individual — suggested initially by Aristotle's self-sufficient, self-loving human being — is invoked. I mean the idea that human beings are thinking, choosing animals who can flourish only by relying on considered action. This idea seems to me to be far more sensible than the Hobbesian, much closer to what we know about human beings.

To secure a foundation for the individualism that capitalism rests on, we need to discuss certain metaphysical and epistemological issues. The most important of the former is the problem of causality. If a Humean version of causality is right, then agent-causality is hardly possible, and ethics, in presupposing human self-respon-sibility, is a bogus concern, on the order of astrology or phrenology.

The first thing to consider is whether causality permits diversity. It would then be possible to consider *persons* (not their wills) as gen-uine causes of their behavior. This would secure a basis for both a naturalistic ethical standard and individual responsibility. As to the former, if we learn that human beings are self-determined in a given respect, this will figure into what we take to be human nature one possible source of the moral standards they should invoke in their choices of behavior. As for the latter, the reason is that, without the possibility of self-determined human conduct, no moral sphere is possible, only a sphere of values which could not be ethical, moral, or political values.

For someone to be morally (or politically) required to act in cer-tain ways, he or she needs to be free to choose whether or not to engage in the appropriate conduct. (This is the main source of the criminal law's insistence that a culpable criminal act be carried out in a state of non-compulsion, volitionally.) The idea that persons are capable of initiating their actions, of genuine free choice, is essential to a moral conception of human personal and social life. The classical individualist or egoist ethics underlying natural rights and the cor-ollary economic system of capitalism rest on the idea of human be-ings as essentially individuals who are capable of choosing their con-duct within a significant sphere of their lives, based on a standard of good applicable to them as human individuals.

We have already seen that a reduction of all causal relations to the mechanical sort is not required by what had been thought to require it, namely, the metaphysics of classical mechanistic physicalism (or by Hume's mentalistic analysis of cause). A different view is justified, namely, one that ties causes to the variety of kinds and types of beings—with their varied causal powers. This view of causality is more consistent with contemporary science, especially neurophysics.

In this chapter we will not concern ourselves with the metaphysical issues but, rather, with the specifically ethical or moral topics. In particular, we will explore whether classical egoism (or individualism) offers a successful moral perspective. Keeping in mind that the criteria of success are themselves controversial, I propose that an ethical theory is a bona fide candidate if it does not contradict the purposes for which ethics exists, if it at least provides a plausible answer to the question 'How should I conduct myself (as the human individual I am)?' It is successful if it answers this question in the best available way—if it solves the problems of ethics more consistently and more coherently than do other candidates.

WHY DOES EGOISM SEEM ABHORRENT?

Why is egoism or individualism found morally objectionable by so many who have discussed it, even to the point that, in moral philosophy, the position is often treated as an instance of anti-morality? Indeed, some moral philosophers define the moral point of view by contrasting it with egoism.

The skepticism about egoism (not just as a sound ethics but even as a bona fide ethical theory) rests, in large part, on arguments which attack the dominant or Hobbesian egoist conception of human nature. This ascribes to egoism a specific conception of the human self, and identifies as egoistic a system of norms which can be derived from that conception. Critics often assume that any egoism must rest on a Hobbesian idea of the self, which they judge to be inherently amoral or even anti-moral, atomistic, and anti-social.

Classical egoism, based on a neo-Aristotelian metaphysics, is not so vulnerable to the standard criticisms. In the revised classical egoist position, the basic principle of morality arises from a consideration of what will guide human beings toward living *their* lives successfully, properly, and thus in the end to *their* benefit, since ethics is seen here to arise in response to the question, 'How should I live my life?'

There is no pretense that, in order to make it successful, egoism can or need be turned into altruism, or egalitarianism, or even utilitarianism. But I do plan to argue that if the human individual or ego is understood correctly, the idea that everyone ought to strive to benefit himself or herself first and foremost in life will not imply that a person's egoistic conduct will result in substantial antisocial, avaricious, callous, or deceptive behavior, as is argued by critics of the standard form of egoism.[10]

Certainly many contemporary moral philosophers hold that the dominant concern of morality lies in determining how one should treat other persons. Restricting the moral to the socially relevant is certainly not self-evidently justified. Philosophers as diverse as Aristotle and Kant disagreed with such a restriction. Standards of an ethically good life will address the question of how one should treat other persons, and some of the questions that arise about conduct toward others will seem at times to center on conflicts between self-interest and the interest of others. But that may not be the best understanding of how morality applies to social life, especially if we consider that the alternative of participating in society is itself one we all face and must decide by reference to ethical standards. This last is just what many post-Kantian ethical theorists deny, mainly because they assume that in some sense self-interested conduct is indeed, as the economic-man model would have it, automatic, as 'natural' as our breathing and the circulation of our blood. The fact that this position presupposes, and developed out of, a metaphysics of mechanistic physicalism does not appear to concern these philosophers. And the reason for this is that in our time it is deemed best (for example by Rawls), to keep ethics strictly independent of metaphysical considerations.

Classical egoism does not address conflicts among different persons by pitting self-interest against self-interest — or, more appropriately, human being against human being. The conflict-of-interest idea is question begging. It assumes that a successful case has already been made for that morality which discounts self-interest as a fundamental standard. And, of course, the concept 'self-interest' is itself problematic. Just what is in one's self-interest is an open issue. Maybe being self-interested is always moral. It might never be in one's genuine self-interest to do the morally wrong thing. In any case, no such loaded sense of 'morally right', for instance what leads to social cohesion, should be adopted at the outset. It clearly flies in the face of Socrates's promising idea, in the *Phaedo* that rational self-interests will coincide: "Just follow my old recipe, my friends: do yourselves concern yourselves with your own true self-interest; then you will oblige me, and mine, and yourselves too . . . . " (115b).

With some of the familiar anti-egoist considerations set aside, let us consider a defensible version of egoism. Since the task here will be to present a theory of morality, it will be necessary to proceed by indicating why this framework of morality makes better sense than do others. In this way, egoism emerges as a better ethical theory than most ethicists believe. Egoism also appears less difficult than one might imagine to reconcile with the concerns of those who opt for other views because they find egoism antisocial, callous, anti-communitarian.

Hobbesian Versus Classical Egoism

The point of the term 'classical egoism' is simple: underlying the egoism of Hobbes and the tradition which follows him, we find a conception of human nature that is reductionist and thus atomistic. The tradition ultimately rejects the objectivity of the classification 'human'. In this tradition each person is ultimately, actually, an aggregation of bits of matter-in-motion, ergo, a pulsating self-aggrandizing blob of matter pursuing — by following the laws of motion — the task of survival.

More developed versions add certain nuances to this idea, but at heart the story isn't changed. Individuals, the 'human' selves or egos, have no specific nature but each is a sort of bare particular. The human individual is not a determinate instance of the objectively established abstract category 'human' but belongs within the human species as a matter of convention, without the benefit of a firm, conclusive justification for that classification. In short, the kind of thing something is taken as is determined by way of a convention or agreement.

This tradition regards the struggle for self-preservation and aggrandizement as central human-character traits. But that fails to distinguish human individuals from other beings, since everything in the universe posseses such a trait. Within this view human nature is the same as the rest of nature. The reductive materialist viewpoint sees all of nature as the same. Nature is composed through and through of matter in motion and human nature is no different. There is no fundamental difference between the kind of entities human beings are and what other things are, except as that has been established by convention. Human beings are not members of a natural kind.

From this tradition we derive a conception of individuality, selfhood or ego, which is not anchored in any firm and stable (human) nature. Thus when by Hobbesian egoistic ethics something is judged to be right, it must be viewed entirely independently of any firm, objective, and independent *universal* standard, and depends wholly on individual (or collectively agreed-to) wants, desires, or preferences.

And here is the rub: Since a collectively agreed-to want or desire can always be changed by someone opting out of the agreement or because the agreement is challenged as unsound, unwise, undesired, or risky it does not provide a rationally binding standard. The updated 'rational' egoistic ethics — still based on an idea of 'rationality' as calculating means to reach preset ends — may add the proviso that 'egoistic' include a long-range perspective on our goals. But in the end this, too, makes little difference since the standard rests again on goals set by the agent, quite subjectively, which makes the standards themselves arbitrary. When co-ordinated with others in a social setting, they suffice only with the aid of effective sanctions, not as rationally persuasive and independently binding guidelines.

The main problem which a Hobbesian egoistic ethics runs up against is that it cannot be reconciled with our general notions about what social ethics involves — non-calculating loyalty, generosity, good will, compassion, and so on. All such virtues could find merely a forced expression in this ethics. Why would anyone be generous on such egoistic grounds, other than because some overt or hidden purpose might be served by it? The same with all the other virtues bearing on social life. The impression would persist from this egoist 'ethics' that the concern of one person for another, even in the limited degree expressed by respecting another's right to life or liberty, could not be based on anything more than a (subjective) advantage, based on idiosyncratic personal preference.[11]

Close personal ties such as genuine love between friends would for Hobbesian egoists be impossible except as those might be anchored in the friend's instrumental or pragmatic value. Here such egoism reduces to a somewhat robust form of hedonism. As John Rawls says, as if it were a self-evident truth, "egoists are incapable of feeling resentment and indignation. If either of two egoists deceives the other and this is found out, neither of them has a ground for complaint." Nor could there be "bonds of friendship and mutual trust" among egoists.[12]

Derek Parfit's recent and important criticism of egoism accepts this narrow conception of the self. Self-interest must necessarily aim at certain future consequences bearing on the unique and essentially same person one assumes one will be in the future. Parfit, of course, intends to deprive this form of egoism of its foundation, namely, of the necessarily stable individual who preserves his or her identity through time. But suppose that the self-interest of an individual rests on abiding by a standard of conduct — rationality perhaps — rather than on serving some future self's desires, wants, or interests (concerns). Suppose that the ego or self to be concerned about divides into a group of near-enough others — in short, by 'ego' something other than a single, unitary, identical-over-time being might be meant, just as Parfit argues. On those rare (logically possible?) occasions where personal identity does not extend through time and one may 'become several' in time, the egoistic conduct consists in doing what is rational. That, in turn, must take into consideration what the individual is most likely to turn out to be in the future. And if he or she is to 'become several', then rational conduct will have to adjust to that prospect, whatever it is.[13]

An ethical egoism that might have a chance of success must be clearly distinguished from the sort discussed by most prominent academic moral philosophers.[14] The term 'classical' aids in this by relocating ethical egoism in the tradition of Aristotelian metaphysical and meta-ethical thought. In that tradition the human individual is viewed differently from the way it is viewed within the Hobbesian framework.[15] (Of course, there is dispute as to whether an Aristotelian metaphysics makes individuality even possible. For now I proceed as if that possibility had been established — that is, as if the idea of an objectively identifiable human nature and the notion of the essential individuality of each human being were fully compatible.)

In reply to Rawls we might begin by noting what Aristotle said on the subject of self-love:

> . . . if a man were always anxious that he himself, above all things, should act justly, temperately, or in accordance with any other of the virtues, and in general were always to try to secure for himself the honorable course, no one will call such a man a lover of self or blame him.

But such a man would seem more than the other a lover of self; at all events he assigns to himself the things that are noblest and best and gratifies the most authoritative element in himself and in all things obeys this; and just as a city or any other systematic whole is most properly identified with the most authoritative element in it, so is a man; and therefore the man who loves this and gratifies it is most of all of a lover of self.[16]

This is the first clue I wish to advance toward a better understanding of classical egoism. But it may be asked, Why call this 'egoism' in the first place? Because in the end the ultimate beneficiary of moral conduct is the agent, in that he or she will be the best person he or she can be. The point of morality or ethics is to provide human beings with a guide to doing well in life, to living properly, to conducting themselves rightly.

WHY MORALITY IN THE FIRST PLACE?

We have already touched briefly on why morality should matter to us at all. Morality or ethics identifies the standards for living properly or well. This purpose immediately suggests that ethics must be understood as in some sense an egoistic system. The reason is that living, for human beings, is, at a crucial juncture, an individual task. (Both Rawls and Nozick begin with the thesis that some kind of self-interested motive plays a vital role in the determination of the nature of a just society. Rawls's participants in the original position make self-interested choices that generate the correct rules of justice. Nozick assumes individual rights but then explains the emergence of the state by reference to the self-interested choices of those in the state of nature.)

A human being is by nature an individual, a being whose life is crucially in the power of the actual person one is. Whatever level of capacity for self-determination one possesses, such self-determination is an integral part of his or her being human. As a rational animal, a living being with the distinctive capacity to engage in conceptual thought and the need to be guided by such thought in its conduct, human beings instantiate their very humanity in their individual *choice* to be attentive to their lives.

Of course this is an emergent aspect of a person, one that needs to be sustained and developed initially by others (society), but there is evidence of this individualist role in life from the earliest stage of human existence. The formation of ideas, and co-ordination of behavior, the planning of life—this is distinctive of human animals. They behave thoughtfully, and this fact about them is inescapable. This is true, of course, only of those not crucially incapacitated. And it is irrelevant that some signs of such conceptualization are evident in other kinds of animals—their successful living is generally not dependent on exercising such a capacity. Moreover, borderline cases are not decisive.

Ethics is part of human life because such life embodies a fundamental role for a system or code of *standards*. It is something we need *as human beings*, given our nature as free and independent living agents (vis-à-vis what we *do*). We must choose to act, and we need some guideline or source for distinguishing between better and worse alternatives in life. Whereas the rest of the animal world can rely on instincts or innate drives, we cannot.[17]

True enough, some people appear to get along perfectly well without reference to moral standards. They appear to be amoral, unconcerned with questions of moral right and wrong. Here, too, however, interpretations can differ. When seriously considered, only sociopaths seem to fit this characterization. Even in such cases some conception of rightness appears to be indispensable, because for all human beings, insofar as they are not driven by forces independent of their wills, choices made from among a variety of alternatives require a system of ranking. Just because some seem to be choosing randomly this does not mean that they are not guided by a standard of sorts, even if in the end it turns out to be an inappropriate standard. Its inappropriateness, however, could show its results in certain conflicts that the person experiences. The racist who nevertheless truly respects some members of the race he regards as generally inferior will likely find himself experiencing inner conflict, for example, when he insists that his friend be admitted to a club that is barred to those of his friend's race. Likewise the thief who wants to insist that what he has stolen not be taken from him by his fellow thieves. For a rational being such conflicts are debilitating; they are not as a rule productive of his or her particular wellbeing, since they create inconsistencies in the way one believes one may conduct oneself. If it is a condition of human success that one exercise one's faculty of reason, one's rational capacity, in a competent, skillful, unimpaired fashion, then the kinds of conflicts that are involved in immorality will rob one of the chance for flourishing as a human being. No doubt survival is possible under such conditions, just as it is possible with a broken leg or a bad heart, but in a similar way, moral shortcomings are debilitating, undermining one's prospects for maximum happiness.

The freedom to choose, the moral independence at issue here, deals with the fact that no one or nothing drives or moves a person to take many of his or her most significant actions — nor is anything or anyone else responsible for them. Faced with such a state — as far as we know unique to human beings — persons require moral standards or what appear to be substitutes for them (for instance, pragmatic rule of thumb, such as 'Go with the flow'). And when they try to do without a consistent moral system, or when they inconsistently apply it, they are very likely to suffer adversity in their lives. Such conduct thwarts their human flourishing.

Let me now present some of the naturalist meta-ethical grounds for the classical-egoist position I am defending here. This will be useful because such a base offers some hope of reaching agreement among potential members of human communities. The approach to identifying basic rights by reference to human nature may face problems, but not problems like those faced by intuitionism or those based on religious faith. In nature there is at least some prospect of finding common ground — barring deep-seated skepticism stemming from the desire for absolute, timeless certainty. And in political matters this prospect is especially important, since the truths of politics have to be accessible to all manner of persons, not merely to members of some order or sect.

I begin with what we have already discussed in Chapter 1, namely the idea of distinct, though not necessarily mutually exclusive, ontological domains, such as the physical, chemical, social, musical, and ethical realms. The idea parallels what is often expressed in terms of the idea of categories, only in the present instance it is the metaphysical side of the distinctiveness of types that is emphasized. Reality exhibits both monistic and pluralistic features. On the one hand the fundamental, integrative principles of the laws of identity, noncontradiction, and excluded middle (as ontological facts of existence) unite all of existence into one realm. On the other hand the indefiniteness of what must exist opens the possibility for unlimited types and kinds of concrete beings.

Second, human existence suggests a distinctive ontological domain, different from all others. All animate beings face death (in the biological sense at least), but human beings can also choose either to reject or to pursue life and this introduces the distinctive domain of self-determination. We should now recall that ethics rests on the need to concern ourselves with a good human *life*. There are factors and processes that can contribute to, while others detract from, good human life. But because people are self-determining beings, they constitute an essential element for purposes of establishing whether they will promote a good or a bad life. Here is where the ontological shift from goodness to moral goodness or virtue occurs. A claim that factors suitable or good for life exist applies to nonhuman living beings; the claim that one is individually responsible for factors that are good for life does not (as far as we know).

The domain of moral responsibility is ontologically distinct. This accounts, in part, for the fact that moral judgments can be true without anyone actually following them in life (which would give phenomenal or empirical evidence for such conduct), at any moment of such judgment. A moral judgment (for example, that one should conduct oneself justly) can be true when many do not so conduct themselves — unlike a claim pertaining to a (sound) principle of chemistry which, even while it isn't always instantiated clearly, is never violated.[18] The element of choice unique to human existence can make this difference something that our moral knowledge and our account of how we obtain it will have to take into account. Any possible 'correspondence' between moral truth and the facts of human morality will thus be very different from such correspondence between, say, a truth of structural mechanics and the facts of the behavior of physical masses.

As to the 'is-ought' dichotomy, once the above perspective is taken as the proper framework from which to approach the issue, we can take account of the fact that a human individual is metaphysically free to choose to pursue living. This, in turn, must mean — keeping in mind the earlier points about what 'must' means in these kinds of nonformal cases — that such a choice implies that the life of a certain kind of being has been elected for pursuit. Inescapably, a human being can choose between human existence or no existence, that is all. Since human life at its best contains indefinite possibilities, the choice is not a limiting one. Yet, on the very broad issue of choosing either a human life or not choosing such a life, there is no other alternative for individual persons. And the choice of the former implies certain very broad limits spelled out by morality. (This is where existentialism is partly correct and partly wrong; the impossibility of escaping human freedom points to this fundamental fact of the nature of human life.)

Life is the ontological base of values — it is always a life of some kind that some course of conduct, or condition, or item is good or bad for. The concept of 'good' cannot rationally be divorced from the phenomenon of life. Unless the phenomena of sustenance, growth, and effort to persist in the state of living be taken as the base, we cannot make conceptual sense of the idea that something is good or bad for some being. So viewed, a concrete or factual basis for knowledge of values is available, leaving various intuitionist, or revelatory ideas of 'good' theoretically inferior to it. And the issue here is not that some uses of the term 'good' or 'value' may not fit within this analysis of the meaning of 'good' but that the most complete and consistent analysis ties goodness to the fact of life, so that those uses not consistent with this analysis must be viewed with suspicion.

If one chooses to live, this choice implies (in an open-ended sense) that one will pursue the means or requirements of one's life. Starting with the grounding of value in life, and adding the choice a human being can make to live, we can appreciate the (tacit) commitment made to take action that will enhance or realize the values associated with one's human life. In other words, from having chosen the objectively good life of the kind of being one is, we can derive the (moral) commitment to pursue conduct that will enhance one's own human life. (This may be likened to the taking of a professional oath on entering medicine or teaching. The choice expressed by the oath commits one to the ethics of the profession.)

If a human being is a rational animal, the individual human being's choice to live implies the choice to conduct (the individual's life) rationally, consistently, in line with the facts of reality — including one's nature as a rational, biological organism and the particular individual one is. For human individuals this is the sort of life that is, in the most general and universally applicable terms, rationally the highest value. And because in the case of individual human beings that value must be pursued by choice — "reason is but choosing", to quote Milton — to lead this kind of life is to lead a *morally* good life.

The 'is-ought' issue is not so problematic here, granting the above account of morality, because moral truth is a type or category of factual truth. Morality is 'instrumental', in a fundamental sense, by facilitating the kind of life implied by one's choice to embark on one's (human) life. Ethics spells out the general facts of how individuals, groups, and their various activities and institutions, will (most probably) contribute to the value of their human life processes. (We may model this on facts in the fields of engineering or medicine.)

It may be objected that the present analysis makes the morally good into a what some contemporary moral philosohers pejoratively call a merely 'prudential' good.

By 'prudential' is usually meant that a putative ethical system consists of principles of conduct that are instrumental or productive of a desired form of life. This contrasts with categorical or deontological moral principles, ones pertaining primarily to the quality of the intention or will underlying actions. But this post-Kantian preference for a *bona fide* morality consisting of purely deontological principles seems to me unjustified. (In Kant it made sense only because of the significance of the noumenal/phenomenal distinction in Kantian metaphysics and epistemology.) Accordingly, in response to the charge of prudentialism it will be necessary to bite the bullet. If a prudential type of ethics is what makes the best sense of the moral dimension of human life, why complain? No doubt, language exhibits numerous alternative attempts to make sense of 'morally good', yet the mere (even if widespread) wish to have a different, more 'elevated' or distinctive — some might say 'otherwordly' — account of morality does not suffice to invalidate an earthbound or realistically tenable account of it.

The human life process is not something arbitrary, indefinite. At bottom only one basic choice contains the moral commitment, namely, the choice to live rather than not to live one's individual human life.

Consider the conception of morality advanced in this book by analogy with principles of good health or perhaps good driving. In the latter case there are innumerable places to which one could quite unobjectionably be headed, yet some basic principles apply just as soon as one takes to the road. The principles do not issue in particular results. But they do issue in competent driving wherever one is headed. Although factors outside one's control can pose obstacles, even totally disrupt the task, these are beyond the management of anyone and the principles of competent driving are not identifiable by reference to such unforseeable matters. In ethics, too, we are concerned with principles of competent human living, and the end we seek may be very different, perhaps, for all of us. The major difference between the two cases is that for most of us driving is little more than a means to some end, quite often achievable by other means. This is not the case with living a human life. Moreover, one of the goals of the actions we take is to make the life we lead a good one, or, as the ancients might have put it, to achieve our happiness. The relationship between the value each person has chosen by choosing to live his or her human life and the principles adherence to which will result in the realization of that value, is not to be conceived as a mechanistic means/ends model, whereby the means can be separated from the ends (as in the driving/getting-there example). This is the truth in the ancient idea that virtue is its own reward, at least for an individual with moral integrity, who sustains his rational plan of living in all his conduct.

The main problem with illustrating this ethical approach is that although the goal sought by way of the moral life is the rational life of the individual, that itself admits of innumerable variety. Indeed, the evident variety of the sort of life that qualifies as perfectly decent tends to suggest moral relativism to most people. That in India a good person may live very differently from one in Cleveland, Ohio, or that in a Yorktown section of New York City a good person may carry on quite differently from the way one does in Greenwich Village, seems to be clear evidence of the hopelessness of finding some common standard of good. Only when we turn to certain despised forms of behavior, such as apartheid in South Africa, the extermination of Jews by Nazis, or the incarceration of dissident poets in the Soviet Union, does the idea of some general moral perspective begin to strike people as inviting.

There could be some basic principles of morality—some 'ought' judgments—whose truth could be demonstrated by reference to human nature (as it can be realized in most normal and stable circumstances)—for example, that human beings should be honest, productive, generous, independent, courageous, prudent, or temperate. Yet their specific application to differently situated human individuals might differ significantly from case to case. This could even require different ways of explaining them. Why should John tell the truth on this particular occasion, even though it may seem that so doing will have unwelcome results? In general, because for human beings to tell the truth is to keep in touch with reality, and to make their social interactions consistent with this project; and in particular, probably because, for example, although striving to achieve welcome results is itself a valued task or good, the value of achieving something that is welcome at the expense of honesty is seriously diminished while the results of dishonesty are demonstrably unwelcome for most human individuals. But this has to be filled in with the specifics or particular of John's case.

I will return to some objections to classical egoism and its foundations later in this chapter. Now, however, we need to turn to the more substantive elements of the position.

EGOISM REVISED

The egoist begins by observing that life is the source of all value. Egoism then predicates any further considerations of what standard one should live by on the fact that only for those who can choose, and have chosen, freely to pursue life are standards of value of *moral* concern. Further, egoism notes that the life that one chooses is necessarily a human life, one's own. The issue that arises next is what is implied in the choice to live one's human life. 'How should I (this particular *human* being) live my life?' To which the ethical egoist's answer is:

> To evaluate the alternatives facing one with respect to the (implicit) decision (or choice) to live one's life, one should invoke the criterion: 'Whatever will most effectively contribute to one's happiness (that is, success as a human individual).'

This answer, put a bit laboriously to satisfy our analytic purposes, means, in essence, that given that the life one has chosen to live is that of a human being, a rational animal, one ought to carry on one's life by considering its nature and its circumstances in a careful, sensible, rational fashion and guide oneself in the light of the results.

Why is that the right answer? Because it provides human beings with the best available means for conducting themselves successfully, coherently, without inherent complications (though not without sustained effort and attention). It satisfies 'ought implies can' by pointing at a feasible life goal.

An ethical theory is correct if it best serves the purpose such a theory has, namely, making it possible to solve all clearly identifiable (but not including all merely conceivable) problems within its area of concern. That is what makes not only an ethical but any theory the best among those advanced.

To tell which ethical theory is the best one — which is all we can ask for at any time — existing ethical systems would need to be fully compared and we would need to see which of them will serve human beings best in pursuing the human good. Before that we would need to determine what is the human good and even before that, what is the good?

This won't be attempted in full here. The discussion in Chapter 1 regarding the relationship between science and ethics must be kept in mind. Without it, many aspects of the present thesis would appear to be untenable.

Our central point in Chapter 1 was that a naturalist, scientifically consistent, conception of human life could make room for morality or ethics. By rejecting reductive, mechanical materialism in favor of a more plausible and supportable pluralistic naturalism, the emergence of a living being that can cause and has responsibility for its actions can be seen as compatible with modern science. At this point we need to supplement the discussion in Chapter 1 with the more sharply-focussed examination of the conception of value or goodness, as well as moral goodness, that is needed for embarking on a development of a substantive ethical framework.

The problem of 'good' arises in response to a concern with ranking in relation to some end, goal, or purpose. This is how value or good is tied to living, first of all, which is an end-oriented, goal-directed process. (This is what we found in our discussion in Chapter 1 when we considered Popper's explanation of the objectivity of values.) A good hunt, a good meal, a good pine tree, a good summer, a good business, and a good apple — all these rank a particular life-related matter along a continuum between the worst and the best of its kind. And the way something will be located on that continuum is determined by whether it is more or less fully in accordance with its nature as a certain kind of living being or as an artifact that pertains to some process of living. A good hunt must most consistently and precisely accord with the nature of hunting, and so on with a good meal, pine tree, summer, business, or apple. In each we are dealing with some ranking in terms of a natural (or assigned) end, goal, or purpose. And of course there is much controversy about a natural end.[18] But the main thrust of the idea can be grasped by reflecting on the way we might judge a certain species of sapling in a forest—to wit, by reference to how well it is doing as that kind of sapling. Here there is also a plain enough way to appreciate the difference between a doctrine of exclusive versus dominant excellence in things and processes. We can tell that a sapling requires nutrition or light for its flourishing, but just how much of these or what exactly they must be would be determined by the context of the individual sapling's existence. The botanist would be the one to give us the best advance information about that topic. Similarly, we can in general terms tell the conditions of good health for any well-understood living thing, yet admit that when it comes to spelling out the details there can be drastic variations. The human good can be appreciated somewhat along these lines—as neither absolutely fixed, nor simply subjective or relative.

Clearly, there are such cases as good news, a good state of affairs, good morning, good tidings, good fortune. In each case, however, analysis indicates that the term 'good' is employed in the sense indicated above, even if in a less than direct fashion. 'Good news', for example, means that in terms of our aspirations in life, that is, given our goals and wellbeing, what we hear is ranked as welcome. 'Good morning' means that we find things as desired, as far as the condition of the day's beginning is concerned. And so forth. And in each case we need to have a clear enough idea—or at least a familiar one—in terms of which we can make sense of our ranking. (We make use of such terms as 'good' in all kinds of casual, even frivolous ways, in those cases where attempting to perform a strict analysis would be artificial and unnecessary.)

As to natural ends, we can say that, for our purposes, only living entities possess them. Only a living entity depends for its flourishing or perishing on innate drives (instincts), or self-determination. Given its nature as a living entity, and given the kind of living entity it is, some forms of behavior will serve, others hinder its natural end—that is, its success in life as the sort of thing it is. The basic alternative to this natural end is its demise (before its time, as it were). But there is also the less than full attainment of its end, which is a kind of failing.[19]

It makes sense to designate this as the core of the concept of good: being in a position to complete the nature of what something is makes that something a good one of its kind. The human good, at its most complete, would be the most fully, consistently realized manifestation of *human* nature. We would have an excellent human being if we found one who most fully and consistently realized human nature. The distinction between this view and Aristotle's may be noted here: we are resting human goodness on human nature, not merely human essence. Aristotle's Platonic intellectualism came from his essentialist rather than naturalist conception of the human good. Human nature is richer, less specialized than human essence. When we consider human nature, then, a person's individuality is of as much significance as his or her common humanity.

Every human being is a rational animal — the only rational animal, so far as we know. Any other rational animal would also find itself to be morally bound by edicts derived from its nature — including both its characteristic of being an animal and that of being rational. Being a different sort of animal from a human being would make a considerable difference to the content of the ethics by which it would be bound.

Since any animal must be a determinate being — a specific living, biological entity — human beings must by nature be at least numerical individuals. But beyond this, because of the constitution of their consciousness — namely, as a faculty capable of self-motivation or initiation of its own functions — individuality in human beings is a central characteristic. The nature of human life is necessarily that of an actual, active individual human being. (The failure to heed this point has lead thinkers like Marx to endorse a conception of human nature that requires all of humanity — species beings — as its full manifestation. This is why the debate between the individualist and the collectivist is at heart a metaphysical debate: What is the nature of the human being, individual or collective?[20] And while rebutting the Marxists will in itself not secure a sure footing for individualism, that task is in our time essential for gaining that footing.)

How does ethics relate to the broader area of value theory, to the nature of the good? It does so by virtue of the fact that the human good is tied to human nature which involves both life, the source of values, and freedom of choice or of the will, the element of responsibility.

What we call moral or ethical goodness is a special category of goodness because it involves choice. A good pine tree can be identified as such without any relationship to what the pine tree has chosen to do. The same goes for a good knife, sunset, worm, owl. All these things can be good or bad, but that has nothing to do with any *choices they might have made.*

In contrast, the distinctively human good has everything to do with what individual persons *choose.* Not only are some persons good or bad, as can be pine trees or grizzly bears — that is, they are good specimens of that kind of thing — but they may be morally good or evil, meaning self-responsibly engaged in their own human goodness or badness. It is this special characteristic of self-responsibility that gives rise to the distinctively human good, that is, ethics or morality. The morally good is, then, the distinctively human good, or, more precisely, that aspect of the human good subject to determination by the person, or open to choice.

I shall leave aside for now the question of whether some other way of conceiving of the distinctively moral or ethical good is possible. I am aware that there are many who avoid any reference to free choice in their explanation of morality. However, I see no way of distinguishing between value-theory and morality without introducing the fact of self-responsibility, something I mentioned earlier. Furthermore, discussion of the moral status of animals and even plants, not to mention their possible possession of basic rights, seems to me to presuppose the invalidation of the thesis that human beings are the only known species of animals capable of making free choices at a fundamental level of behavior.

Now the question arises which conception of the human moral good makes the best sense. We have thus far noted the broad, so-called formal characteristics of that good, but we need to learn something of its substance, as well, before we can proceed to the connection between ethics and politics.

Classical ethical egoism holds that the best conception of the human moral good is (in answer to the question 'How should I live my life?') everyone's individual human happiness, *within the context of his or her actual life.* Rationally navigating through one's concrete circumstances, developing oneself and one's intimate fellow human beings — as far as they consent — is the most that can morally be expected of persons. Any more concrete statement would necessarily involve some more special conception of human goodness, applicable to some but not to all persons.

Why is this the answer to the central ethical question? Or why is it the best answer to that question?

First, because, since the human moral good is intimately tied to what a person chooses to do, each individual can only make a determinate, definitive contribution to his or her own moral goodness. One can merely offer to others some opportunities for being good — for example, one's children, for whom one can be a 'role model' or good example. (This is the element of truth in the claim that morality cannot be taught or instilled.) Second, knowledge of oneself is most available to oneself, thus who is more likely to be in a position to observe the standards of human moral good, namely human nature, which includes one's own individual identity? Third, because no one else pursues one's own moral excellence, no one else is in the position to make a choice to do the right thing outside of the agent whose actions such a choice would initiate. Offering help in this matter is not of sufficient causal significance, since the subject of that help could choose to reject it. It would be his or her responsibility whether to use or not use the help. For one's own life one has a clear responsibility, while others have responsibility for theirs. All of this suggests that from the moral point of view one is responsible to make the best of one's life as an individual *human* being.

But in terms of what standards? Being human, and thus a rational animal, a standard will require the use of reason as well as the satisfaction, mostly through that use, of one's needs and purposes in life as determined by one's humanity *and* individuality.

'Rationality' is meant here in the sense of 'thinking clearly, being perceptive and aware of what we should do and how we should act.' In choosing to live rationally, we are committing ourselves to being thoughtful, to applying ourselves to concrete tasks in a basically principled fashion. Family life, work, communication, integration of goals, choice of friends and country, taking long views and laboring for long-term results, are the concrete and varied moral tasks of every individual human being with the distinctive capacity of rationality.

The classical egoist sees acting rationally, choosing to think clearly and logically and thus following the dictates of one's best understanding of nature, including one's life, as the central moral task. This can produce decisions, attitudes, and policies quite different from the 'selfish' ones commonly associated with 'egoism'. They are nevertheless egoistic, as I conceive egoism, because by choosing to live rationally, one is fulfilling one's nature as a human being most fully. Thus one becomes a good individual human being. One thereby succeeds at the (implicit) task one has set for oneself.

A central characteristic of rational living is to consider available alternatives thoroughly, consciously. Should I attend a lecture or go to my scheduled exercise session? Should I, with a limited budget, purchase a video for the whole family or a chemistry kit for my son? Should I invest my earnings in bonds or send funds to some group fighting a tyrannical government? Should I spend more time with my wife or work longer hours? But before one can select from alternatives, one has to be in focus, has to be aware of them. This state of awareness is not automatic — as the expression 'Dammit, I didn't think' reveals. A crucial feature, then, of rationality is that it is a capacity that is exercised when one initiates the power of thought, of awareness, of reflection.

QUESTIONS ABOUT MORALITY

Among the numerous criticisms of naturalistic ethics, including ethical egoism, one is especially worth mentioning, mainly because it aims to cut very deep. This criticism holds not simply that egoism is unsound but that any ethics which conceives of objective moral values based on human flourishing is misconceived.

Gilbert Harman has levelled this charge most directly. He argues that an ethics of flourishing — including classical ethical egoism — implies "moral relativism, since what counts as 'flourishing' seems inevitably relative to one or another set of values."[21] He adds that "it is difficult to see how one rather than another conception of flourishing is to be validated simply in 'the nature of things' or in the 'nature' of persons — except in the sense in which different sets of values yield different conceptions of nature or of the nature of a person."[22]

Our discussion earlier meets some of the points Harman raises, as does, I hope, my response to him elsewhere.[23] But I query here whether he can rest the conclusions of a natural-rights doctrine on his conventionalist approach. If there is a serious problem about that, then the present ethical-egoist stance is a more promising doctrine in defense of the right to liberty Harman supports. (Of course, there are other theories besides egoism that conflict with Harman's conventionalism, but they are not our concern here.)

Harman seems to hold that negative rights — to life, liberty, property, the pursuit of happiness, or however else such libertarian principles have been spelled out — rest on the social agreement which we may suppose has been reached among us, persons with very different frameworks of value:

The basic protections of morality have arisen as a result of bargaining and compromise, sometimes after serious conflict and even war. For example, ordinary morality draws an important distinction between the weighty "negative" duty not to harm others and the less weighty "positive" duty to intervene to help prevent others from being harmed. So a doctor may not seize and cut up a healthy visitor to the hospital in order to save the lives of several patients by distributing the visitor's organs where they would do the most good. The harm to the visitor is not permitted morally even in order to prevent more harm to others. The healthy visitor has a "right" not to be harmed by the doctor. The patients who might be saved by this organ distribution do not have an equally strong "right" to have a corresponding harm to them from disease prevented. I suggest that this distinction in ordinary morality is a consequence of the fact that morality is a compromise between people of different powers and resources.[24]

In Harman the agreement which gives rise to morality arises out of a kind of social clash. It is a sort of mechanical result of many people's automatic pursuit of their self-interest. This clearly harks back to Hobbes's idea of natural law, as the result of an instrumental rational assessment of how we must cope with the imposibility of simply pursuing our raw self-interest.

Such a neo-Hobbesian view banishes morality rather than clarifies it. There is no genuine choice left to people when they are prompted to develop their rules of interaction, their system of rights. But if, as I think one would have to accept, 'ought (largely) implies can', then morality cannot be analyzed into this kind of mechanistic sociology. By Harman's account we hold 'moral' values roughly as a fox may entertain certain strategies of catching the hen or the elephant may have come to live harmoniously with the birds who feed off the lice on its skin.

Furthermore, if we admit to genuine choice in human life, then the possibility of such choice would have to be admitted for the circumstances people find themselves in prior to reaching any agreement among themselves. Indeed, whether to join in the effort to seek such agreement would also have to be open to moral assessment, yet since no convention has yet produced Harman-like rules, we would lack any moral principles enabling us to do so.

Furthermore, to say that people have reached a compromise — which, after all, is possible even between a murderer and a totally innocent potential victim — is different from saying that this was a sound, morally proper resolution among them. People can reach bad agreements. Conventionalism assumes, without any further argument, that the actual agreement people have reached — or the one we might hypothetically expect them to reach — is somehow worthy for that reason alone. This is, like a preference for unlimited majoritarianism, an unwarranted faith in the outcome of agreements.

Even accepting various standards of value is something different from the view that we have certain rights. So although people might have reached the agreement that they wish to be free, it is another thing entirely whether this freedom is something they possess by right.[25]

Also, when people show differences in frameworks of value, they could be mistaken, they could be stubborn, they could be rationalizing their perverse aims and objectives — or they simply may be focussing on the diverse, often idiosyncratic implications of what could well be an objective and universal standard of value, binding on us all.

If social agreement could not be the ultimate ground for the existence of basic rights, as Harman supposes, why would people have these rights? (Although the concept of basic human rights has gained currency only in modern times, there are traces of it in ancient political thought. And simply because a concept was not developed to the level which it has since achieved, it does not follow that it has not always been valid.)[26]

The reason that the negative rights to life, liberty, and property are those supported by ethical egoism is that each of us should choose to attain our happiness, and among others this can be realized only if each has a sphere of sovereignty, his or her moral space in society where he or she can strive to live, to be creative and productive, and to attain the kind of happiness suited to human beings. This includes provisions which the right to private property can secure intact through the complex institution of property law. But more about this in Chapter 4. The doctrine of natural rights — first described by John Locke and further developed by others — enables us to lay the foundations for and maintain that system of moral space for all individuals. Despite efforts to convince us that Lockean natural rights are alienable,[27] these rights are indeed something human beings have as human beings — in virtue of their inherent moral nature.[28] That may help to explain why they have been a source of political optimism and inspiration to millions in the hope, possibly, that their clear understanding would fend off those tyrannies which have sought for centuries to enslave them.

It might be thought that there is a suppressed premiss here which is really too strong for the Lockean natural rights account, namely, that 'One has a right to anything required for one's happiness'. But the premiss here is much weaker: 'One has a right to anything required for the pursuit of one's happiness.' That is a rather minimal content for a doctrine of rights. It involves only negative rights, since once such negative rights are secured, either by voluntary respect or by government protection, the sort of individuals we have argued human beings are can proceed to pursue their happiness in the diverse ways they should.

The ethical egoism that undergirds the free market has now been outlined and defended. One of its main features can be stressed by recalling Adam Smith's observation on the motives for virtue:

> It is not the love of our neighbor, it is not the love of mankind, which upon many occasions prompts us to the practice of . . . virtues. It is a stronger love, a more powerful affection, which generally takes place upon such an occasion, the love of what is honorable and noble, of the grandeur, and dignity, and superiority of our own character.[29]

Once the content and essential soundness of classical egoism is appreciated, we can also see why it supports the kinds of free institutions that make capitalism possible. But we can go further than that. There are some implications of classical egoism that support certain of the distinctive characteristics of a free-market capitalist system. (I will discuss these in Chapter 4.) Where the essential or natural moral concerns of human beings must take into account their individual values — where the true individuality, not true collectivity (à la Marx), is the human essence — a market system, which reflects and responds to individual differences to the greatest possible extent, is morally suitable and a planned system is morally objectionable.[30]

Peter Winch offers an important objection to the naturalist meta-ethical approach underlying classical egoism.

> One very common approach to ["the difficulty about what cases we are going to call cases of a 'moral outlook' and about what is involved in so calling them"] . . . is to try to locate the moral in certain alleged features

of human nature, to say what human needs morality answers to and to refer to such needs as criteria for what can be accepted as a moral concern and what cannot. These needs are used to give content to a notion of 'human good and harm', and the claim is that all genuine moral judgments involve a reference, though sometimes more explicitly than at other times, to such a notion. But the undoubted attractiveness of such a move is considerably lessened if we notice what has been suggested by some critics of the 'neo-naturalist' movement, that the identification of these human needs — at least in many important cases — may itself be a matter for dispute of a kind which is hard not to characterize as a moral dispute.[31]

It seems that Winch has charged 'neo-naturalists' with producing circular arguments on the foundation of moral principles. If the features of human nature that give rise to moral concerns are but disguised moral features, one cannot derive from them moral standards because the conclusions would simply restate the premisses, thus carrying no new information and leaving the premisses unsubstantiated.

First, features of human nature giving rise to moral concerns are not necessarily human needs.[32] Admittedly, reference to such needs is troublesome since needs rise in connection with prior judgments as to values or purposes worth pursuing. Strictly speaking, a person's needs, basic or not, arise from the goals he or she seeks to attain, and unless these purposes or goals are first established as right, what is needed to fulfill them cannot be given moral support. If art is of value, then the need for artistic sensibility will help to indicate 'human good and harm' but not without shifting the issue to whether indeed art is valuable.

Second, Winch is confusing value with moral value — a problem frequently encountered in contemporary moral philosophy. But although some feature of existence may be a value, it may have nothing to do with morality. For instance, independently of any moral considerations it may be noted that the sun is a value to growing plants. Without the sun or some equivalent, the plants will not flourish. This in no way involves morality. If we now observe that the life of a human being requires rational thought, again we have only *implied* something about morality. Without unearthing the implication, all we have said is that the realization of some value requires some process, period. Since in examining the process of rational thought we discover that it must come about by way of a willful choice — that is, that thinking must be initiated — unlike the organic processes of growth in a plant, we do have occasion to classify the sort of good that this process brings about as a *moral good* — the self-generated, self-determined enhancement of the good of the human life in question. As I have emphasized, it is the element of choice involved in the seeking of something objectively good that introduces the moral dimension.

Third, the existence of disputes about whether something is indeed a good is not enough to rule out the existence of that good or the possibility of objectively identifying it. Disputes permeate the human world, bearing on everything from whether some subatomic phenomenon is evidence for a particle or wave to whether this or that philosopher is better when it comes to discussing moral problems. Not much can be said against the possibility of firmly grounding moral concerns on human nature simply because disputes arise in the process, even disputes with a distinctly normative tone.

Another criticism, advanced by John Gray, is more tricky. He believes that an unresolvable paradox arises from the broad meta-ethics of natural law: "Let us suppose we are in a position (one we may well occupy in the middle future, given the possibilities of genetic engineering) to alter the content of man's nature or essence: how could the natural law ethic of realizing man's distinctive powers help us here?"[33]

Natural law theories are concerned with the agent's realization of *his or her distinctive essence* (or nature, as I prefer to put it). Gray's 'paradox' rests on misunderstanding what it means to say that one ought to realize one's distinctive essence as a human being. Gray equivocates between one's choosing to realize the essence of a human being *in one's own case* and one's choosing to bring about the realization of the distinctive human essence as a separate project (that is, in some other being). But no natural-law ethics ever advocated that we ought to run around trying to produce a lot of human beings with their distinctive essences realized. No one is responsible for manufacturing a bunch of self-realized persons. If the issue arises whether one ought to genetically alter oneself, that choice will have to be made in line with the ethical-egoist idea that one ought to succeed as a human being. To the extent that the genetic alteration intrudes on this project, it would be wrong. If it enhances it, then it would be morally acceptable. But the details of such a case cannot be determined ahead of time. Each of us should indeed realize his or her human essence (or, as I would prefer, nature), and when we find ourselves faced with the choice to gene splice or not to gene splice something to turn it into a human or non-human being, then we must consider whether doing one or another thing is what most fully realizes our distinctive human nature. Such a problem is not essentially different from other moral choices, and doesn't involve any paradox, though naturally the details of a concrete situation of this sort may raise formidable difficulties.

QUESTIONS ABOUT EGOISM

We now need to discuss some of the issues that arise when considering any variety of egoistic ethics. These are often the substance of criticisms levelled at the capitalist society that egoism supports.

First, why should anyone seek happiness first and foremost? Second, why should we focus on promoting our distinctive human nature? Third, why should one single oneself out as the beneficiary of one's actions? Lastly, how does this manage to support natural-rights theory?

Let us grant that to live is a matter of (implicit) first choice. Of course, in one respect this is obvious — we could commit suicide. But we could also just let ourselves waste away. What is crucial is that such a choice is a fundamental one, not itself justified by some other reason but a first choice, initiated by a person. This choice gives reason, therefore, for the rest of one's actions and requires no reason for itself. It is the primary reason, the *first* one, which then creates the need for morality. My point here is conceptual rather than chronological.[34] First one tacitly, implicitly, chooses to live. By the nature of human life, starting as it does with infancy, the 'choice' at first can only be tacit. Later it becomes more explicit, though usually not taken explicit note of, just as the bulk of one's intentional activity is volitional yet not taken note of. Yet the law, for example, recognizes that all such intentional activity is chosen and open to blame or praise. Throughout one's life one is faced with how to go about carrying out that choice or commitment, how to do well at living. And this is where ethics or morality, a concern with principles of conduct, emerges as a central concern of human existence. Were we, as presumably other living beings are, equipped with instincts or genetic prompters, there would be no need for morality. There would then be no place for a standard of conduct that we ought to abide by but can, if we choose, ignore.

In the context of classical egoism the point or explanation of morality is that human life requires it. As Adam Smith notes, "[in] ancient moral philosophy the duties of human life were treated of as subservient to the happiness and perfection of human life."[35] And here happiness means not hedonistic or even utilitarian pleasure but Aristotelian *eudaimonia*, the success of a human being at the task of living his or her individual human life.[36]

To ask why one should pursue happiness is comparable to asking why, if one has set out for New York City, one should choose to get there efficiently. The choice to be happy — which means, roughly, 'to succeed at one's task of human self-fulfillment within the range of available possibilities' — is implicit in the choice to live. One makes the commitment to do so successfully just by choosing to do it in the first place.

As to why that initial, fundamental choice should be made, the question reveals a misunderstanding of the classical egoist position. One either does or does not make it. Not making it poses no moral problems unless one has already made the choice and then changes one's mind, which would then be a default on a commitment and would ordinarily involve the neglect of other [perhaps related] persons to whom one has also made commitments. But if initially the choice is to bow out of life, then, to the best of our knowledge, one needs no moral guidelines.

To the question, why should I be moral?, the 'answer' is: Well, you, a living human being, are inescapably involved in morality, by your choice to carry on with life. As Quentin Lauer has put it, "The answer, it would seem, is that it is the rational thing to do; to be a human being and not a morally good human being is not to be human, not to be rational."[37] At least, it is to be a defective, incomplete, unfulfilled human being. Human life and morality are inextricably linked.

In several psychotherapeutic schools there seems to be little hesitation about taking this classical egoist approach to the betterment of the psychological health of clients. The human-potential, the self-actualization, and the self-esteem movements are always stressing that persons have to seek self-fulfillment in order to gain optimal psychological health. That the precise meaning of 'human self' is assumed without much scrutiny in their discussions (though there are exceptions, for example, in the writings of Carl Rogers and Nathaniel Branden) indicates a widespread confidence in the commonsense understanding of this idea.

Third, one singles oneself out as beneficiary of one's actions because the central, essential benefits one can reap in life are worthwhile only if one has personally, intentionally achieved them. At this point we can appreciate the Aristotelian overtones of the present ethical theory: to be morally meritorious, the right course of conduct must be *chosen.* This is true of career, close friendships, artistic excellence, great wealth, reputation, health, friendship, romance, and even citizenship. To benefit another in cases of dire need or in emergencies can provide some necessary but never sufficient support for the attainment of that person's good human life. Also, of course, one can be benefited by having values provided by others, but such benefit is always conditional upon what one then does with what one is given, whereas one's own rational achievements are always and necessarily a source of moral pride, even when unappreciated by others.

FROM CLASSICAL EGOISM TO NATURAL RIGHTS

If one chooses to be part of human community life, one is implicitly consenting to the necessary conditions for such association, namely, respect for other people's sovereignty over their own lives and the reasonable securing of those conditions, that is to say: enforceable basic rights. So we approach natural rights by way of egoism.

Rational persons — ones who choose to use their minds — treat doors as doors need to be treated and learn what doors are; eat food that is digestible, and acknowledge that the moon is not made of green cheese. Similarly, when rational persons voluntarily, intentionally interact with other rational persons, their nature as moral agents — free and equally morally responsible agents who require 'moral space' for living their lives in line with their natures (as the human individuals they are) — will be a condition of that interaction. Rational persons would also have to admit to the anticipated response to the violation of these conditions. Respecting the moral nature of persons and how they ought to guard the conditions for living the life of moral agents will be a binding condition for interaction with them. They have implicitly agreed to be so bound.

This moral obligation to succeed in one's particular life as a rational agent through the voluntary choice to interact with essentially similar others who also ought to (and may be expected to) want to refrain from undermining their moral nature, will bind each person to rationally respect everyone's moral space. If, then, egoism requires that one be rational, and rationality produces a recognition of the equal moral nature of others (which, if denied, would invalidate any blame attaching, for example, to bigots or racists), this justifies anticipating their choice to resist intrusion upon them. Their choice to live a human life, a life of rationality also commits them to a system of enforceable principles that protects and preserves the requirement that all persons obtain the moral space for their moral nature. (This is one way in which it becomes clear that natural rights are, in another respect, also civil rights.)

Numerous thinkers, including Samuel Scheffler, Sidney Hook, and John Gray, object that there isn't a chance we could find mutually consistent, compossible ways for all human beings to pursue excellence or happiness in life. The world, they maintain, simply leaves us with basic, unresolvable moral and political dilemmas.

This objection, as we saw, rests on a fundamentally antimetaphysical approach to ethics. If, however, one realizes that the good human life is as much a part of the natural order of reality as any other part of reality, doubting the possibility of a mutually compossible life of excellence is not different in principle from doubting the possibility of a mutually compossible set of true propositions in the description of reality. One wonders how some skeptical philosophers would respond to the plea of a witness in some court case to have his self-contradictory testimony admitted as credible. 'But why could I not have been both in Los Angeles and London on the night of January 17th, 1986, your honor? Why do you hold me to the law of the excluded middle? Have you not heard that philosophers are constantly questioning this law?' In fact, however, the courts are right not to treat such testimony as credible. It would similarly be hazardous to assume that moral truths applicable to human beings can be mutually contradictory.

What is true, of course, is that few people actually live a fully moral life, a life without lapses of rationality, without any negligence, evasion, denial, betrayal. Once the moral order is disturbed, it is no longer reasonable to expect of it a perfectly smooth development in the rest of one's life. Rather, recovery can occur, more or less extensively, with luck often playing some role in reducing the impact of certain lapses. Nevertheless, once a person has lapsed in the moral life, a certain range of results will very likely follow. Slavery, apartheid, and tyranny may all be traced to the moral lapses of individual persons. It is not insensate nature that presents us with confusion, conflict and inconsistency, but rather, human choices.

Whereas ethics guides us individually, socially, professionally, and in other personal, voluntary relations, politics provides guidelines vis-à-vis our conduct toward strangers in whom we take a less personal interest.[38] Even if we know nothing of another, the fact that this other is a human being imposes certain obligations on us — for have we not chosen (at least implicitly) to carry on life within their vicinity?

The principles that we need to inform us about the requirements of proper conduct vis-à-vis our fellow humans are just those individual rights, which, as Ayn Rand notes, "are conditions of existence required by man's *nature* for his proper survival."[39] And since human nature implies that our conduct in life be rational, our rational social life commits us to respect the equal rights of all persons to live by their own choices as they ought to. This respect implies, also, that we accept that others may fail to choose as they ought to. As lamentable as that may be, it would destroy moral life altogether to fail to respect the sovereignty of their choices in regard to the conduct of their own lives.

Classical egoism holds that all persons ought to exercise their rational capacity fully, that is, to realize their distinctive human capacities in the course of living their natural, individual lives. The exercise of rationality, something that is a matter of primary choice and virtue, requires a suitable setting. By their nature they more or less have available this setting, namely, the natural world that surrounds them and on which they can act thoughtfully, productively, generously, moderately — that is, morally. It is this world that is capable of being understood, navigated, and manipulated.

Other human beings, however, are not always so accommodating or predictable. They may have freely chosen to deny to others their necessary "moral space", in Nozick's words.[40] Provisions are therefore needed to secure their co-operation or at least compliance.

WHY IS CLASSICAL EGOISM RIGHT?

Ethical egoism is one serious candidate in providing the fundamental standards of human conduct. But it has been seriously misconceived. The underlying conception of the human self is mostly to be blamed for this. Once this conception is revised and we see that the human self is much richer in its dimensions—for example, sociality is inherently human, implicit in human nature, provided it is a matter of rational choice—much of what is lamentable about egoism disappears. What remains, however, is that morality must ultimately enhance the life of the individual who practices it. As Adam Smith says, "the perfection of virtue . . . [would be] necessarily productive to the person who possessed it, of the most perfect happiness in this life."

Karl Marx, among others, suggested that ethical egoism implies, for social life, that a system of natural negative rights should govern individuals in their relations with others (although egoism itself implies a much richer social ethics when friends, relatives, colleagues, and even neighbors are involved). We will consider the specific nature and justification of those rights in Chapter 4.

The central theme of classical ethical egoism is that everyone ought to strive to become the best individual human being possible. Egoism will not morally tolerate the sort of 'moral' code which makes of individuals resources for others, even for those who are in great need. From the outset, ethical egoism makes this point clear (and that in part may explain its lack of *popularity*). When we consider the political principles which ethical egoism implies, its intolerance of subjugating some persons for the benefit of others becomes even more manifest.

To consider whether ethical egoism is ultimately the best ethical system would require comparing it with all other live options. There is no room here for that very extensive project.

Ethical egoism or individualism is not an ethics of greed, ambition, or power, but one of self-development. Its political dimension, the doctrine of natural rights, is concerned with making as much room for such self-development in as peaceful—though not necessarily fraternal or familial—a context as can reasonably be secured.

This may not seem as inspiring a vision as that offered by those who prophesy the remaking of human nature in order to solve the problems actual human beings face. Those who have focussed their imagination unswervingly on such a prospect will no doubt find classical ethical egoism lacking in the kind of grandiose vision they associate with morality. But in the last analysis, classical ethical egoism is congruent with the actual nature of human life, as well as with a measured conception of what that life can be and ought to be for human beings.

GROUNDING 'LOCKEAN' RIGHTS

WHY 'NATURAL' RIGHTS?

The distinguishing feature of natural-rights theories in the literature on basic human rights is that they purport to rest their conclusions about the existence and nature of rights on a consideration of human nature. The bulk of contemporary rights theories are not advancing a case for natural rights. This includes Robert Nozick, who embraces 'Lockean' rights but whose *argument* is not Lockean—he does not derive his idea of individual rights from a consideration of human nature but merely assumes the existence of such rights. Nozick advances the 'argument from best explanation' as well as certain Kantian intuitions about persons in making his libertarian case. The first element of his approach exhibits a Hobbesian analysis of how the state will emerge from the state of nature.[1] He concludes that a society respecting certain Lockean rights would be just since rational, calculating individuals would prefer it to other kinds and act to seek to protect it.

More recently Russell Hardin has argued for a version of a utilitarian case for, as he calls them, "morally defensible rights", rights that Hardin insists are "sensibly grounded in a concern for consequences."[2] From such views it is easy to arrive at the conviction that "Obviously, if there are several rights to be protected, their exercise may come into conflict."[3]

The natural-rights tradition, however, would aim at securing a foundation and explication of individual human rights that avoids any suggestion that genuine, bona fide individual rights can conflict either (a) among each other, for any individual, or (b) among each other between different individuals. Thus, for example, the right of A to do *s* (for example, speak in favor of communism) may conflict neither with the right of A to do *r* (pursue the study of ancient literature) nor with the right of C to do *s* (speak freely) or the right of D to do *t* (seek to live a life of religious worship).

In any case, the natural-rights approach to identifying individual human rights aims to provide these rights with a solid foundation in human nature. By grounding these rights in something they take to be as stable as human nature these theorists advance an understanding of rights based on metaphysical naturalism. Within such a conception, any system of human rights would have to be self-consistent, since the basic laws of existence or nature—viz., the law of identity, the law of non-contradiction—extend into the realm of morality and politics which are aspects of human life and thus very much a part of nature. So by the natural-rights approach the ascription of basic rights to human beings must never involve fundamental conflict.[4]

In any case, my plan here is to present a case for the existence of basic human rights of individuals within the natural rights framework, not some other. I realize that the position I wish to defend faces enormous resistance today, just as does ethical egoism. Hardin gives a good clue when he notes that "Anyone who tries to defend an unvarnished right of contract for any two parties to do whatever they want to do under any circumstances will be met with vacant stares from most moral and political theorists today."[5] Of course, no one—other than perhaps Max Stirner[6]—who is not associated with the Lockean natural-rights tradition—has ever advanced the view that anyone has the "unvarnished right" to contract to do just anything—the very idea of a contract as a pact between various parties implies specific conditions and thus is incompatible with the idea of doing "whatever they want to do under any circumstances". So the only sensible exclusion Hardin could have in mind is the libertarian view of unregulated contract between two or more parties bearing on just the lives and properties of those parties—on what they have the right to contract about. In short, Hardin claims that no defense of the basic right, for example, of two people to do with themselves or their own as they choose can be sensibly contemplated, never mind defended! Yet this seems to me to rule out of court a very powerful and important tradition of moral and political philosophy.

Even in our complex times intellectuals remain sympathetic to a principled viewpoint, as when they criticize Richard Nixon's 'pragmatism' or would not tolerate any utilitarian approach to a topic such as, say, rape, which would require reserving the condemnation of the practice to cases where the rapist's gain from the 'encounter' was outweighed by the victim's loss. It would be arbitrary to withhold the utilitarian test from rape but apply it to violations such as theft. Considering that most people in most times probably viewed rape with horror, to reduce it to a utilitarian calculation reverses the order of moral priorities. One would have to possess moral understanding of a certain sort to do so — note how some men have to be persuaded to look with horror upon rape within marriage. Certainly a utilitarian approach could hardly induce or sustain the feeling of horror. If I realize that a woman is a sovereign person, not a play- or sex-object at someone's else's disposal, then when I encounter rape I will be horrified. (Slavery was wrong before people were horrified at the idea.)

The best one can do in this huge area of human concern is to offer a system that provides the best prospect for successful problem-solving. If it is possible to give this a successful treatment, it should not be resisted, even with vacant stares.

Moral and political principles may be seen as in some respects analogous to principles of good health. Some very general propositions may be applicable to all individuals in the universe where they aim to hold true. But there is room for individual variation. Yet even with a few exceptions we need not abandon the general principles. (The constant haggling over borderline cases seems to me to have gotten much of philosophy off the track. Theories outside metaphysics and, perhaps, logic, cannot be expected to meet the standard of absolute universality. None of us is blessed with omniscience — if, indeed, that would be a blessing.)

Numerous challenges have been put to those who have tried to demonstrate the existence of human rights. Most recently, as we have seen, Samuel Scheffler has complained that natural-rights theorists have not explained "what they mean by assigning rights to people" and have not said enough "about the source of these rights" or dealt successfully "with a variety of epistemic questions."[7] The very idea of the *existence* of such rights is often challenged. What is it for a right to exist anyway? As Henry Aiken put the issue, this matter is confronted by most theorists

> . . . *simpliciter*, out of any context of inquiry or concern [and will] entangle you in a murky swamp of speculation about the nature of being *qua* being, or reality as reality . . . .

and he adds,

> . . . such speculations . . . turn out invariably to be disguised queries about the meanings, or better, the uses and roles in our discourse of the words 'being,' 'existence,' and 'reality.'[8]

Others, such as Kai Nielsen, question the existence of our knowledge of human rights, on grounds of various skeptical points about what can be inferred from an idea of human nature that is widely disputed and rejected by prominent philosophers,[9] or about the legitimacy of deriving any *ought* judgments from *is* judgments.[10]

One could continue endlessly with the list of recorded and imaginable objections to developing an adequate natural-rights theory. In the end, however, all that would be really fruitful would be to attempt the construction of such a theory and compare and contrast it with others addressing the same general problems in political philosophy. My plan here amounts to exactly that.

In my efforts to reach some fruitful understanding about human rights I will make use of a program spelled out by Martin P. Golding in his paper 'Towards a Theory of Human Rights'.[11] In the next two chapters I will address the main obstacles which are generally agreed to face any natural-rights theorist. Here is the program as Golding presents it:

> For someone to ask me to concede something to him as a human right is implicitly to ask whether I admit the notion of a human community at large, which transcends the various special communities of which I am a member; whether I admit him as a member of this larger community; and whether I admit a conception of a good life for this community. Without these admissions on my part I will not allow the pertinence of his claiming; once I make these admissions I must allow the pertinence of his claiming.[12]

By asking for "the notion of a human community at large" and by speaking of "a member of this larger community" Golding might be taken to be treating mankind as a group or collectivity on the model of a football team, a club, a commercial or scientific enterprise, or a professional association. In the present context this appears not to fit Golding's meaning. Membership in such communities is normally assumed at will. No one, however, is a member of the human community by having chosen it over against, say, the communities of fish or of rocks. Golding is, then, referring to membership not in a community but rather in a species or classificatory slot, identifying 'this kind of entity'. At least this seems to me the most sensible way to take him, and that is how I will be understanding him in my discussion. What Golding is after and what I will try to provide is a sound idea of human nature. By this I mean a suitable place in an objectively sound scheme of categories which serves best, as far as we can tell, to identify what we are aware of in reality.

I plan to meet Golding's first requirement by outlining a theory of objective classification which makes the idea 'human nature' palatable without invoking some actual entity that is designated by the term (such as a concrete universal, along Platonistic or Hegelian, lines). This will require that there be (rational) warrant for regarding the classification 'human' as required by the evidence. It will also require the meaningful organization of this evidence in some nonarbitrary fashion. To put the matter differently, Golding's requirement can be met by showing that human nature exists.

Golding next requires that it be possible to apply knowledge of human nature to actual cases, that it be possible to identify individual human beings. Whether I admit someone as a member of the human community at large requires first of all that the criteria of membership be known. But more is required than that, namely, a justification for identifying some entity as a human being. In ordinary cases this requirement might seem to be superfluous, but there are enough hard cases to warrant a detailed discussion of the problem, especially in light of some concerns voiced recently about the possibility of subsuming classification within mutually exclusive but equally palatable schemes.[13] Since Golding refers to "this larger community", his challenge would have to be understood in such a way that a theory of human nature and an accompanying account of rationally justifiable identification of individuals, as fitting the class of human beings, would have to satisfy him. Since I have attended to several aspects of this problem in earlier sections, as well as in previous works,[14] my aim here is merely to indicate the direction in which Golding's requirement could be met.

Finally, in his last requirement Golding asks for a theory of the human good — "a good life for this community". Here again an ambiguity may appear. But, following the previous interpretation, I take Golding to be concerned with a conception of the human good rather than the common good or the good of the community. (I will discuss the nature of the political good in the next chapter, where I also take up challenges from alternative conceptions of the political good or the just society.)

On Nature and Human Nature

It needn't be argued in detail that the contemporary philosophical consensus evinces skepticism regarding the existence of natures, for example, the nature of trees, the nature of planets, or the nature of medicine. While notable exceptions can be found, prominent philosophers (with one or two recent exceptions) look askance at the view that beings possess natures in anything other than a conventional, instrumental, stipulative, or otherwise provisional manners.

This skepticism is partly justified. Given the salient traditional conceptions of what it would be for there to be natures in the relevant sense, it is very likely that natures do not exist at all. Put plainly, if to know the nature of something we must identify some 'timeless, unchangeable, fixed being' that individuals with this nature are supposed to share, then it is no wonder that we could never know of such natures. We could never learn that such a fixed nature had been correctly identified, since we would have to exist to the end of time to confirm that what we took to be the nature of anything was indeed forever fixed. Since we can carry out confirmations for a limited time only, the claim that there exists a fixed nature of anything simply cannot be demonstrated. The onus of proof lies on those making the claim, and this they could never achieve if by 'the nature of' we have to refer to an eternally fixed nature.

The central problem with talk of human or any other sort of nature stems, as noted in Chapter 1, from the artificial standard that has been thought to be required of a theory of the natures of things. If such a theory had to make out that a fixed nature exists for any item at all, such a theory was foredoomed. The question is whether such fixity is indeed a prerequisite for developing a theory of the natures of things. I think not. It seems to me quite unnecessary to commit oneself to the idealistic characterization of natures. Indeed, ordinary discourse persists in relying on talk of the nature of this or that precisely because no one actually expects that in doing so one is endorsing impossible ideals, changeless forms of things, or timeless essences.

It is an interesting question whether the nature of some being can retain its metaphysical standing as an objective, real aspect of whatever has this nature, given that it cannot be fixed in the fashion envisioned by Plato and perhaps even by Aristotle. I will not attempt to answer this question but I do wish to suggest that the metaphysical standing of the nature of something may be secured without this timelessness or changelessness. I have argued before and will reiterate that what we best mean by 'the nature of X' is the rationally justified place in a system of categorization of the various beings known to us. But this does not imply the identity of some actual statement of the definition of a concept and what it identifies, namely, the nature of whatever is being meant by that concept. Rather the nature of the thing meant by some concept is constituted by those aspects of each being with that nature which serve as the reason for the categorization. Those aspects are not only cognitively registered, and thus serve to identify the nature of the being—they serve as well to develop a statement of the definition. They exist independently of cognition. And when one identifies them as indeed the nature of some being, that identification is true within the context of our most up-to-date information in the realm of inquiry in question. For example, if the correct defining features of the concept 'human being' were 'rational animal', then 'human beings are rational animals' would state this definition and each person's characteristics of possessing a capacity for reason and having a biological constitution would be his or her nature. By 'nature' one means 'whatever something must be so as to be a certain kind of thing'. This 'must' should not be taken in an idealistic, noncontextual sense. It is often but quite artificially so used by philosophers, perhaps because they import their criteria for metaphysical certainty into branches of philosophy other than metaphysics. It seems clear enough what is commonly meant by the nature of some being and it is evident that in this sense everything has a nature.

Thus an alternative to the prominent traditional account of what the natures of things amount to is available to us. I want to explore whether this account can withstand challenges to the general notion that natures exist.

Surprisingly few philosophers actually pose direct challenges to naturalism or essentialism. (I prefer 'naturalism' to 'essentialism' because by 'essence' some people mean only the distinguishing characteristic[s] of what is being talked about.) There are exceptions, notably Popper, Quine, and Hampshire.

Popper lists three main problems with essentialism: (1) problem of distinguishing clearly between a mere verbal convention and an essentialist definition which 'truly' describes an essence. (2) The problem of distinguishing 'true' essential definitions from 'false' ones.

(3) The problem of avoiding an infinite regression of definitions.[15] Although Popper's quarrel in *The Open Society and its Enemies* was with Platonists, Hegelians, and Marxists,[16] it seems clear that even if one rejects the naturalist views of these philosophers one will have to answer his challenges.

Quine, as a nominalist, discusses the idea of the nature of entities rather infrequently. His most direct treatment goes as follows:

> Mathematicians may conceivably be said to be necessarily rational and not necessarily two-legged; and cyclists necessarily two-legged and not necessarily rational. But what of an individual who counts among his eccentricities both mathematics and cycling? Is this concrete individual necessarily rational and contingently two-legged, or vice versa? Just insofar as we are talking referentially of the object, with no special bias towards a background grouping of mathematicians as against cyclists or vice versa, there is no semblance of sense in rating some of his attributes as necessary and others as contingent.[17]

It needs to be noted at once that Quine is conflating the problem of whether things can have natures and the problem of whether something can have a property both necessarily and contingently.[18] As far as naturalism is concerned, there is no commitment in the position to anything about necessity and contingency. The issue of whether the nature of some being is something necessary about it or not is to be treated separately—one might say as a matter of discovery about the nature of that thing. I will say more about this later. As to Hampshire's position, I have discussed it in Chapter 1 and merely remind the reader that Hampshire reiterates in more contemporary terms the well-known Kantian objection to the possibility of metaphysics and thus any stable and objective grounding of categories.[19]

Contemporary thought is rife with objections to the very idea of a 'nature of man or of human beings'. In philosophy proper, so influential a book as *Principia Mathematica* informs us that "a definition is, strictly speaking, no part of the subject in which it occurs" and that "definitions are theoretically superfluous" even if sometimes they "convey more important information than is contained in the proposition in which they are used."[20] Others challenge, not so much the general notion of the nature of something, but rather the idea of human nature specifically. Ernest van den Haag complains,[21] in con-

nection with natural-rights theorists in general and Dworkin's effort
to defend objective moral rights in particular, that

There is no chance of agreement on what is 'suited to human beings
essentially.' Gandhi, Hitler, Professor Machan, Billy Graham, Mao
Tse Tung, Ayn Rand and I would not agree. Nor do we have a method
or experiment to settle our disagreement.[22]

And Larry Briskman, in a review essay critical of some of my ideas,[23]
even contends, following Karl Popper, that

Essentialist political argumentation . . . speaks with a forked-tongue, so
that if one's aim is to defend the value of individual liberty it is far better to avoid introducing any essentialist considerations at all. In fact, it
seems to me that traditionally essentialism has been one of the intellectual bulwarks of collectivism and totalitarianism, so that in fighting
such views we may actually find ourselves forced to criticize essentialism.[24]

All these are very serious points and need to be met. Golding is
right. Without meeting them, or avoiding their sting by some suitable
counterpoints, there really isn't much to be said for natural-rights
theory from the start. If, as Quine says, "A definition, strictly, is a
convention of notational abbreviation",[25] and if by 'convention' it is
understood that there is no objective warrant for the manner of abbreviation which is the result or product of the convention, then any
idea that human beings may have rights in view of their human
nature amounts to nothing more than an unsupported desire to stick
to one's convention rather than, say, that of Karl Marx, Adolf Hitler,
or, to pick Kai Nielsen's example, used to refute the prospect of
universal human rights,[26] Friedrich Nietzsche. It is just this kind of
vulunerability to relativism that undermines the human-rights
theory of the late Bill Blackstone, who wished to tie human rights to
our "desired ideals".[27]

Most of those associated with the critique of essentialism focus
not so much on what is wrong with the doctrine but on how their
own non-naturalist or conventionalist view may escape objections.
Quine, for example, admits that "Although signs introduced by
definitions are formally arbitrary, more than such arbitrary notational convention is involved in questions of definability; otherwise

any expression might be said to be definable on the basis of any expression whatever."[28] Popper, too, has been called a modified essentialist[29] because he takes care to maintain features in his position that will do the job everyone knows that natures were introduced to do. So while at first anti-essentialism seems brutal, soon much of its bite is removed.[30]

Yet I disagree with those who would remake Popper and Quine, for example, into defenders of real definitions under different colors. It seems clear to me that an outlook such as Popper's ultimately leaves us dangling in mid-air, without the anchors that may tie us, however delicately, to reality.[31] Similarly, the absence of any ontological commitment, or rather the disturbingly permissive attitude taken by Quine as to what commitments we might ourselves choose to make — these approaches to philosophy are ultimately direct threats to the idea of objective moral and political principles. After all the fine nuances have been taken into account, there remains the clear impression that Popper and Quine want to be free to have it any way they choose. Standing within the classical liberal intellectual, moral, and political tradition, they hope — clearly in Popper's case and probably also in Quine's — to forestall any attempts by minor or major zealots to advance claims about our categorical duties, in the name of which we might be made prisoners. Briskman's complaint, quoted above, makes the point explicit.

I, too, am troubled by the point Briskman raises. First, however, let me explain that my approach is not to set out to defend anything, including the value of individual liberty. I attempt, as best I can, to see what is what, and what may be inferred from that. (It seems to me that once one has proceeded some way with inquiries, and found that a certain viewpoint is more convincing than others, it is absurd to claim that one is rethinking everything anew each time a challenge arises.) I also think that any sort of holistic conception of the nature of something, such as man, is indefensible. Between these two admissions, so to speak, I have found something that is a *bona fide* naturalism and this is what I wish to defend here. I will do this by first spelling out, in very general terms, some of the characteristics of the nature of a thing. Then I will return to the points raised by critics to see whether my characterization of naturalism succeeds in overcoming their objections and fears.

The most serious obstacle to the development of a theory of definitions is provided by Hampshire in the passages we discussed in

Chapter 1. He states that it is an error to "suppose that there must be some independently identifiable ground in reality, independent of the conditions of reference to reality." I take this objection to amount to the denial of what Aristotle identified as first principles of being. The idea is put bluntly by Mansel, explaining Kant, when he states that "The conceptions of the understanding as much depend on the constitution of our thinking faculties, as the perceptions of the sense do on the constitution of our intuitive faculties. Both *might* be different, were our mental constitution changed; both probably *are* different to beings differently constituted. The *real* thus becomes identical with the *absolute*, with the object as it is in itself, out of all relation to a subject; and, as all consciousness is a relation between subject and object, it follows that to attain a knowledge of the real we must go out of consciousness."[32] While there is dispute about whether Mansel correctly understands Kant, it is clear enough that many neo-Kantians whose influence we now experience in philosophy did so understand him, the later Wittgenstein and Hampshire being prominant examples. While I have already touched on some of the problems associated with the neo-Kantian critique of metaphysics, I wish here to note two additional difficulties.

First, the way in which Hampshire, Mansel, and in less explicit ways many other contemporary philosophers, wishing to avoid 'the error of the pre-critical metaphysicians before Kant', understand the conditions of reference or the constitution of our thinking implies that these are *obstacles* as distinct from *means* or *instruments* or *facilities*. It is as if the fact that we must understand reality in some definite manner amounted to the very obstacle of understanding reality. The very facility of reaching understanding, because it must be some process distinct from other processes, stands in the way of understanding. Ayn Rand's criticism by way of an analogy is useful for purposes of highlighting the confusion of these post-Kantian philosophers:

No one would argue . . . that since man's body has to process the food he eats, no objective rules of proper nutrition can ever be discovered — that "true nutrition" has to consist of absorbing some ineffable substance without the participation of a digestive system, but since man is incapable of "true feeding", nutrition is a subjective matter open to his whim, and it is merely a social convention that forbids him to eat poisonous mushrooms.[33]

Second, what is called our evidently theory-laden understanding of reality is mistakenly taken to be an understanding which might for that reason alone contain distortions — as if 'distortion' could even make sense in that kind of framework. As if there could not be a theory that is sound. But that idea is itself defended on Kantian grounds, so the argument is circular. It says that we cannot know that we know reality. Why? Because our knowledge is theory-laden. So what? Well, theory-laden knowledge is inadequate. Why? Because if the knowledge is always laden with theory, we have no way of independently checking the knowledge, that is, in a way that will avoid the possibly distorting influence of a theory. We cannot know because theory-laden knowledge is not knowledge proper. But this is question-begging. Only if being laden with theory is an obstacle would the point hold. There's no reason to think that knowing by some means — theory-ladenness — need involve any obstacles at all.

As noted before, this is a view that suffers from a misconception of knowledge in that it makes the criteria for knowing anything inherently unsatisfiable. Yet that is itself a hopeless position in its own terms, because if there cannot be any well-grounded knowledge, then knowledge of the criteria of knowledge is equally impossible. This kind of circularity can only be escaped by reconceiving what human knowledge is, which is what we have suggested in Chapter 1.

A system of concepts, the mode of our understanding of reality accurately, has as its point the facilitation of awareness of what there is. It has a cognitive function — it is the means by which we know the world. This is exactly what is denied, extremely paradoxically, by those who accept the force of the Kantian critique. They hold that our concepts, especially the most basic ones — even at their best or most carefully developed — serve in part to pose obstacles to accurate, confirmed awareness. At least they pose the problem that we cannot be sure that they don't obscure reality rather than help us become aware of it.

In turn, this view calls into question definitions of concepts — or statements of the nature of beings — which are the more specialized, more streamlined means for obtaining and increasing our knowledge of reality. Just as Hampshire argued, once it is doubtful whether the basic framework helps or hinders our awareness of reality, the same will hold for whatever gains some of its footing in that basic framework including science, ethics, and political theory. In the present case we are concerned only with ethics and political theory. Given the conclusions arrived at by those prominent philosophers who stand in the Kantian and neo-Kantian skeptical tradition, all discussion of the nature of human beings and, consequently, of natural human rights must become contaminated with that pervasive skepticism. Is there an objectivist alternative to this tradition?

As noted in Chapter 1, the understanding of knowledge as requiring necessary and sufficient conditions that *must forever* constitute its nature, has prejudiced the issue of whether objectivity is possible. It has placed in doubt whether we can know things-in-themselves; whether, in short, reality can be identified. The sort of knowledge which is absolute, final, infallible, incorrigible, formally necessary and sufficient in its defining conditions is, of course, uniquely limited. This is then unjustifiably taken to amount to a general limitation on us, on our capacity to know reality as it is.[34]

Such a limited standard may apply at best to the biblical sense of 'knowing'. This really amounts to *being-one-with*. It does not mean what anyone's knowing anything could conceivably be, where knowing that *p* or that *s* is true is concerned, except, perhaps, for knowing oneself in the respect that one-is-onself. By taking this one form as the true and only model of knowledge, the sort of skepticism we have found expressed in the neo-Kantian tradition is openly invited. (It seems to me that just this fact is exploited by a radical skeptic like Peter Unger.[35])

A final point: Hampshire says that "In order to show that elements in reality could only be distinguished for the purposes of language in one familiar way, we would have to show that nothing else would count as 'distinguishing elements in reality for the purposes of language'."[36] But to show this we would have to carry out a process of elimination to infinity, an impossible task. Yet is there any justification for assuming that to show that something "could only be" requires such an impossible achievement? The very terms being used would have to be inapplicable in any actual context if this were the case; yet "could only be" is frequently used, for example, when no grounds for supposing that anything else could be are available, for example, in law.

One might object that such grounds *might* be found, even though no one has found them to the present. But it is not clear what this 'might be' amounts to. Some philosophers would argue that it amounts to the claim that there isn't any contradiction, not outright at least, in claiming that there could be this or that, however true it is that no reason exists for even supposing it. But this again invokes a sense of knowing that makes it a general requirement for knowing something that it be a self-contradiction to deny what is claimed as being known. Why is that a general requirement? (I don't like to refer again to what might appear an obsessive search for metaphysical rather than contextual certainty, but is the suggestion so outlandish?)

There is a conception of the adequacy of what is to count as knowledge, as a definition, as objectivity, and the like which is often left unexamined within the frameworks where skepticism is expressed about the very prospects of endeavors to answer the questions. As Renford Bambrough observes, "It is self-defeating to attempt to impose a requirement which must necessarily fail to be satisfied by every conceivable attempt to provide a justification. . . . " Yet Bambrough also poses the objection which is most compelling against the position I am advocating here. He puts the matter as follows:

> If we are to escape from the mazes and dilemmas of traditional epistemology, whether in its general form or in its specifically moral variant, we must follow the arrow that points upwards to the top of the blackboard from the particulars to the principles, and not the arrow of deductive logic that points downwards from the so-called axioms or principles to the particulars.[37]

He goes on to argue that just as we can locate things in an inexhaustible physical space, "An enquiry may be inexhaustible without being inconclusive. It may be possible to go further and still not be necessary to go further . . . . There is always something for the sceptic to say, and always something to say to him in reply . . . . "[38]

First, the axiom or principle of the law of identity or noncontradiction *is* the result of having paid heed to particulars—each particular, every fact, whatever there is, gives ground for it, embodies it, if this means that the nature of anything is such that to deny of it what it is (as its identity is affirmed) is rationally impossible. This shows the fact of the law and the law is exhibited by the fact.

Second, as the law (incorporated into a conceptual scheme) is stated, it has to be a universal in some sense, yet it is also a particular since it is of existence as such, of any and all of it. The universality of some judgment does not deprive it of particularity. What is added by its being universal is the range of applicability to particulars—it applies to all of them.

Finally, while the skeptic can go on saying something, it is questionable that he can mean anything beyond a certain point, so no reply is warranted from there on. Whatever the skeptic might wish to mean always requires that certain facts be admitted as known. Yet skepticism is just the denial of that possibility; thus it undercuts its standing as justified or reasonable doubt.

We can now turn briefly to the question of what fundamental facts there are for us to know. I have previously argued that the law of noncontradiction is indeed such a basic, rationally undeniable substantive fact.[39] My arguments were advanced in an effort to counter Peirce's view that absolute certainty, exactitude, and universality cannot be attained. Peirce's point is similar to what Hampshire and others have said, and, like them, Peirce does not show that it is true. Moreover, he also suggests why it is false, when he says:

> A logical principle is said to be an empty or merely formal proposition because it can add nothing to the premises of the argument it governs although it is relevant; so it implies no fact except such as is presupposed in all discourse.[40]

And the law of noncontradiction is just that sort of fact, namely, one the doubting of which presupposes it. This much is conceded by some philosophers who still wish to express some hesitation, for example R. M. Dancy:

> One might deny the law of non-contradiction for all sorts of reasons. None that I have seen strike me as good reasons. But neither do I see any reason for saying that there never *could* be good reason for denying it.[41]

But this point, namely that there is no ground for ruling out some good reason for denying the law, cannot be cogently made out in the last analysis, so it is unacceptable. As I noted earlier, unless an interpretation of *"could* be good reason" is offered, such that the law could be dispensed with and the interpretation would stand as meaningful, Dancy's point that he sees no reason that there never could be good reason for denying the law is an empty, even self-refuting musing. I suggest that Aristotle's observation stands unrefuted, namely, that "it won't be possible for the same thing to be and not to be, where that isn't just a matter of the word — but where it's a matter of the thing."[42]

Since the denial of this most comprehensive and yet always and everywhere thoroughly instantiated fact itself presupposes the fact being denied, our awareness of it provides as firm a link as can reasonably be asked for between the thinking and philosophizing someone might want to engage in, and reality, ultimately the subject of such thinking. Granted the link is fragile — for it requires extreme care as it is invoked and must weather sustained assaults (from Pyrrho, Hume, Kant, Russell, and Unger). Yet if it is kept in mind, utilized properly and judiciously as a court of the very last resort (instead of being abused by making it carry too much burden in argumentation via the overuse of the *reductio*), then such a basic datum will achieve what various philosophers who take their clues from skeptics think cannot be achieved, namely, it will serve as the link between human awareness and what we want to know.

There are many other requirements for making progress in the next stage of this book's argument. Most significantly, the identification of reality requires the dependability of the human sensory organs, since it is by their use that we find the premises for our reasoning, theorizing, and decisions. I won't deal with the issue here other than to observe that the dependence is so basic that here too, at this general level of discussion, no skeptical thesis concerning perceptual awareness can even be advanced without itself presupposing this dependability.[43] Here too a denial omits from consideration what function our thinking and discourse has when considering these matters, namely, to become aware of reality. But beyond this negative or dialectical support for the validity of perceptions, the comprehensive development of a naturalistic view of definitions, as against the prevalent nominalist views, requires an analysis of conceptual knowledge. In particular, a defense of the possibility of nonpropositional knowledge would be of significance here. The nonarbitrary character of concepts and, concurrently, of definitions hinges, in large part, on the possibility of and actual knowing of existents, and of having this knowledge available in organizing them.

About conceptual knowledge my account owes a great deal to reflection on the analysis provided by Rand[44] and to considerations prompted by confronting the difficulties brought to light in the works of J. L. Austin, L. Wittgenstein, S. Cavell, and Thomas Kuhn. I will not provide a full explication, let alone defense, of the analysis here. Very briefly, I regard concepts as *means* by which human beings are aware of reality. They are the results of the activity of human reason, the faculty by which human beings integrate and differentiate the materials provided by the sense organs. And if the purpose served by the use of these means is accomplished—that is, the correct identification of aspects of reality is achieved—then in connection with them human beings are correctly said to possess conceptual knowledge. It would then be a further cognitive stage to know that we do have such knowledge via concepts, something that would issue in propositional knowledge, which is the elaboration and explication of conceptual knowledge. So viewed, the special character of the theory of definitions underlying the present natural-rights account will be less difficult to appreciate.

Let me now outline the features of the present account of the nature of a thing, and its statement, namely, its definition, so that later my more particular concern with human nature can be guided and checked in terms of them:

(1) A definition (or statement of the nature of a thing), given in propositions of the form: "X is a, b, c, . . . n," states those objective aspects of (some) beings by virtue of which one is rationally warranted in differentiating these beings from all others, as well as integrating them within a scheme of classification of reality.

(2) The defining characteristic(s) of some being is objective, such that the claim that it is existent (given the suitable context) can be shown true, by methods most appropriate to date for this purpose, beyond a *reasonable* doubt, i.e., soundly established doubt.

(3) A definition states what the characteristics of some being are, what the nature of a thing is, without implying that these *must* be metaphysically or in some existential respect separable features of the being whose nature is under consideration. In short, no commitment to 'inner natures' or 'innate essences' is involved in the view that true definitions can be produced. (Of course, these features of some beings might be separable, for example, when certain chemical compounds or mechanical contraptions are at issue.)

(4) The definition of some concept, for example, human being, is contextual, not necessarily unchanging, timeless. If the nature of a is A, at time t_1, it is not logically necessary that it will be A at time t_2; yet any change in the nature of some being must be explainable by reference to objectively identified causes or reasons.

Although the position in epistemology that best succeeds in supporting the theory of natures or definitions summarized here was advanced by Rand, her views haven't received attention from many contemporary philosophers outside of Nozick,[45] Matson,[46] and, especially, Den Uyl and Rasmussen, editors of a recent volume on Rand's philosophical works.[47] Because the 'testing' of philosophical views is best carried out in the course of discussions within the philosophical community, this is unfortunately not possible in the present situation. In developing the present position I give expression to the objectivist foundations of natural-rights theory, using the terminology familiar in mainstream philosophy whenever possible, without, I hope, permitting this to distort the position at hand. Still, there is enough in common in these approaches to philosophy to carry on.

To highlight the central insights of the objectivist position, the following quotation from Rand's epistemological work will be extremely useful:

On the pre-verbal level of awareness, when a child first learns to differentiate men from the rest of his perceptual field, he observes distinguishing characteristics which, if translated into words, would amount to a definition such as: 'A thing that moves and makes sounds.' Within the context of his awareness, this is a valid definition: man, in fact, does move and make sounds, and this distinguishes him from the inanimate objects around him.

When the child observes the existence of cats, dogs and automobiles, his definition ceases to be valid; it is still true that man moves and makes sounds, but these characteristics do not distinguish him from other entities in the field of the child's awareness. The child's (wordless) definition then changes to some equivalent of: 'A living thing that walks on two legs and has no fur', with the characteristics of 'moving and making sounds' remaining implicit, but no longer defining . . . .

When the child learns to speak and the field of his awareness expands still further, his definition of man expands accordingly. It becomes something like: 'A living being that speaks and does things no other living beings can do.'

But this ceases to be valid at about the time of the child's adolescence, when he observes (if his conceptual development continues) that his knowledge of the 'things no other living beings can do' has grown to an enormous, incoherent, unexplained collection of activities, some of which are performed by all men, but some are not, some of which are even performed by animals (such as building shelters), but in some significantly different manner, etc. He realizes that his definition is neither applicable equally to all men, nor does it serve to distinguish men from all other living beings.

It is at this stage that he asks himself: What is the common characteristic of all of man's varied activities? What is their root? What capacity enables man to perform them and thus distinguishes him from all other animals? When he grasps that man's distinctive characteristic is his type of consciousness — a consciousness able to abstract, to form concepts, to apprehend reality by a process of reason — he reaches the one and only valid definition of man, within the context of his knowledge and of all of mankind's knowledge to date: 'A *rational animal*.'[48]

This integration of the contextualist conception of definition with the problem of defining the concept 'human being' in stages of development helps us to understand something about the way conceptual changes as well as changes in the definitions of things can come about without upsettng objectivity. Barry Stroud explains how this may be fruitfully thought of, in connection with his discussion of Wittgenstein's view of 'logical' necessity, which, Stroud says, for Wittgenstein:

. . . is not like rails that stretch to infinity and compel us always to go in one and only one way; but neither is it the case that we are not compelled at all. Rather, there are the rails we have already travelled, and we can extend them beyond the present point only by depending on those that already exist. In order for the rails to be navigable they must be extended in smooth and natural ways; how they are to be continued is to that extent determined by the route of those rails which are already there. I have been primarily concerned to explain the sense in which we are 'responsible' for the ways in which the rails are extended, without destroying anything that could properly be called their objectivity.[49]

It seems to me right to define human beings as rational animals, but I will discuss this at greater length when we come to the second requirement posed by Golding's program (since I will have to talk at length there about conceptual consciousness or reasoning).

Turning to Popper's three main problems with essentialism, how is one to distinguish between "a mere verbal convention and an essentialist definition which 'truly' describes an essence"? First by noting that "mere verbal" is ambiguous — does it refer to the fact that different sounds and notations can be used, or does it refer to some alleged relativity of the concepts we express by these sounds and notations? Second, "mere verbal" may refer, for example, to a statement that, though an item isn't known to be a carrot, it will be *called* a carrot. Later, when we have identified it as indeed a carrot, we may note, 'By Jove, it really is a carrot!' The former may be a verbal definition, but that seems a somewhat honorific title, while in the latter case we identify it correctly, given what the concept of carrot is expressed by in English. The distinction rests on the genuine option between a mere verbal designation and a true definition. As Rand puts it, "A definition is the condensation of a vast body of observations — and stands or falls with the truth or falsehood of these observations."[50] If the series of observations-abstractions on which a definition is based can be justified in terms of procedures themselves based on true fundamental metaphysical principles, then the prospect of true definitions is no mere philosophical dream. The procedures vary, of course, depending on the subject matter (the context) — for example, those suited to physics will not suit sociology, due to the ontological distinctiveness of the two domains.

As to the distinction between " 'true' essential definitions [and] 'false' ones", when the purpose is to state those characteristics of some beings by virtue of which they are to be classified as beings of some kind, and this is achieved by ill-conceived means, we obtain what may awkwardly be termed false essential definitions. The falseness can, of course, stem from numerous sources, just as any falsehood can.

Finally, still in answer to Popper, "the problem of avoiding infinite regression by definitions" may be solved in view of the role played by the basic principle(s) of metaphysics, namely, as the last point(s) of reference in any enquiry. In identifying such a basic principle, the organizing standard of the best conceptual scheme within the context of available human knowledge has been secured. That for the basic principle(s) it is not possible to offer further verbal definitions need not imply at all that other, less fundamental ideas do not require them either. To put it another way, the being of which we are aware when we affirm the truth of the law of identity or noncontradiction is being *as such*, existence; and what we are aware of in this very broad and fundamental sense is that it is whatever it is. In Aristotelian terms, 'A is A'. Using, alternatively, the expression Ayn Rand coined in propositional form, 'Existence exists'.

Because the proposition is fundamental, it is not like other ideas; it does not serve either to integrate or differentiate various elements or features of existence. But its fundamental character explains this and there's no reason why other ideas would have the same character. Yet by a *reductio*-type argument, quite appropriate in the context of metaphysics, it can be shown that the idea is sound and indeed fundamental or axiomatic, which makes it eminently fit for the purpose it serves.

In Quine's objections, too, what ultimately stands in the way of the prospect of finding objectively essential characteristics is Quine's rejection of the possibility of an objective tie to reality, namely, his ontological relativism. Quine, Popper, Hampshire, Kuhn, Feyerabend, Winch, and Rhees all share this standpoint. They owe a greater debt to Descartes than to Kant in this matter. Since Descartes, consciousness alone has been expected to carry the enormous burden of reaching an understanding of anything. Hence subsequent philosophical reasoning rejected the very possibility of any anchorage for developing the framework to comprehend and, ultimately, cope with reality. Frederick Will makes this point succinctly as applied to the problem of definitions:

> It is not . . . the project of defining 'good' or 'probable' that is the object of criticism here, when, in contrast with the nominal, linguistic connotations of this way of referring to the project, what is sought under the title of 'definition' is nothing so restricted as the isolation of some linguistic fact. This title is also sometimes employed to refer in a compressed way to the project of developing a comprehensive view of a wide domain of human practice, a whole institution or set of institutions, which, not in any narrow, strict way, but in a genuine philosophical way, may be taught to be the *designatum* of the terms in question. Then the term 'definition' itself refers to the endeavor to develop a systematic critical view of these practices and institutions which will serve to provide, not only understanding of them as they stand at any given time, but also, and closely consequent upon this, a basis for the criticism and rectifiction of these institutions, as the need for these repeatedly arises. Definition, so understood, signifies a process and result that are indispensable, and indeed central, to the philosophical vocation.[51]

ABOUT DISCRIMINATION

What is needed, in part, is a conceptualization of existence such that no imposition is made concerning the character of possible beings apart from conformity with the basic facts of reality, with, as Aristotle put it, first principles. Outside that monistic element, there is ample room for pluralism, which in turn allows for the possibility of different standards of knowing something, depending, in crucial respects, on the general type of being that one seeks to know.

Golding's second requirement assumes, rightly, that whether I (rationally) admit someone as a member of the human community at large—that's to say, correctly identify some being as a *human* being—depends on the availability of the criterion of membership. But can we have justified confidence in our judgment concerning the classification of some entity?

Golding's challenge appears to be directed at difficult cases. In most identifications of human beings problems of discrimination are absent. Determining when something has become a human being—during conception, at some stage of the woman's pregnancy, at birth—or, alternatively, when some being ceases to be human—following brain death, at the loss of a certain IQ level, when the physical organism as a whole dies, or at senility—can be a complicated matter, and there is far more than academic philosophical interest in this. And it is just such problems that face natural-rights theorists when their view is said to be most capable of giving direction to concrete legal and political problem-solving and decision-making. At this stage of following out Golding's program more is required than to have ascertained the possibility of identifying the nature of something and, thus, the possibility of identifying human nature. It is necessary, of course, to have done this, but once the nature of something has been identified, it becomes crucial to consider what use if any can be made of such a definition. The meta-ethical challenges to this view have already been discussed in Chapter 1.[52]

In most cases criticisms focus on various epistemological issues surrounding the classification of individuals: this individual as a human being or as something else. Thus some thinkers despair because we can make mistakes, or do make them frequently. And if these thinkers are right, what Golding asks cannot be provided.

But critics here assume that the claim that some entity is a human being must be irrefutable—certain beyond a shadow of doubt—in order for it to be true or correct. This is an impossible requirement. All that is actually required is that such a claim be defended to the most complete and comprehensive extent, given what human beings have achieved to date in this area of inquiry. The skeptic's impossible task need not be taken up. The identification of an entity as human imposes the obligation, from the epistemic point of view, that this claim be shown true beyond any reasonable doubt about the matters involved in its possible truth.

That we *can* make mistakes in various cases of admitting some entity as a human being does not prove that we *cannot* ever be right — and *know* that we are right. Nevertheless, a suggestion does emerge from what has been argued thus far concerning the more constructive task of defining the concept of human beings.

The skeptic accepts that we can make errors. The idea of error seems to him valid. This commits him to a distinction between erroneous and correct identifications (concerning whether some entity is a human being) which has itself been formed by human beings. Otherwise how could the distinction be made at all? Both failure and success in handling difficult cases of class-inclusion have been encountered throughout human history, suggesting that we can, in the relevant sense of 'can', know that some particular being is a human being, has a human nature. We can also know that in the past some have made mistakes and even evaded the fact that some beings were human beings. (Both honest error and willful error would be ruled out if the skeptic were right — itself an odd notion on his own terms. Too much skeptical talk capitalizes unfairly on how tolerant we all wish to be about not closing the book on various issues. Moreover, there is a general moral bias against anything smacking of arrogance, even when that degree of conviction is warranted. All this seems to make the skeptic's mission a simpler one. Yet skeptics are by no means always paragons of humility.)

Although warranted judgments of inclusion and exclusion are sometimes made, are these objective? Don't they occur within a framework or paradigm that isn't demonstrably true? Once again Kantian doubts about knowing things in themselves based on our dependence on *the* human way of understanding, a way that we cannot independently test, need to be considered. In a recent version, due to Thomas S. Kuhn,[53] a somewhat different analysis suggests these doubts, giving credence to skepticism about the capacity of human beings to arrive at objectively correct judgments, or even to reach 'inter-subjectivity'.[54]

I have tried elsewhere to meet the Kuhnean criticism of the possibility of objectivity.[55] For both Kuhn and Kant an impossible ideal governs the epistemic inquiry into what knowledge of various features, aspects, parts, and so forth, of the world must be. The same applies to Kant's and Kuhn's criteria of truth. The inability of human beings to satisfy this impossible ideal is then taken as decisive evidence against the possibility of objective knowledge and truth.

Kuhn maintains that we can never justify the paradigm which governs our procedure for identifying what is the case in some situation. Paradigms serve as justificatory bases. There is nowhere further to go, yet paradigms may change, so ultimately we are ungrounded, unanchored, unconnected to reality. All that we can claim is that *within a framework* we are right, but not that we have learned the truth about something. In these kinds of cases what is to count as a successful determintion of truth or a correct identification of reality falls prey to the flaw of requiring a *guarantee* against error now and any time in the future. Accordingly, the sort of criticism we find in J. L. Austin, pertaining to the revisability of concepts, and to their role in truth-claims, is an apt response here.[56]

The idea of knowledge as some sort of copy (picture?) of what is known, a kind of replica in the mind, must be abandoned. And the view that true judgments or statements are timelessly final must also be rejected. Concepts as tools of cognition *for the time being* — which preserves the distinction between falsehood and truth, or ignorance and knowledge, without demanding of the latter of the two pairs an impossible result — will do the job.

Another matter bears significantly on Golding's second requirement. This is whether human beings as such could accomplish what is required for purposes of learning that something is or is not a member of the class of beings at issue, for example, human beings. Are they such that they could do this? Two tasks will be considered here. The question posed just now will be answered. At the same time the definition of the concept 'human being', that is, the nature of man, will be further discussed and defended. Success in the first task will help us make progress in the second.

If we assume that human beings are compelled to think as they do think — to believe what they do, to behave accordingly, and so forth (for 'compelled *thinking*' might be a contradiction in terms) — then any judgment of inclusion or exclusion (within or from a community of human beings at large, for example) will be a matter of imposition upon someone's convictions or beliefs, not an achievement of that person. In short, if (hard or soft) determinism — (excluding self-determinism) — is true and human beings cannot initiate their thinking and, thus, the discriminating processes, then Golding's second requirement cannot be satisfied. Why do I say that determinism implies that individuals can't initiate their thinking? Well, to initiate in this context means to start the process, to begin it. Determinism of the sort that is at issue here denies that human individuals start any processes — each event for the determinist is the product of a previous event, and so on endlessly, with individuals as mere points of juncture (as B. F. Skinner would have it). One might ask, don't we want our beliefs to be determined by the facts? Yet this sense of 'determined by' means 'determined by reference to' so that here the issue of who or what has determined the belief by reference to the facts is left open. Facts alone clearly do not determine beliefs. If they did, no one would fail to believe facts; and where no facts could be found, no beliefs would be found either. The facts would not be there to determine them.

The requirement that we initiate our thinking processes cannot be met if we do what we do because we are caused by various forces not under our direction to reach 'conclusions'. Under such compulsion we could never take the needed objective stance to demonstrate the soundness of these 'conclusions', precisely what Golding's second requirement asks us to do.

The relationship between the capacity for rationality, including objective assessment of arguments, and freedom of the will is intimate — the two are really distinct aspects of one faculty, namely, the mind, human reason. To show, then, that we can do what Golding requires of us, it is necessary to show that a human being is just the sort of being that is capable of rationality, of conceptual differentiation and integration, and of the justification of the results of these. Of course, it could be that such a capacity is not distinctively human and Golding's request could still be fulfilled. As a matter of fact, though, there is no reason to believe — despite allegations about monkeys, porpoises, or, most recently, some birds using language — that nonhumans exhibit distinctive rational capacities, much less that their distinctive form of consciousness, by which they guide their conduct and flourish, is conceptual. The reason is that in human beings this capacity serves to explain the greatest number of their other characteristics, while this is not the case with respect to the conceptual capacities ascertainable in these other animals.[57]

Since a definition is a classificatory device, not denoting some separable being of any variety, there is no threat to it from borderline cases. The issue facing a definition is whether, given the best schematization along lines spelled out earlier, the occasional exceptions can be explained without upsetting the scheme. If this is not possible, changes in the scheme are objectively warranted. This will still enable us to preserve the idea that changes themselves must be explained by reference to the natures of things because in such a case a change of a definition is explained by reference to the nature of the large scheme on which it is based by reference to the requirements of parsimony and consistency.

Although identifying human nature is crucial in the present project, I shall not take a long detour so as to rediscover, as John Kekes put it, "what everybody knows anyway". Instead I will address the problem of whether, in terms of the view of definitions outlined earlier, the claim that human nature consists of some entity's being a rationally (and thus volitionally) conscious animal can be defended against familiar objections. This will be our test.[58]

First, it is by virtue of the characteristic of rationality that we can differentiate human beings from the broader category of existents, namely, from animals; the capacity for rational thought best explains the overwhelming number of distinctive characteristics of human beings, warrants their integration into the scheme of classification of reality as a group of a kind. As writers, builders, scholars, plumbers, politicians, cheats, liars, friends, bigots, soldiers, husbands, believers, researchers, economists, composers, oppressed, tyrants, clergy, Germans, and so forth, human beings are united by virtue of depending on their rational minds, their capacities for creative conceptual thought and imagination.

Second, reason is an existent faculty and its exercise an existent process, and it is possible to defend this against such challenges as those by behaviorists or physicalists who view thinking as *nothing more* than brain processes. The thinking I have in mind here is supposed to be an activity *via* my brain resulting in conceptual understanding, which is itself a relationship between reality and ourselves, who entertain beliefs and may gain knowledge of reality in consequence of that thinking. The characteristics of reason serve to best explain what human beings can do as such, while efforts to substitute, for example, verbal behavior for thinking (in the manner of B. F. Skinner) fail to achieve this task. What such recasting of consciousness into physicalist language does is to impoverish our conceptual framework and render it impossible for us to consider numerous phenomena that simply cannot be discounted — dreaming, *déjà vu*, memory, reaching conclusions, changing our minds, discarding notions, and so on.

This indispensability of the thinking process as a self-initiated essential activity of human beings, tied to the biological facilities of their brains, demonstrates the objectivity of the defining characteristic(s) of human beings.

Third, the above may be true without its truth having to be impervious to modification, as would be required by a doctrine of 'inner natures' or 'inner essences'. Future change in knowledge could prompt such modification, and actual changes in reality (such as a mutation producing some new entity) could lead to altering the classificatory scheme which had been correct to date.

The fourth provision is basically a restatement of the third, stressing the open-endedness of the definitions or statements of the natures of various things, events, activities, institutions, and so forth, without denying their objectivity in the slightest. Accordingly, each of the four requirements laid down before, which a definition must meet, can be met by the definition of the concept at issue here. What follows from this in regard to Golding's second requirement, concerning whether a fetus is a human being, whether someone with extraordinarily low IQ scores is one, whether brain death causes the extinction of life for human beings, and so forth?

For the present approach borderline cases do not pose the sort of stubborn problem they pose to metaphysical essentialism according to Plato or even Aristotle.[59] If no final picture but the best available classificatory place is understood to be the aim of a correct definition, based, nevertheless, on facts in evidence gathered by looking and thinking, the problem of borderline cases is something that is no longer threatening. While the cases listed above do not become unproblematic individually, the fact of the existence of such cases ceases to be a threat to the soundness of the account of definitions along present lines.

There can be instances of something being closer to one place in a scheme than to any other, yet not fully satisfying the requirements of fitting exactly within that spot—a broken chair won't fulfill the role of chairs, yet it is still best identified as a chair. Similarly with a chair in a museum that may no longer work as chairs ordinarily do. We also develop modifiers, as for example, 'toy' chair. The point holds as well with reference to entities that are not made by human beings and thus do not lend themselves to so much variety—for instance, a human 'vegetable', albeit not quite a human being, is still not wisely classified as anything else. A fetus in its early stages would deserve a different classification from one in later stages of pregnancy, given various factors such as the development of the cerebral cortex, but near birth it would be unjustified to treat the fetus and the baby as different kinds of beings.

Gray areas can be accepted and instant solutions may not be forthcoming for yet another reason that does not intrude on the basic rationality of the outlook we are considering. The fact of human volition — for example, stubbornness, oversight — can account for some of the indecisiveness about how reality should be organized and classified.[60]

In any case, Kuhnian-type problems concerning the erratic development of concepts, aren't hereby fully disposed of. But they can be given a distinctive account in the present approach.[61] At the borders everything is difficult and maybe only those doing the work there are in a position to say, upon reflection, what justifies the choice of a given solution and not some alternative. As with desert-island or life-raft cases in ethics, the problems which are actually (or have been formulated so as to stand for) very difficult cases require extensive scrutiny and cannot be handled, by their very extraordinary character, with the reiteration of general principles. Yet, the confidence for construing all this as manageable, in the last analysis, comes from handling some cases in detail and from noting the inadequacy of arguments which defend the pessimist stance. For example, although much controversy surrounds the abortion issue, which gives the appearance that there is no solution possible, there is a resolution that appears superior, namely, one that locates the initial existence of a human being at the point where the fetus acquires a cerebral cortex.

Nor does it follow from existing difficulties that the problem must remain intractable, although living in the world confronts us with ample challenges, some of which may incline one to give up hope that some human problems are indeed manageable by human beings, most particularly in the spheres of science and epistemology.[62]

Given these considerations and arguments, it is now possible to move on. Golding's requirements have been met — the first two in this chapter, the third in the previous chapter where classical egoism was defended. I turn now to tying these features of a theory of human rights to the overall conclusions about human community, that is, to politics. In short, how does all this provide us with natural rights?

RIGHTS AS NORMS OF POLITICAL LIFE

ENTER POLITICS

Aside from the answer to the question, 'How should I live my life?', advanced in the field of ethics, supported by meta-ethics, we also need a response to 'How should we live in the company of other people?' The scope of this question includes interactions with strangers, people who are members of our larger communities, but not family or friends. That is where politics arises — organizing a community so as to provide standards for living with others whom we know only as human beings. The polity is that community of human beings wherein principles of interaction pertain only to our mutual humanity and common citizenship. Principles of political justice touch on the problem of what we must do — what indeed we may be made to do — so that our community will be home to all manner of persons, groups, clubs, families, enterprises, teams, religious orders, experimental communities, and so forth.

It is to learn what these principles are that political philosophy has emerged. One of the candidates in the discussion of possible answers is the natural-rights school. Proponents of this school suppose that theirs is a good answer to the question that is to be answered in political philosophy.

HUMAN NATURE AND HUMAN GOOD

As we learned from Golding, at this point we must turn to the immediate grounds of human rights. Is there a conception of the human moral good that is correct? Can we then show that such a conception, combined with a reasonable understanding of the circumstances of human social life, gives rise to certain political principles?

As I attempt to satisfy this requirement, it will be necessary to keep in mind all that has gone before. While Golding's guidance is very helpful in the present inquiry, it isn't possible to take what he says entirely at face value. "Human community at large" in Golding's discussion should be understood to refer to human nature, as noted earlier, because of the function the phrase has in its present context. When Golding refers to "the good life for this community", he can be fully understood only if we take him to mean human nature, since communities in the sense of clubs, countries, or doctors are not the sort of entity with a *life* that could be good or bad for them. Human nature, on the other hand, as spelled out above, amounts to nothing more nor less than the actual human beings (in respect of their defining characteristics). So the good life of the human community at large is the good life of the individuals of that community. Strictly, there is no other life to speak of here.

The major meta-ethical obstacle to fulfilling Golding's third requirement has, of course, been the notorious 'is/ought' controversy, which I have already touched upon. Essentially the issue is that, whereas there are judgments or statements containing the copula 'is' that are capable of being shown true, judgments containing the copula 'ought to' are not capable of being shown to derive by means of valid inference from the former. Since the truth of claims, judgments, and so on, is supposed to be established by reference to evidence that could only be referred to in judgments containing the copula 'is', only if the derivation of 'ought' from 'is' could be accomplished would it be possible to produce true judgments containing 'ought'.

Accordingly, the most influential factor sustaining this controversy has been Humean and post-Humean empiricism, although there are philosophers who have explicitly denied any intimate link between the controversy and its alleged epistemological background. Be that as it may, the prominent home of the controversy is empiricism, with its insistence that all judgments concerning what is the case get their base or ultimate support from sensory impressions. If no such impressions can be produced, in principle (to cash out the meanings of the terms of the judgment — which prevents the empirical verification of the judgment's truth), the claim is not meaningful. For the present what I wish to do is to object to the strict empiricism on which, when closely scrutinized, the bulk of the arguments alleging an 'is-ought' gap rest. (I confess it puzzles me how the connection between empiricism and the alleged gap could be denied. Is it that since no other argument for skepticism seems to work well, but empiricism has been pretty much discredited, this denial is the only hope of the skeptic? It seems a curious mission to me, rescuing skepticism at all costs. But some libertarians, who mistakenly take it that if we know what is morally right, we are immediately authorized to make it happen, may see it as a worthy crusade.)

On the strict empiricist view all true judgments of fact or to what is the case have as their referent something that is a static datum, a certain state of awareness. It isn't well enough appreciated just how special this state of awareness had been for Hume and how strong an impact that fact had on Hume's epistemological and meta-ethical views. The model of the unit of sensory impressions can best be called to mind in connection with a minute snapshot, a static image imprinted on the human mind combined with other such images in a variety of configurations. All judgments pertaining to what *is* the case must, therefore, be judgments which, if true, would stand for some such configuration of images. In Hume there is no justification for the claim that we are aware of what the static images depict. There is only a passing allusion to some secret causation[1] which may exist beyond the sensory impression. On the metaphysical side, however — meaning objectively, apart from consciousness — for all we know, there is nothing. The only kind of stuff that exists is whatever kind the snapshots are pictures of, namely, some kind of state of consciousness (which later became the prime concern for logical atomists).

What makes the above position alluring is that it advances the ideal of the prospect of certainty along empiricist lines, as distinct from the rationalist lines Descartes stressed. But both, of course, support skepticism, including skepticism about knowing whatever should or ought to be done by human beings. Once this background has been abandoned, the 'is/ought' gap resulting from it in most moral skeptics' minds lacks support. With different metaphysical underpinning, as well as a much more open idea and broader scope for what can be objects of knowledge, one can't preclude the possibility of our knowing what is good, right, wrong, or bad and what we should or should not do.

Some, as noted, deny that the 'is/ought' dichotomy depends mainly on empiricism. Kai Nielsen puts the point as follows:[2]

Those who argue that we cannot 'derive an ought from an is' (to put it in slogan form) need not be committed . . . to a Humean 'atomism of

sense-data'. One can accept . . . that there are real interconnections between events without committing oneself to the belief that *moral*
statements can be derived from purely factual *statements*.[3]

Nielsen goes on to deny that "moral terms 'name complex relations',"
as some philosophers claim, and asks, rhetorically, whether for any
relation that 'ought' might name, say X, "could we not ask whether X
ought to have that relation?" He says that "Since this always remains
an open question, is this not a name of that relation?" He continues
by speaking of words or terms that "stand for" something or other
and he claims that any view that proposes that "good" or "ought"
stands for something is not "capable of confirmation" because "there
are no facts corresponding to . . . moral statements" so that any such
correspondence might be "ostensively teachable."[4]

    Granting that Nielsen's empiricism is more tolerant than the
"atomism of sense-data", his endorsement of the 'is/ought' gap still
relies on a distinctly empiricist element in the theory of language,
meaning, and knowledge. To wit, the meaning of words (or ideas of
concepts) *must* be teachable *ostensively*, words 'stand for' relations,
and claims of such relations must be confirmable. So I am not convinced that there is much else to the 'is/ought' gap than an empiricist
philosophy of meaning and confirmation.

    Does the use of the Moorean open question argument show what
Nielsen wants it to? First, for Moore 'good' must refer to 'qualities or
properties' and so his view precludes that 'good' might mean some
relationship (as suggested by the predominant use of 'good' in contexts specifying what something is good *for*). (Much of what Moore
says suggests this, although this is in dispute.) Second, the idea that,
because we may ask of some purported definition of 'good' whether
the definiens really is good, this definiens cannot be the definition of
'good', has unacceptable implications. For example, a scientist who
proposes that 'antimatter has the properties of koinomatter but in
reverse' could be asked, 'Is antimatter the reverse of koinomatter?'
When the definition is in dispute, or in circumstances in which one is
teaching it to someone, such questions are in order. Once the definition has been established as correct, it would serve no purpose to ask
the question. But in an ongoing controversy questions will always be
asked that have the character of open questions. Nothing definitive
follows from our being able to make sense of such open questions
concerning some proposal advanced and being put to the question.

In connection with the concept 'good' we may expect such questions to arise all the time. In normative spheres there will be many who will reject any purported definition. The likely existence of human evil would suggest this. And we need to acknowledge the philosophical propensity to raise questions about anything, even when some of the questions are ultimately without foundation. This is even more likely when what many take to be a discredited idea of what 'good' means is advanced — very probable if a naturalist/essentialist analysis is proposed. (Yet it would be naive to believe that philosophers *qua* philosophers never advance irresponsible and sophistic questions, objections, doubts, or, indeed, theories, positions, hypotheses, and arguments. Certainly already in Plato we see that some philosophers, e.g., Thrasymachus, were not beyond reproach. Any reading of contemporary analytic philosophy will corroborate this.)

It is now time to carry further the attempt to satisfy Golding's third requirement, namely, to provide a conception of the good life for human beings as such and to relate this conception to the task of developing a theory of natural rights.

HUMAN GOODNESS
AND NATURAL RIGHTS

As we saw in Chapter 2, my own view is that a certain (classical) form of ethical egoism or what David L. Norton has called "eudaimonistic individualism",[5] does provide the content of the natural-law ethics Locke said governs the state of nature — that is to say, should guide our conduct prior to considerations of civil law.

Let me very briefly sketch here, once again, the ethical egoist approach to supporting Lockean natural rights and the view of justice which rests on it. I have already discussed some of the meta-ethical issues which must be handled and the results will serve us well in the present project. As I have already suggested, the standards of truth in ethics need not apply to all fields — for example, they do not require irrefutability of the truths achievable therein, whereas in metaphysics the standards would include the requirement that no counter-example can be imagined, since metaphysical facts are comprehensive, covering past, present, future, and possible existence.

For ethics the special requirements include that all human beings must be able to identify and to make use of the moral position proposed as the right answer to the basic question of ethics, namely, 'How should I live my life?' Otherwise the proposed system would not even be a candidate for doing the work expected of it, to guide human conduct as such. (Borderline case problems are, of course, involved in these requirements, but the question is not how this is to be avoided but, rather, which system provides the best grounds for supposing that these can be kept to the minimum.) If people who are not crucially incapacitated cannot practice and/or identify the central principles of a proposed ethical system, cannot live by it, then the system cannot be a candidate for the right ethics.

The central moral principle of the ethical egoist is that in the choice to live a human life, one commits oneself to such conduct as will enhance his (human) existence in the particular case that is his life. Since in the case of a human being this comes down to the claim that one has chosen a human life, the first egoistic virtue, as we saw earlier, is the choice of rationality as one's guiding mode of life. The rest of the virtues would all emerge from this choice, if made constantly, if sustained.

What bearing does this have on social life, law, and politics? The (implicit or explicit) choice to live among others which (social) individuals may be presumed to have made can be well founded. Social life is of enormous value to an individual, and to choose such a life is commendable in most cases. But not just any social life will do. Only when social life makes possible the (comparatively) maximum engagement in self-determined rational conduct can it be regarded as a good prospect. A good society must include provisions that make the choice to be a good human being possible. In society the option to establish these provisions is present because human beings can choose the condition of their social existence, even if only gradually, incrementally. Nonhuman obstacles to a self-determined, rationally conducted life will of course persist and will have to be dealt with individually and in co-operation with others. But even this can be accomplished in a morally commendable manner only if the basic conditions required for living a morally good life are present in society. The obstacles to such a life ought to be removed, and they can be removed. To put the matter in familiar terms, members of a community ought to establish and preserve a constitution of natural human rights. To flourish to the maximum, it would be necessary (though not sufficient) to establish and preserve the natural human rights that fix the principles of human interaction suitable for moral excellence in society.

Of course, if human nature were different from what it is, the principles themselves would be different — although it is difficult to imagine what they would amount to. This point needs to be kept in mind when we consider those philosophers who would rest rights not on human nature but on various consequences human beings might value. The thesis advanced by Russell Hardin, mentioned in the previous chapter, is a clear example of a flexible, indeed unstable, approach to 'principles' of human social life. Yet, if as Hardin and other utilitarians seem to hold, there is no stable human nature from which to derive principles, then indeed human rights will be subject to constant recasting and thus lose their function as principles of justice and law. This is well illustrated in the human-rights theory of William Blackstone, cited earlier. It also invites the kind of relativism that disposes of morality and, more pertinently, of a constitutional politics that looks to predictable guidelines for social conduct. Instead, judges and legislators may cook up their agenda in the light of currently preferred goals, preferences, values. The value of the kind of consequences most utilitarians endorse — namely, subjective preferences — is too variable to provide us with lasting standards of moral and political conduct and institutions.

The challenge put before us by Golding has, I think, been met thus far. In the next sections of the present chapter I will refine the points advanced in this defense by reference to some prominent objections advanced against naturalist ethics and politics, specifically libertarian natural-rights theories. Many of the critics are most concerned about the justification of the right to private property. I will, however, take up this topic only in Chapter 5. Some of the points below may appear ad hoc. Yet the purpose of the following sections is to examine at a relatively abstract level the merits of the present theory, as well as to contrast it with the critics' positions.

SOME REPLIES TO CRITICISMS

The human rights that we all possess because of our humanity are principles of conduct. It is by reference to them that we can answer the political question: 'How should we live our lives as human beings in the company of one another?' or: 'What are the standards of justice in a human community?' Natural-rights theory is not some alternative to a theory of justice. Rather it is a competing theory of political or legal justice. It concludes that instead of, say, fairness to or equal concern for all others, political justice consists of the systematic respect for the moral and political sovereignty of others, defined in terms of those rights individuals have by virtue of being human.

As we saw in Chapter 1, rights are principles defining a range of social reality within which a person ought to be treated by others as the sole judge, jury, and executioner (unless he or she, by continuing citizenship, has consented to the appropriately limited delegation of this posture — for example, to a government). In short, rights specify the sole personal authority of someone to judge and the jurisdiction to act. Others require one's permission to have a morally effective say as to what will happen within one's sphere of rights. These others could be fellow citizens, administrators of governments, or even foreigners who may thus gain entrance to one's community.

The Right of Contract: Obsolete?

First I will return to Russell Hardin's comment that "Anyone who tries to defend an unvarnished right of contract for any two parties to do whatever they want to do under any circumstances will be met with vacant stares from most moral and political theorists today." As I have already noted, the only sensible exclusion Hardin could have in mind is the libertarian view of unregulated contract between two or more parties bearing explicitly and unavoidably on just their own lives and properties — on what they have the right to contract about.[6]

Let us start by recalling that it is arbitrary to bar Hardin's utilitarian approach from being used in analyzing rape, while applying it to violations of property such as theft. But perhaps one could argue that the inviolability of personal sovereignty must be built into the utilitarian calculus in a very fundamental way, so that any breach of that inviolability would have to be taken as a priceless loss.[7] This may be behind the doctrine that whereas personal or human rights are correctly taken to be inalienable, property rights must often be traded for other values. So while rape is categorically wrong, since it violates a person, theft and breaches and limits of contract — as in rent control measures which intrude on the contract between owner and tenant — can be justified whenever the benefits of them are greater than respecting ownership.

Yet the arbitrariness of the distinction between personal or human and property rights still obtains, despite these maneuvers. No doubt my car is related to me physically differently from my body, yet why should that be morally significant? If the car's continued existence and usefulness come about largely by my taking care of it, and if it is necessary for my human dignity — my 'moral space' — then there is no morally significant difference. Nor is there any as far as my stocks in IBM or my apartment house are concerned, to the acquisition and maintenance of which I have devoted an appreciable portion of my life. If one does it the 'old-fashioned way', that is, one *earns* one's wealth, to see it treated as if it were a common resource is, practically speaking, to see confiscated a portion of one's life. (As to just how ascription of property rights should be accomplished, I'll turn to this in Chapter 5.)

It makes more sense to consider property rights as one of the several human or basic rights every individual possesses. Starting with Locke, it has been argued that since people's lives are inexorably connected to nature, to divorce human rights from property rights is no more justified than divorcing human rights from the right to life or liberty. Indeed, the former is just the necessary extension of the latter two so that these can be defined and protected in operational — practical legal — terms. [8]

It seems that the following more accurately sketches the story on rights than what we got from Hardin: The right to life signifies that murder is intolerable, the right to liberty that assault or kidnapping are, and the right to property that theft, robbery, and so on, also ought not to be tolerated. Thus the right to life imposes on the government the restraint against conscription for military purposes or any other sacrifice of individuals to certain desired ends. The right to liberty requires governments to abstain from paternalistic policies such as forcing people not to drink or eat certain items or engage in certain sexual acts. And the right to property prohibits the seizing of people's belongings, by theft, taxation, robbery, burglary, and so on. If the last is denied, the borders between people that let us determine when breaches of the former have occurred will vanish. (Marx realized this but then denied that we ultimately ought to have those borders.)

The entire list of basic rights has deontological force except in the rare circumstances that there are conflicts between them, in which case the right to life is prior, the right to liberty secondary, and the right to property follows these. (Yet, since without the right to property the implementation of the other rights is rarely possible, such conflicts would be rare.)

Utilitarian approaches to basic rights seem to rest on the

widespread preference by people for not violating rights and on the frequent but changing social utility of assigning these rights. Consider that the so-called personal rights of children used to be freely violated for what could easily be taken as utilitarian reasons:

> To us today the revelation of the legal murders and cruelties connected with the trial of children are revolting. We have become so habituated to the kindly and even anxious atmosphere of the Children's Courts, that it is hard to believe that the full ceremonial, the dread ordeal, of the Assize Courts could have been brought into use against little children of seven years and upwards — judges uttering their cruel legal platitudes; the chaplain sitting by assenting; the Sheriff in his impressive uniform; ladies coming to the Court to be entertained by such a sight — the spectacle of a terrified little child about to receive the death sentence which the verdict of 12 men, probably fathers of families themselves, had given the judge power to pass.[9]

Whether children have rights or not would seem, in at least the sophisticated utilitarianism of Hardin, to depend on how much benefit we obtain in the aggregate — including, of course, the children — from treating them with respect for their humanity. If we deem it unimportant to consider their humanity and focus on the value of deterring them from bad behavior, then talking of the rights of children makes no sense.

The Nonexistence of Basic Welfare Rights

James Sterba and others maintain that we all have the right to "receive the goods and resources necessary for preserving" ourselves. This is not what I have argued human beings have a right to. They have the right, rather, not to be killed, attacked, and deprived of their property — by persons in or outside of government. As Abraham Lincoln put it, "no man is good enough to govern another man, without that other's consent."[10]

Sterba claims that various political outlooks would have to endorse these 'rights'. He sets out to show, in particular, that welfare rights follow from libertarian theory itself.[11] Sterba wishes to show that *if* Lockean libertarianism is correct, then we all have rights to welfare and equal (economic) opportunity. What I wish to show is that since Lockean libertarianism — as developed in this work — is true, and since the rights to welfare and equal opportunity require their violation, no one has these latter rights. The reason some people, including Sterba, believe otherwise is that they have found some very rare instances in which some citizens could find themselves in circumstances that would require disregarding rights altogether. This would be in situations that cannot be characterized to be "where peace is possible."[12] And every major libertarian thinker from Locke to the present has treated these kinds of cases.[13]

Let us be clear about what Sterba sets out to show. It is that libertarians are philosophically unable to escape the welfare-statist implication of their commitment to negative liberty. This means that despite their belief that they are only supporting the enforceable right of every person not to be coerced by other persons, libertarians must accept, by the logic of their own position, that individuals also possess basic enforceable rights to being provided with various services from others. He holds, then, that basic negative rights imply basic positive rights.

To Lockean libertarians the ideal of liberty means that we all, individually, have the right not to be constrained against our consent within our realm of authority — ourselves and our belongings. Sterba states that for such libertarians "Liberty is being unconstrained by persons from doing what one has a right to do."[14] Sterba adds, somewhat misleadingly, that for Lockean libertarians "a right to life [is] a right not to be killed unjustly and a right to property [is] a right to acquire goods and resources either by initial acquisition or voluntary agreement."[15] Sterba does realize that these rights do not entitle one to receive from others the goods and resources necessary for preserving one's life.

A problem with this formulation of the Lockean libertarian view is that political justice — not the justice of Plato, which is best designated in our time as 'perfect virtue' — for natural-rights theorists presupposes individual rights. One cannot then explain rights in terms of justice but must explain justice in terms of rights.

For a Lockean libertarian, to possess any basic right to receive the goods and resources necessary for preserving one's life conflicts with possessing the right not to be killed, assaulted, or stolen from. The latter are rights Lockean libertarians consider to be held by all individual human beings. Regularly to protect and maintain — that is, enforce — the former right would often require the violation of the latter. A's right to the food she has is incompatible with B's right to take this same food. Both the rights could not be fundamental in an integrated legal system. The situation of one's having rights to welfare, and so forth, and another's having rights to life, liberty, and property is thus theoretically intolerable and practically unfeasible. The point of a system of rights is the securing of mutually peaceful and consistent moral conduct on the part of human beings. As Rand observes,

> "Rights" are . . . the link between the moral code of a man and the legal code of a society, between ethics and politics. *Individual rights are the means of subordinating society to moral law.*[16]

Sterba asks us — in another discussion of his views — to consider what he calls "a *typical* conflict situation between the rich and the poor". He says that in his situation "the rich, of course, have more than enough resources to satisfy their basic needs. By contrast, the poor lack the resources to meet their most basic needs even though *they have tried all the means available to them that libertarians regard as legitimate for acquiring such resources.*"[17] (my emphasis)"

The goal of a theory of rights would be defeated if rights were typically in conflict. Some bureaucratic group would have to keep applying its moral intuitions on numerous occasions when rights claims would *typically* conflict. A constitution is workable if it helps to remove at least the largest proportion of such decisions from the realm of arbitrary (intuitive) choice and avail a society of men and women of objective guidelines that are reasonably integrated, not in relentless discord.

Most critics of libertarianism assume some doctrine of basic needs which they invoke to show that whenever basic needs are not satisfied for some people, while others have 'resources' which are not basic needs for them, the former have just claims against the latter. (The language of resources of course loads the argument in the critic's favor since it suggests that these goods simply come into being and happen to be in the possession of some people, quite without rhyme or reason, arbitrarily [as John Rawls claims].)[18]

This doctrine is full of difficulties. It lacks any foundation for why the needs of some persons must be claims upon the lives of others. And why are there such needs anyway — to what end are they needs, and whose ends are these and why are not the persons whose needs they are held responsible for supplying the needs? (Needs, as I have already observed, lack any force in moral argument without the prior justification of the purposes they serve, or the goals they help to fulfil. A thief has a basic need of skills and powers that are clearly not justified if theft is morally unjustified. If, however, the justification of basic needs, such as food and other resources, presupposes the value of human life, and if the value of human life justifies, as I have argued earlier, the principle of the natural rights to life, liberty and property, then the attainment or fulfillment of the basic need for food may not involve the violation of these rights.)

Sterba claims that without guaranteeing welfare and equal-opportunity rights, Lockean libertarianism violates the most basic tenets of any morality, namely, that 'ought' implies 'can'. The thrust of ' "ought", implies "can" ' is that one ought to do that which one is free to do, that one is morally responsible only for those acts that one had the power either to choose to engage in or to choose not to engage in. (There is debate on just how this point must be phrased—in terms of the will being free or the person being free to will something. For our purposes, however, all that counts is that the person must have [had] a genuine option to do X or not to do X before it can be true that he or she ought to do X or ought to have done X.) If an innocent person is forced by the actions of another to forgo significant moral choices, then that innocent person is not free to act morally and thus his or her human dignity is violated.

This is not so different from the commonsense legal precept that if one is not sound of mind one cannot be criminally culpable. Only free agents, capable of choosing between right and wrong, are open to moral evaluation. This indeed is the reason that many so-called moral theories fail to be anything more than value theories. They omit from consideration the issue of self-determination. If either hard or soft determinism is true, morality is impossible, although values need not disappear.[19]

If Sterba were correct about Lockean libertarianism typically contradicting ' "ought" implies "can" ', his argument would be decisive. (There are few arguments against this principle that I know of and they have not convinced me. They trade on rare circumstances when persons feel guilt for taking actions that had bad consequences even though they could not have avoided them.)[20] It is because Karl Marx's and Herbert Spencer's systems typically, normally, indeed in every case, violate this principle that they are not bona fide moral systems. And quite a few others may be open to a similar charge.[21]

Sterba offers his strongest argument when he observes that ' "ought" implies "can" ' is violated "when the rich prevent the poor from taking what they require to satisfy their basic needs even though they have tried all the means available to them that libertarians regard as legitimate for acquiring such resources".[22]

Is Sterba right that such are—indeed, must be—typical conflict cases in a libertarian society? Are the rich and poor, even admitting that there is some simple division of people into such economic groups, in such hopeless conflict all the time? Even in the case of homeless people, many find help without having to resort to theft. The political factors contributing to the presence of helpless people in the United States and other Western liberal democracies are a hotly debated issue, even among utilitarians and welfare-state supporters. Sterba cannot make his argument for the typicality of such cases by reference to history alone. Arguably, there are fewer helpless poor in near-libertarian, capitalist systems than anywhere else—why else would virtually everyone wish to live in these societies rather than those where welfare is guaranteed, indeed enforced? Not, at least originally, for their welfare-statist features. Arguably, too, the disturbing numbers of such people in these societies could be due, in part, to the lack of consistent protection of all the libertarian natural rights.)

Nonetheless, in a system that legally protects and preserves property rights there will be cases where a rich person prevents a poor person from taking what belongs to her (the rich person)—for example, a chicken that the poor person might use to feed herself. Since after such prevention the poor person might starve, Sterba asks the rhetorical question, "Have the rich, then, in contributing to this result, killed the poor, or simply let them die; and if they have killed the poor, have they done so unjustly?"[23] His answer is that they have. Sterba holds that a system that accords with the Lockean libertarian's idea that the rich person's preventive action is just "imposes an unreasonable sacrifice upon" the poor, one "that we could not blame them for trying to evade." Not permitting the poor to act to satisfy their basic needs is to undermine the precept that ' "ought" implies "can" ', since, as Sterba claims, that precept means, for the poor, that they ought to satisfy their basic needs. This they must have the option to do if they ought to do it.

Another case that supposedly shows that Lockean libertarianism wrongly restricts the state to protecting only rights to life, liberty, and property is provided by Nancy Davis, concerning the "lonely, shy, and insecure individual" who is being taken advantage of, with her consent, by "a charismatic charmer." Here Sterba asserts: "This example seems to be a clear case of where a person is being used even though, in her present circumstances, she has freely agreed to be so used."[24] This case seems to support the thesis that despite the presence of full, informed consent, the terms of interaction between some people is immoral and, presumably, may be prohibited or regulated by the state. (Why the state? Why not some wise, decent, powerful next-door neighbor? Perhaps because that would violate legal and political rights. But why is that so important in these cases?)

The possibility of such situations is supposed to support a version of paternalism,[25] one feature of welfare-state liberalism. Securing a justification of this practice would certainly assist the anti-libertarian, statist argument. For if we are generally justified in taking care of other adults without permission from them individually, then, prima facie, state officials may do this too.

When people defend their property, what are they doing? They are protecting themselves against the intrusive acts of some other person, acts that would normally deprive them of something to which they have a right, and the other has no right. As such, these acts of protectiveness make it possible for men and women in society to retain their own sphere of jurisdiction intact, protect their own "moral space."[26] They refuse to have their human dignity violated. They want to be sovereigns and govern their own lives, including their own productive decisions and actions. Those who mount the attack, in turn, fail or refuse to refrain from encroaching upon the moral space of their victims. They are treating the victim's life and its productive results as though these were unowned resources for them to do with as they choose.

Now the argument that cuts against the above account is that on some occasions there can be people who, with no responsibility for their situation, are highly unlikely to survive without disregarding the rights of others and taking from them what they need. This is indeed possible. It is no less possible that there be cases in which someone is highly unlikely to survive without obtaining the services of a doctor who is at that moment spending time healing someone else, or in which there is a person who is highly unlikely to survive without obtaining one of the lungs of another person, who wants to keep both lungs so as to be able to run the New York City marathon effectively. And such cases could be multiplied indefinitely.

But are such cases typical? The argument that starts with this assumption about a society is already not comparable to the libertarianism that has emerged in the footsteps of Lockean natural-rights doctrine, including the version advanced in this book. That system is developed for a human community in which "peace is possible". Libertarian individual rights, which guide men and women in such an adequately hospitable environment to act without thwarting the flourishing of others, are thus suitable bases for the legal foundations for a human society. It is possible for people in the world to pursue their proper goals without thwarting a similar pursuit by others.

The underlying notion of society in such a theory rejects the description of human communities implicit in Sterba's picture. Sterba sees conflict as typically arising from some people producing and owning goods, while others having no alternative but to take these goods from the former in order to survive. But these are not the typical conflict situations even in what we today consider reasonably free human communities — most thieves and robbers are not destitute, nor are they incapable of doing something aside from taking other people's property in order to obtain their livelihood.

The typical conflict situation in society involves people who wish to take shortcuts to earning their living (and a lot more) by attacking others, not those who lack any other alternative to attacking others so as to reach that same goal. This may not be evident from all societies that team with human conflict — in the Middle East, or Central and South America, for example. But it must be remembered that these societies are far from being even near-libertarian. Even if the typical conflicts there involved the kind Sterba describes, that would not suffice to make his point. Only if it were true that in comparatively free countries the typical conflict involved the utterly destitute and helpless arrayed against the well-to-do, could his argument carry any conviction.

The Lockean libertarian has confidence in the willingness and capacity of *virtually all persons* to make headway in life in a free society. The very small minority of exceptional cases must be taken care of by voluntary social institutions, not by the government, which guards self-consistent individual rights.

The integrity of law would be seriously endangered if the government entered areas that required it to make very particular judgments and depart from serving the interest of the public as such. We have already noted that the idea of 'satisfying basic needs' can involve the difficulty of distinguishing those whose actions are properly to be so characterized. Rich persons are indeed satisfying their basic needs as they protect and preserve their property rights. As I shall argue in Chapter 5, private property rights are necessary for a morally decent society.

The Lockean libertarian argues that private property rights are morally justified in part because they are the concrete requirement for delineating the sphere of jurisdiction of each person's moral authority, where her own judgment is decisive.[27] This is a crucial basis for the right to property. And so is the contention that we live in a metaphysically hospitable universe wherein people normally need not suffer innocent misery and deprivation — so that such a condition is usually the result of negligence or the violation of Lockean rights, a violation that has made self-development and commerce impossible. If exceptional emergencies set the agenda for the law, the law itself will disintegrate. (A just legal system makes provision for coping with emergencies that are brought to the attention of the authorities, for example, by way of judicial discretion, without allowing such cases to determine the direction of the system. If legislators and judges don't uphold the integrity of the system, disintegration ensues. This can itself encourage the emergence of strong leaders, demagogues, who promise to do what the law has not been permitted to do, namely, satisfy people's sense of justice. Experience with them bodes ill for such a prospect.)

Normally persons do not 'lack the opportunities and resources to satisfy their own basic needs.' Even if we grant that some helpless, crippled, retarded, or destitute persons could offer nothing to anyone that would merit wages enabling them to carry on with their lives and perhaps even flourish, there is still the other possibility for most actual, known hard cases, that is, seeking help. I am not speaking here of the cases we know: people who drop out of school, get an unskilled job, marry and have kids, only to find that their personal choice of inadequate preparation for life leaves them relatively poorly off. ' "Ought" implies "can" ' must not be treated ahistorically — some people's lack of current options results from their failure to exercise previous options prudently. I refer here to the 'truly needy', to use a shop-worn but still useful phrase — those who have never been able to help themselves and are not now helpless from their own neglect. Are such people being treated *unjustly*, rather than at most uncharitably, ungenerously, indecently, pitilessly, or in some other respect immorally — by those who, knowing of the plight of such persons, resist forcible efforts to take from them enough to provide the ill-fated with what they truly need? Actually, if we tried to pry the needed goods or money from the well-to-do, we would not even learn if they would act generously. Charity, generosity, kindness, and acts of compassion, presuppose that those well enough off are not coerced to provide help. These virtues cannot flourish, nor can the corresponding vices, of course, without a clearly identified and well-protected right to private property for all.

If we consider the situation as we are more likely to find it, namely, that desperate cases not caused by previous injustices (in the libertarian sense) are rare, then, contrary to what Sterba suggests, there is much that unfortunate persons can and should do in those plausible, non-emergency situations that can be considered typical. They need not resort to violating the private-property rights of those who are better off. The destitute can appeal for assistance both from the rich and from the many voluntary social service agencies which emerge from the widespread compassion of people who know about the mishaps that can at times strike perfectly decent people.

Consider, as a prototype of this situation on which we might model what concerns Sterba, that if one's car breaks down on a remote road, it would be unreasonable to expect one not to seek a phone or some other way of escaping one's unfortunate situation. So one ought to at least try to obtain the use of a phone.

But should one break into the home of a perfect stranger living nearby? Or ought one instead to request the use of the phone as a favor? ' "Ought" implies "can" ' is surely fully satisfied here. Actual practice makes this quite evident. When someone is suffering from misfortune and there are plenty of others who are not, and the unfortunate person has no other avenue for obtaining help than to obtain it from others, it would not be unreasonable to expect, morally, that the poor seek such help as surely might be forthcoming. We have no justification for assuming that the rich are all callous, though this caricature is regularly painted by communists and by folklore. Supporting and gaining advantage from the institution of private property by no means implies that one lacks the virtue of generosity. The rich are no more immune to virtue than the poor are to vice. The contrary view is probably a legacy of the idea that only those concerned with spiritual or intellectual matters can be trusted to know virtue — those concerned with seeking material prosperity are too base.

The destitute typically have options other than to violate the rights of the well-off. ' "Ought" implies "can" ' is satisfiable by the moral imperative that the poor ought to seek help, not loot. There is then no injustice in the rich preventing the poor from seeking such loot by violating the right to private property. ' "Ought" implies "can" ' is fully satisfied if the poor can take the kind of action that could gain them the satisfaction of their basic needs, and this action could well be asking for help.

All along here I have been considering only the helplessly poor, who through no fault of their own, nor again through any rights violation by others, are destitute. I am taking the hard cases seriously, where violation of ' "ought" implies "can" ' would appear to be most probable. But such cases are by no means typical. They are extremely rare. And even rarer are those cases in which all avenues regarded as legitimate from the libertarian point of view have been exhausted, including appealing for help.

The bulk of poverty in the world is not the result of natural disaster or disease. Rather it is political oppression, whereby people throughout many of the world's countries are not legally permitted to look out for themselves in production and trade. The famines in Africa and India, the poverty in the same countries and in Central and Latin America, as well as in China, the Soviet Union, Poland, Rumania, and so forth, are not the result of lack of charity but of oppression. It is the kind that those who have the protection of even a seriously compromised document and system protecting individual negative human rights, such as the U.S. Constitution, do not experience. The first requirement for men and women to ameliorate their hardship is to be free of other people's oppression, not to be free to take other people's belongings.

Of course, it would be immoral if people failed to help out when this was clearly no sacrifice for them. But charity or generosity is not a categorical imperative, even for the rich. There are more basic moral principles that might require the rich to refuse to be charitable — for example, if they are using most of their wealth for the protection of freedom or a just society. Courage can be more important than charity or benevolence or compassion. But a discussion of the ranking of moral virtues would take us far afield. One reason that many critics of libertarianism find their own cases persuasive is that they think the libertarian can only subscribe to *political* principles or values. But this is mistaken.[28]

There can be emergency cases in which there is no alternative available to disregarding the rights of others. But these are extremely rare, and not at all the sort invoked by critics such as Sterba. I have in mind the desert-island case found in ethics books where instantaneous action, with only one violent alternative, faces persons — the sort we know from the law books in which the issue is one of immediate life and death. These are not cases, to repeat the phrase quoted from Locke by H. L. A. Hart, "where peace is possible". They are discussed in the libertarian literature and considerable progress has been made in integrating them with the concerns of law and politics. Since we are here discussing law and politics, which are general systematic approaches to how we normally ought to live with one another in human communities, these emergency situations do not help us except as limiting cases. And not surprisingly many famous court cases illustrate just this point as they now and then confront these kinds of instances after they have come to light within the framework of civilized society.

Let me finally and briefly turn to the case Sterba borrows from Nancy Davis and explain why it does not suffice to defend any kind of paternalist statist interference, assuming that this is why the case was introduced in the first place.

It seems to me that we (including, especially, a powerful government) owe it to the "lonely, shy and insecure individual" not to interfere beyond the bounds that respect her autonomy, lest we relegate her to the status of a child, which by the example given she clearly is not. There are, of course, some people who are psychologically vulnerable to con-artistry. Most of us have encountered marriages and other relationships similar to the kind Davis and Sterba offer in their example. Yet I do not understand why such situations make it morally permissible to take the responsibility for sound behavior out of the hands of the vulnerable person. If there is any meaning to the idea of human dignity it surely must be that any adult who is not crucially incapacitated — *incapable* of rational judgment in terms of the disciplines concerned with determining criteria for this — ought not to have her power of choice taken from her. Doing so is a kind of kidnapping, assault, and consequent dehumanization.[29] It seems to evidence considerably less confidence in human nature, and in individual human beings, seriously to entertain the idea that some of them need to have their judgments made subservient to others. Moreover, it is a self-defeating idea since if some could require this, surely others might also, and those who do the interfering are not immune. (Here we should note the economists' insight that failures of the market are rarely if ever remedied by political means, since failures of politics tend to be far more costly and irreversible.)[30]

Gewirth's Rights to Liberty plus Well-being

In a recent paper[31] Douglas Den Uyl and I argued that "the egalitarian assumptions behind Alan Gewirth's conception of welfare rights give freedom a *de facto* conditional value — that is, freedom is a value only if it does not stand in the way of egalitarian concerns."[32] Gewirth responded by denying that he is a radical egalitarian, concerned with equality of results. He said that "it is not 'egalitarian concerns' in general but equality of opportunity that figures in my discussion of additive rights to wealth and income,"[33] rights which Gewirth insists he can derive from the necessary conditions of human action, to wit, that one requires well-being (and knowledge) in order to be able to pursue one's objectives. Anyone's human agency implies that everyone has the rights to freedom and welfare.[34] He then added the following point with which I will be concerned here:

> Moreover, like "equality," "freedom" should not be used as a global, undifferentiated concept. There are distinctions between occurrent or particular freedom and dispositional or long-range freedom, and also between different objects of freedom. A temporary interference with a relatively minor freedom, such as a traffic light, is morally less important than a long-range interference with the freedom to perform some highly valued action. Hence, if the affluent are taxed so that a relatively small part of their wealth is removed in order to prevent the destitute from starving, this is a far less significant interference with their freedom than would be the case if they were forced to surrender most of their wealth or were prohibited from supporting political parties, religions, or universities of their choice . . . . [35]

There are numerous criticisms on record aimed at Gewirth's ideas involving the claim that human beings have the right to freedom and to well-being — to be left free to do what they choose and to be provided with what is needed for them to exercise this freedom. He has replied to some of the objections raised against him but he certainly has not admitted that there is anything wrong with his basic view. This view defends the right to (negative) freedom and the right to well-being—which together support a kind of welfare state that mixes the institutions of capitalism with those of socialism (or, in some cases, fascism, which is more inclined to regulate than to seize property). Briefly, Gewirth sees the lack suffered by some people in society as so severe that anyone's wanting to be an acting agent—thus to not suffer this lack—would be impossible without implying that everyone's right to freedom may be circumscribed to the extent that this lack will be eliminated by the equal right to well-being. But the right to well-being is equally subject to being circumscribed because each requires negative freedom to pursue moral objectives.

This is a rationalist, neo-Kantian attempt to derive both the right to freedom and the right to well-being. It is, of course, one candidate for establishing the existence of human rights. If it succeeds, then the welfare state is indeed the just society. If, however, there is a lacuna somewhere in the deductive process, then that endangers the entire edifice.

There is no room here to review the entire question of which of the systems, Gewirth's or some other, is the best for establishing the principles of political justice. I do want to consider here Gewirth's admonition that " 'freedom' should not be used as a global, undifferentiated concept." I am concerned with this remark in part because it is the sort of point that serves to make it appear that some viewpoint has the virtue of moderation, balance, lack of dogmatism, suggesting, in turn, that critics fail to advance views with those virtues.

I want to show that Gewirth's remark only appears plausible but misses the point in the context of discussing rights. It is possible that Gewirth's mistake stems from some people speaking loosely about equality and freedom rather than of *the right* to freedom or liberty. The crucial issue is not whether 'freedom' but whether 'the right to freedom or liberty' is indeed a global, undifferentiated concept.

When one argues with radical libertarians, it is tempting to stress, with Gewirth, that freedom is not an absolute good—there are other goods which evidently may be traded for it. I may trade my freedom to run red lights for the value of safety in traffic. Or I may trade my freedom to be a playboy for the value of a happy home life. A journalist may trade his or her freedom to sell to any bidder for the stability of a secure position with a good newspaper.

Now none of the above is odd usage—people do use the concept 'freedom' in just those ways, so the radical libertarian will appear stubborn and obtuse insisting on the absolute highest value of freedom *per se*. Yet to the libertarian the issue is really not so much freedom as *the right to freedom or liberty*. The view is that within a socio-political context it is paramount to secure this right or its corollary, the right to private property (which effectively secures the right to freedom for every individual).[36] If by restricting 'freedom' we include what happens when one stops at a traffic light, and so on, then libertarians would combat the obvious in opposing the value and justice of restricting freedom. What the libertarian is concerned about is the source of this restriction — is it consensual or not?

The example of the traffic light is a very appealing device for showing the absurdity of some "global, undifferentiated concept" of "freedom". Yet it is also argumentatively unfair, just as it would be unfair to argue against the thesis of the basic right to well-being by noting that in innumerable cases people risk their well-being for the sake of freedom — as when they escape from slavery to seek a very uncertain, possibly unsafe free life, or when 'boat people' embark upon the open seas. These are trade-offs people choose to make and some of them are indeed perfectly sensible, as anyone who has faced complex choices will be able to confirm.

When we speak of trading freedom, what we have in mind is not the right to freedom — the right not to be intruded upon when we carry out our life plans, make our decisions, choose our ways — but some opportunity to do one thing that is excluded if we select a different option. Two senses of 'freedom' are at issue: a right not to be forced to act and an opportunity one may choose to forgo.

The issue between Gewirth and libertarianism is not that well-being is often traded for freedom and freedom may be traded in for values. The issue is whether the right to freedom may be traded in for the right to welfare. This right is something that would have to be traded on a collective basis, by a whole legal order, not by some individual in the course of making various choices regarding his or her life. Moreover, the right to freedom implies the right to engage in trade with willing parties, so trading freedom for security already presupposes the right to freedom of trade.

Rights are not the sorts of things we can trade, any more than we can trade a moral trait of character. We can trade goods for other goods — a refrigerator for a televison set, an opportunity to go bowling for one to go fishing. But to speak of trading off rights is a category mistake.

The libertarian objects to the welfare state's legal structure and public policies not because freedom has been traded off but because in a welfare state the right to liberty is being violated. It is to this issue — not to the one about personal trade-offs — that Gewirth must be understood to address his point that the right to liberty is not a global, undifferentiated concept — that is, not a universal, fundamental, and absolute principle within the context of a political system. This is the thrust of his objection, despite its expression in terms of the value of freedom and its evident availability for morally justified trade-offs. In short, we are discussing here whether the rights human beings possess are best seen as basic principles of political life or mere rules of thumb, to be abandoned whenever some other value is to be vigorously pursued. We are touching on the question, discussed already in this work, whether we ought to see matters in a utilitarian, value-pursuing, consequentialist way or instead in a way that is more principled, less dependent on the uncertainties of a great many of the particulars about any person's and any society's future.

What is the right to freedom? In some respects this is a confusing matter because a right is often understood as a kind of freedom. If one has the right to the use of faculty dining facilties, this means that one ought not to be interfered with when choosing to use them. In short, the right is a kind of freedom — freedom from others' intrusion. This is true of negative and positive rights. If one has a right to a welfare check or to proper health care, it means that in case one should elect to obtain such a valued item or service, no one may interfere (which will translate into others' having an enforceable obligation to deliver such items or services upon the right-bearer's choice).

So the notion 'the right to freedom' embodies a redundancy. It is worth observing that the U.S. Declaration of Independence speaks of "the right to liberty", and although this in itself won't yet help, it gives a hint that this right — what Gewirth and many others, including some libertarians, call the right to freedom — is not unreasonably treated as a global, undifferentiated notion. Liberty, asserts Webster's *Unabridged Dictionary* (1978) in the first definition given, is "freedom or release from slavery, imprisonment, captivity, or any other form of arbitrary control." One way out of the problem of redundancy is to interpret the right to liberty to mean the right to take actions that one chooses to take, not those *others* might wish and force one to take. In that case we could understand by such a right the moral and political imperative never to intrude on other people's actions, to leave them at liberty.

There are of course those who would reject any broad or global conception of the right to liberty. H. L. A. Hart, among many other contemporary legal theorists and political philosophers, makes this pitch:

> We must also substitute for the blindingly general use of concepts like 'interference with liberty' a discriminating catalogue which will enable us to distinguish those restrictions on liberties which can be imposed only at that intolerable cost . . . . How can it be right to lump together, and ban as equally illegitimate, things so different in their impact on individual life as taking some of a man's income to save others from some great suffering and killing him or taking one of his vital organs for the same purpose? If we are to construct a tenable theory of rights for use in the criticism of law and society we must I fear ask such boring questions as: Is taxing a man's earnings or income which leaves him free to choose whether to work and to choose what work to do not altogether different in terms of the burden it imposes from forcing him to labour?[37]

While we can appreciate the worry shown by Hart, there is an equal if not far greater worry of leaving it to some representative democratic assembly, a court, or appointed bureaucrats to decide such matters rather than to individual persons. If one notes, for example, that taxation is the nonconsensual deprivation of someone of some of the earnings he has obtained by spending a considerable portion of his life at a certain task, then perhaps the reason for concern with "blindingly general uses of concepts like 'interference with liberty' " will be appreciated.

Now we can apply this understanding of the libertarian concern with liberty to Gewirth's position that we must trade off one right against another. This sounds like a very reasonable, realistic, practical insight, but is it really?

It is misleading to argue that complying with traffic laws is acceptance of the limits of liberty. The reason is, in part, that such compliance is either (tacitly) voluntary or indeed grudging, under some protest. Consider how often other rules of the road, such as helmet or seat-belt laws, are taken to be infringements of one's liberty. The explanation for that is very likely that the state's management of the roads is not fully understood nor again fully accepted when understood.

Arbitrary control can be imposed on someone only by other beings capable of choice, that is, other persons. The rest of nature does not have the option to exercise justified versus arbitrary control; persons do.

When we now consider the two concepts, 'freedom' and 'the right to liberty', we see that while the former may indeed not be appropriately used as a global, undifferentiated concept, the latter lends itself to such use much more readily. In short, it is plausible enough to maintain that one has the right to liberty even while admitting that one often trades one's freedom—that is, taken as one's opportunity to do something—for this or that other value: security, stability, family life, and so forth. In this sense the term 'freedom' means something akin to spontaneity, the absence of any self-restraint. As such no libertarian principle is violated in the process of trading off one's 'freedom', so long as the right to choose to do it is not violated.

Consider also that to trade something off for another thing, one is assumed already to have a right to it. But this would then lead us to the peculiar idea that we have a right to the right to freedom and thus to the right, in turn, to trade that right off. All this loose talk about trade-offs commits the fallacy of the stolen concept, invoking an idea that can only make sense if we admit what it is used to deny. Engaging in legitimate trade requires the right to liberty, its recognition, and so that right could not itself be subject to trade-offs. When the Founders called certain rights "inalienable" in the Declaration of Independence, they seemed to have been well aware that such rights were of the kind that could not be given up or away or traded off or otherwise disposed of by human beings.

Earlier I used the example of the journalist who trades the freedom—again, the opportunity—to sell to any bidder for the stability of a job with a good paper. No one would think that this in any way impinges on the freedom of the press—which is a shorthand way of referring to the right to liberty enjoyed by those in the profession of journalism. But if the journalist is subjected to governmental clearance of the copy to be sent off to the paper he or she works for, that would appear to be a case of impinging on the right of the liberty of the press. Here arbitrary control is imposed, whereas trading the status of a free-lancer for that of a stringer does not involve a relaxing of one's right to liberty.

Gewirth is not the only critic of libertarianism who invokes the trading or giving up of the freedom to do some particular act as a purportedly clear case of morally innocent compromise of the right to liberty. Ronald Dworkin says "the vast bulk of the laws which diminish my liberty are justified on utilitarian grounds [so] I have no political right to drive up Lexington Avenue [a one-way street headed down]."[38] Claiming that such traffic laws diminish liberty, he says that "they nevertheless do not take away from me anything that I have a right to have."[39]

If we look a bit closer at the two cases, Gewirth's and Dworkin's, we notice a telling similarity. In both the laws are themselves unlibertarian but not because they involve trading freedom but because they involve government monopolies. While Dworkin does refer directly to the right to liberty, his case, as Gewirth's, presupposes the unquestioned state ownership and management of the roads, a presupposition that in a philosophical context one should certainly subject to scrutiny.

Could Dworkin's objection apply to private roads? Not if we understand that liberty or political freedom does not mean opportunity but the absence of intrusion upon one's life by others, the refraining by others from making decisions in one's life. If I have decided to accept the conditions of driving in the Indianapolis 500, then the imposition of the various rules of that race do not constitute deprivation of my freedom, only perhaps my opportunity to drive in ways I might now and then wish to drive.

It is a difficulty of libertarianism that so few of its critics sympathize with it. The case for Marxist communism — which projects some remarkable states of affairs, including human beings with a radically reformed human nature (such that profit, competition, and acquisition will no longer interest them) — is heard out without upsetting in the slightest those examining it. In contrast, the libertarian's presentation of unfamiliar scenarios is received with disdain and scoldings about how counter-intuitive they all are. When communism conceives of the withering away of the entire state — that is, total anarchy — this is deemed a fine enough idea, worthy of serious consideration. The notion that all work will be performed for the love of it alone again is received with understanding nods. When universal brotherly love, full employment, global co-operation and the rest are considered by socialists and others as conditions of a political community, again these are understood to be unfamiliar but certainly not impossible scenarios. That behind this entire vision lie bizarre notions seems not to be terribly disturbing, so long as the sentiments are roughly shared.

One would, in any case, suppose the communist's to be the more impracticable ideas—we already enjoy private cities as well as some private roads in political cities.[40] What is involved in adhering to rules of the road is not in principle different from what is involved in any voluntary trade. In Disneyland, for example, or on the Indianapolis raceway, one accepts the rules as the terms of entry or goes elsewhere for entertainment or auto-racing. No violation of the right to liberty is alleged in these cases, nor when one marries and thus forswears the freedom to 'play the field'.

Gewirth should have realized that there is no reason to think that the right to liberty, consistently applied, is violated when traffic lights are enforced. The recognition that a private, competitive road system might exist would have made it more difficult to find an easy objection to the position that it is wrong to violate the right to liberty, even to help the poor. This stance is not entirely dissimilar from one Gewirth may more readily appreciate, namely, that even for the sake of sparing the sensibilities of adamant feminists or puritans, the civil liberties of pornographers must not be violated. The libertarian is concerned to defend the integrity of the system of rights, regardless of the consequences of protecting these rights in particular cases, consequences a legal system—or individual citizens—should not be burdened with having to consider. (One difference between moral and legal systems is their respective attention to particulars.)[41]

Do Gewirth and Dworkin consider this sort of response to their counter-examples about the global, undifferentiated concept of liberty or the right to liberty? In Gewirth's case, no, probably because he was not emphasizing the right to liberty, but only freedom *per se*, which, as we saw, is easily taken as one among many values. The issue is not freedom *per se* but the right to liberty. And while Gewirth does use this locution in his works, he drifts from it often enough to engender the problem I am discussing here. When we realize that every person's right to liberty is at issue, it is less easy to construe it conditionally, relatively, or differentially, such that liberty might be traded off for, say, security.

Furthermore, by emphasizing the right to liberty, not freedom *per se*, the libertarian can insist that the integrity of the legal system would be jeopardized even in cases of minor, morally negligible, violations. The way precedent is used in legal reasoning makes such a danger inescapable. The law must have considerable stability, just as promises and ordinary contracts must if human beings are to develop and pursue their life plans with coherence and consistency. If what today is property or copyright can too easily be changed tomorrow by some legislature or court, what is the point in saying that one has property rights in the first place?

Gewirth does at one point put the matter in terms of "the right to freedom" when he says that it "is not absolute; it may be overridden by other rights such as the rights to life, health, or subsistence, since the objects of the latter rights are more pressing because more necessary for action." But here a different kind of difficulty faces him. My right to life means that none may kill me without justification. My right to health, however, means that I may secure for myself medical aid even when those capable of providing it want to do something other than aid me. The former right requires no more than abstention from performing an untoward act, an act that uses another person without his permission. The latter right does just the opposite — it treats another in such a way that his or her decision as to what to do with his own life, skills, property is not taken into consideration. Gewirth wishes to ascribe both the right to freedom or liberty and the right to welfare or well-being to all individuals. But the two kinds of rights are in conflict with each other. One or the other must be treated as prima facie or conditional. Gewirth's theory results in a lack of integrity in the system of rights he recommends for society.

Gewirth and others wish to escape these objections by references to the nonabsolute or conditional character of all rights. It is not only that the rights Gewirth ascribes to persons are not the familiar Lockean libertarian rights to life, liberty, and property. It is rather that the rights he does ascribe to persons are nonabsolute or conditional — susceptible of override or limitation when the welfare rights he also ascribes to persons come into play. Gewirth and those who share his views on this matter believe that these rights can be "limited only where needed to prevent or remedy interference with other person's necessary conditions of action,"[42] that is, by the welfare rights of others.

It turns out, however, that now we require additional standards to forge a system of laws that helps us in deciding which rights prevail in one situation, which in another. Gewirth's doctrine of rights offers little help in the resolution of conflicts — it will not be sufficient to show that 'A violated my right to property.' One can then raise the question, 'Well, how severe a violation was it and how much is allowed?' But by what standard will it be decided whether the violation was too severe or not nearly severe enough — for example, how much property is to be taken from people in taxes? Where is the objectivity of law in this kind of decision-making? Basic human rights are proposed as just the sort of (constitutional) moral-political principles to guide such social decisions. By not treating basic human rights as basic, all Gewirth and others do is invite some other set of principles we will have to turn to when we need to make principled decisions about what people are free or not free to do. Or, more likely, they leave the matter to the discretion of those who sit as judges in the courts. Indeed, the current legal climate, in which any strong political interest group can secure the protection of some alleged right to well-being — to be provided with medical care, child-care facilities, a museum, the preservation of an historical building, a subsidy, or the imposition of a tariff upon a foreign import business — suggests what can be expected of a welfare state, a system that embraces both the limited right to liberty and the limited right to welfare. The resulting situation is a kind of Hobbesian war of special interests against all other special interests, each demanding the protection of its alleged liberty or welfare rights.

Gewirth, like Gregory Vlastos before him, seems to forget that rights are basic principles of political life and that making them inherently unstable deprives them of their essential character. To make rights nonabsolute within the legal context is to open a Pandora's box of bureaucratic arbitrariness producing the very situation that the moral-political principles we know as human rights were explicitly designed to render impermissible.

Instead of treating human rights as contextually deontological, as principles rather than piecemeal rules of thumb, Gewirth and Dworkin are inviting the elitism that utilitarianism requires — that is, certain leaders whose value-judgments must be imposed on the rest whenever they find it intuitively certain or in some other fashion warranted to override basic human, individual rights.

There is a snowballing effect arising from this kind of utilitarian thinking. Such thinking ought to be avoided and alternatives to solving the problems for which the violations of rights seemed to be justified should be sought. At a different level of argumentation, of course, there is a kind of teleological consequentialism involved in the present defense of libertarian natural rights. That defense is ultimately based on the central goal each person has in life, goals that are, naturally, very different in their concrete manifestations for different persons. Thus they cannot be reduced to that level of utilitarian calculation that speaks of trade-offs.

Gewirth says that "if the affluent are taxed so that a relatively small part of their wealth is removed in order to prevent the destitute from starving, this is a far less significant interference with their freedom than would be the case if they were forced to surrender most of their wealth or were prohibited from supporting political parties, religions, or universities of their choice." Had he said that 'this is a far less significant interference with their *right to liberty* . . . .' his mistake might have become evident to him. For if one were to substitute for his example — which is such a convenient one in a moral climate that has never regarded the pursuit of wealth as something noble or even worthwhile — an example of minor violations of the right to press liberty, or the right to a fair trial, or to one's own religious worship, it is doubtful that the 'intuitive' force of Gewirth's argument would have carried much weight. When people spend long hours in church, one might argue that they deprive many of the benefits of the work they might instead be performing. And when members of the press indulge themselves in reporting trivia, surely it might be intuitively obvious that they could be spending their time on something more worthwhile, something of assistance to the destitute among us. Furthermore, wealth taken from the rich might well have been spent by them to support their church. Taxing them then comes to much the same thing as if their right to freedom of religion had been directly abridged

The Platonic bias against 'mere' earthly aspirations and worldly success is so firmly embedded that libertarians — who refuse to accept it without proof that there is something so inherently wrong with wealth that it may be treated with moral and legal disdain — rarely have their 'intuitions' treated fairly. This is a special handicap in an atmosphere of philosophical argumentation that puts so much stress on intuition — thinking and feeling that comes naturally to people. In the 1800s paternalism toward black slaves in the South was intuitively natural and right, yet few today would hold that those intuitions should have been taken as decisive.

Despite Gewirth's extensive deductive argumentation, he relies for his rejection of the global, undifferentiated nature of the concept of the right to liberty on no more than the intuitive notion that we often trade off freedom for other values, and that soaking the rich in aid of nobler values than they would choose to pursue is morally acceptable. The libertarian defense of the absoluteness of the principles of human rights to life, liberty, and property may not sail easily, but more will be required than such intuition-mongering to sink it.

Gewirth, of course, hopes to buttress his defense of welfare statism from many angles, including the notion that we tacitly consent to being taxed for the sake of the needy. He says that just as the criminal "chooses" the results of his or her actions, including jail, even (we may surmise from Gewirth's reference to the "logic" of the choice) if no intention was formed focussed on that result, so, too, the citizen who interacts with others, has, by his choice, assumed "the duties required . . . including those fulfilled by the supportive state with its protection of welfare rights and its corresponding restrictions on certain freedoms." He thinks that the tacit consent of the thief or murderer to abide by the basic principles of community conduct also applies to the federal tax evader, inspection dodger, or regulation violator.

But, as I argue in Chapter 7, one cannot explicitly or tacitly agree to something that would violate someone else's rights. That kind of authorization or consent involves deciding matters one has no authority to decide. So while it is possible that one should tacitly agree to respect the rights of others, it is not possible that one should tacitly agree to the supportive state, which takes from persons what is theirs against their will. Nor has one agreed to claims against one's own peaceful conduct—e.g., if one produces some wealth, one need not tacitly agree to part with it for others' sake just by virtue of joining others' company. The conditions for joining don't include giving up one's life, liberty, or wealth, but do include not taking others' lives, liberty, or wealth.

Gewirth and other defenders of the welfare state and opponents of capitalism substitute the principle of welfare rights for the virtue of generosity. They believe that the urgency with which some people desire and need support establishes a (politically enforced) right to this support. But someone may need something very urgently, say a kidney, while another possesses two of these, with one enough for reasonable health, and yet no right to such a kidney is established thereby. This is even true when the possession is not a result of achievement, creativity, accomplishment, productivity, or some other chosen conduct but mere accident of birth. The crux of the matter is that we are not slaves of one another in a good society, but live as sovereigns and with limits to what we can consent to, even about ourselves.

In Gewirth's doctrine of human rights there is a failure to ground the political principles in a more fundamental ethical theory. This is a grave oversight. We can ask the question 'How should I conduct myself?' before we move on to the question, 'How does the answer to that question bear on our relationship to other people?'

If we are individuals, not simply members of some natural team or cell, then the logic of this kind of moral inquiry already suggests that when we enter society, conceptually or actually, some unbreachable sphere of personal jurisdiction will have to be recognized for each of us. But to know what the jurisdiction is, we need to have the answer to the first question, to the question bearing on personal, individual conduct. That is why I began the present work with a defense of classical egoism as a sound moral theory. Once we are clear about the fact that every individual ought to strive for a good life for himself or herself, then we know that the conditions necessary for making this possible — but not for guaranteeing it — in society are indispensable conditions of justice.

Between Positive and Negative Rights

One philosopher who has dealt with whether positive and negative rights are capable of being distinguished directly is Henry Shue.[43] In essence Shue holds that all basic rights are really positive rights. This is because he believes that we do not so much have a basic right to life or liberty but to having our life and liberty (or as he calls it, "security and subsistence") protected by the government.[44] To accomplish his task, Shue states the position of those who uphold the positive/negative rights distinction and defend negative rights as dominant:

> Since subsistence rights are positive and require other people to do more than negative rights require — perhaps more than people can actually do — negative rights, such as those to security, should be fully guaranteed first.[45]

But to this understanding of the situation (framed here without benefit of the terminology of actual proponents of the distinction) Shue objects as follows:

> . . . neither rights to physical security nor rights to subsistence fit neatly into their assigned sides of the simplistic positive/negative dichotomy . . . . In an organized society . . . no one would have much interest in the bare rights to physical security . . . .[46]

Shue holds that people have an interest in what "might be called rights-to-be-protected-against-assault-upon-physical-security", which is a positive right in that government must produce protection. Thus, Shue believes, the so-called negative rights, the existence of which even many advocates of positive rights accept, are in fact positive rights.

Shue appears to take his thesis back when he explains that "In any imperfect society enjoyment of a right will depend to some extent upon protection against those who do not choose to violate it."[47] Here Shue speaks of the *enjoyment of a right* depending upon its protection. That suggests that the right in question exists prior to its protection or any 'right-to-be-protected-against-assault-upon-[e.g.] physical-security'. That leaves open the possibility that the right that may or may not be protected is a negative right after all. Of course, talk about "enjoyment of a right" is murky from the start, so Shue might reformulate his claim to read: "My right that you protect me depends upon your actually protecting me." But I am not sure this will help. The language Shue employs suggests that there is some (negative?) right and that could be violated, which generates the further (positive) right to be provided with protection.

Shue, along with Ronald Dworkin and James Nickel,[48] fails to notice that the existence of the government or state—which is supposed to fulfill the duty which is the correlative of the positive right to being protected he believes we all have—is morally problematic. For example, where did the state derive its authority to restrain those who would violate our rights, ones we might enjoy without this violation? And how does its right to use the resources needed to provide protection arise? Furthermore, if, as Shue, Dworkin, and Nickel seem to suggest, we have no basic negative rights which we may justifiably protect, how does the government get its authority to deliver the protection Shue agrees it must deliver? The negative-rights theorist has an answer: the government is voluntarily created to protect negative rights and our positive right to receive its protection is derivative from our compact to have those negative rights protected by someone. Thus the positive right is not basic.

But Shue's case has additional weaknesses. For one, it is not the right to "physical security" that most negative-rights theorists regard as a basic negative right. Rather it is the right to life and, derivatively, the rights to liberty and property. Physical security *per se* is not something anyone has a negative right to because physical security can be threatened and destroyed by other than human agents. Negative-rights theories spell out only such rights as could be violated by persons. They have caused confusion when they have failed to make themselves clear enough, as when they speak of the 'right to life' or the 'right to property', which has been misread to mean 'the right to be provided with life' or 'the right to be given property'.

But perhaps Shue has in mind, when he speaks of the basic right to physical security, the basic rights to life and liberty. These imply, among other things, not only that none may destroy or threaten to destroy one's physical security, but that one may resist any attempt by others to do so. And then a basic right to physical security would amount to a negative right.

Still, the possibility of an ambiguity in Shue's choice of terms needs to be considered because if indeed we have a right to physical security *per se*, whatever the source of threats against it, then this suggests that we possess more than a negative right from the very outset. If one had a right to physical security against, say, the San Andreas Fault or Mount Saint Helens, then to have this right respected, some people may have to engage in some positive actions—such as building earthquake-proof dwellings or lava barriers for everyone. In short, one could read Shue as suggesting that we all have a claim against others to make them do what they can to protect us from such dangers to our physical security.

Thus, in the familiar sense one cannot have a basic negative right to physical security. One can have a negative right, however, to not having one's physical security *taken from one by others*. That is because negative rights are claims against moral agents to refrain from doing certain things, namely, whatever invades one's "moral space", to use the apt phrase of Nozick.[49] However, as is observed in *Black's Law Dictionary*, "wherever there exists a right in any person, there also rests a corresponding duty upon some other person or upon all persons generally." Negative rights are not claims against 'the heavens' or against nature. Yet one's physical security can be imperilled by these far more readily than by other people.

Then again, the view of negative rights against which Shue argues does not support a basic right to physical security but rather one to life or liberty or property. Each of these is supposed to be a negative right because other people could be threatening them, not through failure to act, but through their failure to refrain from action. The right to life means that others must not take one's life, not that one may not be allowed to die. The right to liberty means that other people must not assault or kidnap one, not that one may not find oneself debilitated from disease or natural catastrophe. And the right to property, in this tradition, means that others must not take one's valuables without permission.

Furthermore, in cases of such rights violations government is established in part to properly respond.[50] It is a unique instrument in that its response to rights violations must itself be constrained by due-process considerations, whereas responses to other kinds of threats or injuries — from earthquakes or volcanic eruptions, for instance — does not morally require the exercise of due process (which means proceeding justly).[51] As J. Roger Lee puts it,

> There [is] a set of wrong actions such that, if an individual, A, performs any one of them, as a direct consequence of his so doing, someone else, B, suffers a loss. No man, B, who has a reasonable concern for his own interest can tolerate A's so acting, and consequently each man has the obligation to *defend* himself against others who would act in the way specified. In civilized societies these defense activities are made subject to both the division of labor and the rule of objective law via the institution of government and its police.[52]

For example, one may try to resist earthquakes with any degree of force, but one may not resist robbery with such recklessness. Government — which within the negative-rights framework is established to secure us in our basic rights — has to abide by the very principles which it is established to protect.

If I am simply insulted by another and none of my rights has been violated, I may ask for an apology, refuse ever to speak to the person, ignore the matter, or whatnot, depending on my priorities. It is not the case that I must respond in certain ways, even if I ought to. Thus in making my response, no enforceable due-process considerations arise. (I may not respond with aggression, of course. This is because such a response violates rights.) And one of the signs of the enlargement of the scope of the government's power is that in more and more areas of conduct one is legally bound to conform to considerations of due process. In short, one is not trusted and left fully responsible for the bulk of one's moral life. Due process applies precisely where our conduct will deprive others of their liberty, something they ordinarily have a right to. And we must tread very carefully when we verge on rights violations!

What Shue does is to take government morally for granted. This avoids having to understand its nature in light of its distinctive purpose within the negative-rights tradition. Shue makes government an unexplained part of the environment, not a result of 'contract' or 'compact'. Yet, as defenders of basic negative rights argue, we cannot make sense of the unique moral status of government—e.g., its authority to use force, to impose its edicts, to try and to convict criminals—without reference to the basic negative rights human beings have which they may act to protect via the agency of government.

So the positive "rights-to-be-protected-against-assault-upon" one's autonomy and independence from other people really is not a basic right at all. It is a special political right which, if it developed without the violation of anyone's basic rights—for example, 'with the consent of the governed'—may be enforced, just as terms of other voluntarily created contracts may be. The rights Shue so readily collapses are, in fact, morally distinct and necessarily so. The authority of government to act in behalf of someone—for example, as police, prosecutor, and prison warden—rests on the prior justifiability of hiring such an organization in the first place. And this hiring is justified because we possess the basic (negative) rights we do.

No one who upholds the doctrine of negative basic rights and duties need deny the existence of special positive rights and duties—e.g., those arising from contract or special relationships voluntarily created (parents vis-à-vis children). The point negative-rights theorists stress is that basic rights are negative and subsequent positive rights must square with them—for example, rights arising out of contract must never contradict basic rights to life, liberty, or property. Which means that contracts must rest on consent. That is why involuntary servitude—not, however, voluntary service—would be prohibited in a society which regarded the negative right to liberty as basic.

Among the positive rights and duties viewed as important by negative-rights theorists, we may find all the civil and political rights of citizens of a free society. Once the Declaration of Independence of the new American republic had asserted the existence of basic negative rights, the rest of the detailed work had to be done under the rubric of the U.S. Constitution which, ideally, should have spelled out the various positive rights which emerged from the compact that established the government. Citizens, upon having established and/or consented to live under a government which exists to protect their basic rights, owe their government certain (agreed upon) duties — payments for services, participation in administration, co-operation in crime detection and prevention, offering testimony in the pursuit of justice, and so on.[53] This is not negligible by any means, but it fails to usher in the whole slew of positive duties which Shue and others wish to uphold with their doctrine of the inherent positive nature of all rights. In any case, the positive rights and duties so grounded would not be 'basic'.

One charge, advanced by James Fishkin,[54] against theories of government which rest on basic negative rights has been that so long as rights are not violated, no other moral judgment is relevant to government's conduct. But the negative-rights tradition is by no means committed to accepting only the minimal moral content of political life. Rather, quite outside of politics, it can invoke considerations of moral virtue and vice in any area of human action and institution. All this tradition insists upon is that in a just society the scope of rights and duties (as here understood, namely, enforceable moral imperatives) is limited to preserving the "moral space" of all individuals. That is, everyone has the basic right to his or her life, liberty, and property and the duty not to violate others' similar rights, so that everyone be in charge of his or her moral life. None of this makes it impossible to morally criticize governments which mistreat civil servants, squander resources, implement irresponsible hiring and firing practices, and so on. Government, as other human agencies, can act wrongly in several ways, some involving the violation of rights, which they are prohibited from doing (so that at some point doing such wrongs can lead to the loss of its moral authority), and some involving the breach of various moral principles — courage, prudence, generosity, and so forth.[55]

Since advocates of negative rights are not usually intuitionists, they are usually not that impressed when philosophers have strong feelings about equality of opportunity, racial prejudice, frivolity, waste, obscenity, irreverence, sexual indiscretion, and so forth. These may be valid moral concerns but not ones which justify violating basic negative rights. It can be morally callous to ignore other people's needs or to exhibit pictures of women in degrading poses. But what is to be done about such things is a matter of personal moral responsibility, not of enforceable duty. It does not follow from negative rights theory that public opinion, social pressure, or even ostracism would always be ruled out. Simply because the government's tool of reaching its objectives, namely, physical force, is not available to private citizens with genuine moral concerns, it does not follow that these others are therefore hamstrung. This seems to me to apply to the concerns of both leftist and rightist critics of libertarianism. There are other than political means by which charity can be practiced or soulcraft administered. The libertarian holds that these more peaceful means are indeed more honorable than those his political adversaries propose to employ.

One other way in which the point that Fishkin advances may be put is that in line with the kind of system of economics that natural-rights theory would support, certain important relations among human beings would become rather peculiar. For example, A. D. Lindsay claims that economic or commercial exchange is such a relation. "In it," he tells us, "A gives to B what B wants, in return for B giving A what A wants . . . . A is not responsible for B's wants, nor B for A's; and therefore—in this curious relation not A but B decides what A should do: and not B but A decides what B should do."[56]

But this is to look at the commercial exchange situation without taking into consideration the role of human volition. Say that A gives to B what B wants—James gives Harry some pornographic literature or dope. Now when A gives this to B, does B have to take it? Is Harry forced by James to accept the pornographic literature or the dope? Or, alternatively, does Harry decide that James should give Harry the pornographic literature or the dope? No. Both parties enter the relationship without anyone's forcing them into it. James may offer something for sale, and this is his own chosen conduct; Harry may solicit something from those in the marketplace, and this is entirely his own chosen conduct. (Of course, if one believes that advertising or solicitation determines other people's conduct, then the situation has to be reconceived. But then we lack the needed conditions for viewing it in a moral light from the outset — ought implies can, and if the parties to trade have no choice about what they do, then they cannot be said to be morally responsible.)

Some, of course, wish to argue that if the trade is in rights, so that James is trading his right to X for Harry's right to Y, and if the rights are inalienable, then the trade would be necessarily wrong and this would indict the market economy as inherently morally flawed.

Yet this is a confusion. One cannot trade inalienable rights, since the very conditions of trade presuppose the respect and protection of those rights. If I have a natural, inalienable right to life, liberty, and property, how could I trade this right without destroying the conditions of trade itself, that is, my free agency as a living human being who rightfully owns some valuable items and chooses to offer them for trade? There is no way to reconcile the trading of inalienable rights with the very framework of free trade in goods and services.

There are those who would argue that labor itself is an inalienable value, though this changes the situation because here we are not talking about rights. It is unlikely that any doctrine of inalienable values can be defended, and I am not going to address this issue here. If, however, it should be claimed that one's right to one's labor is inalienble, then what needs to be clear is that when one sells one's labor — or, rather, offers one's skills for conditional use by others — one has not sold, or offered, anything inalienable, since one still retains the right to that labor.

Perhaps the reason this kind of problem arises in connection with contemporary rights theories is that many philosophers conceive of rights in a less principled way than is possible within the natural-rights tradition. If one does not have the natural right to life, liberty, and property but, rather, to certain particular things or kinds of things and courses of conduct — one's car, one's going to church, one's writing of philosophy articles — then it may appear that some of these are alienable, others not. (It will also be theoretically easier to treat the rights of some people — such as those who work in the news-reporting business, those who write novels and philosophical articles — as perhaps inalienable, while treating the rights of others — businessmen, plumbers, physicians — as perhaps alienable. From such a perspective we may believe we see a convenient route to treating different people very differently, simply by virtue of the work they do and how important or unimportant it is for them to do it as they see fit.)

When we consider whether a capitalist, libertarian society is free, whether it secures human beings their right to individual freedom or liberty, we need also to discuss some of the radical Marxian critiques that flatly deny that capitalism respects human freedom of choice. Not only do they criticize capitalism for failing to ensure for us well-being and equality of opportunity. They also hold that capitalism is in fact an enemy of individual freedom. Marx made this point in the

19th century, and in our time many have followed his lead. For example, Professor Larry Preston claims that "a capitalist market, understood as a system in which production and distribution are based on the pursuit of private interest through the acquisition and transfer of privately owned property, generally denies freedom to most participants."[57] His basic defense of this claim lies in his identification of freedom as follows: "Free decisions and actions are identified as those in which an agent's conscious deliberation has played an essential role"[58] and, "The prerequisite of deliberate choice can only be determined with reference to specific activities associated with particular roles."[59] Furthermore, "A choice is voluntary (freely made) if the persons who agree to it possess, before they decide, the relevant capacities and conditions for deliberation regarding the proposed transaction."[60]

Within the Anglo-American political tradition freedom has been perceived differently. As F. A. Hayek observes,

> The original meaning of the word "freedom" means always the possibility of a person's *acting according to his own decisions* and plans, in contrast to the position of one who was irrevocably subject to the will of another, who by arbitrary decision could coerce him to act or not to act in specific ways. The time-honored phrase by which this freedom has often been described is therefore *independence of the arbitrary will of another*. In this sense "freedom" refers solely to a relation of human beings to other human beings, and the only infringement on it is by coercion by other human beings.[61]

In Hayek the emphasis is placed on 'his own' decisions. And in contrast to Preston's characterization of a free decision, Hayek does not insist on deliberation having an "essential role" in free choice. The implicit difference between the two conceptions of freedom seems to be fairly clear. It is that whereas Preston does not stress personal autonomy and self-determination, Hayek does, and while Hayek seems to accept decisions of any sort—whimsical, intentional, negligent, or deliberate—Preston allows only deliberative or self-consciously calculated decisions for a choice to be free.

We can further appreciate the difference between what is meant by 'human freedom' in connection with the feminist movement which has two meanings of 'liberty' associated with it. First, feminism means the *absence of restraints imposed by other people* who would keep women under a yoke or treat them as if they were not of age but in constant need of guidance (from males or from the state). Second, feminism means women being guided to a higher state of consciousness and human emancipation.

Preston holds that 'real' freedom is not the libertarian, capitalist sort. Following a very respected tradition, what his theory proposes is that one can only be really free if one is also on the right path. The famous biblical text, "The truth shall make you free" (John 8:32) testifies to the currency of this sense of the term. A person 'imprisoned' by temptation, false belief, whim, desire, and the rest is in this sense quite unfree. Consider the conception of freedom embraced by Karl Marx, who was following Hegel, who, in turn, was elaborating the tradition of freedom originally developed in Plato:

> [F]reedom . . . can only consist in socialized man, the associated producers, rationally regulating their interchange with Nature, bringing it under their common control, instead of being ruled by it as by the blind forces of Nature; and achieving this with the least expenditure of energy and under conditions most favorable to, and worthy of, their human nature.[62]

Marx was invoking the idea of freedom which ordinary people invoke when they say they wish to be 'free of worry, trouble, hardship, psychological blocks, bad memories, disease'. From the time of Plato this sense of 'human freedom' has been a powerful contender. It refers to our capability of attaining full human flourishing, unhindered by such obstacles as ignorance, illness, or sin. In our day many have in mind this sense of freedom when they refer to the Marxist-Leninist kind of liberation. Unlike the libertarian use of this term 'liberation' here means being guided towards a good life. Compare the liberation of France with the liberation of Poland.

One trouble with Preston's view is that, with such an understanding of 'free to choose', we may end up saying that only those are free to choose who in fact make the correct choice. The "relevant capacities and conditions for deliberation" have to include individual wisdom and the ability to select wisely from among the alternatives, including the absence of any impediments to such wise decisions, such as ignorance or poverty. The tendency then is for unwise choices to be treated as evidence of absence of choice.

A deliberation is, furthermore, a rare process. Most people proceed through their days without much deliberation, yet acting *inten-*

tionally, that is, fleetingly thinking of their objectives and almost automatically using the means to attain them, as when they switch on a light as they enter a room. The intentional character of such actions may be gleaned from the fact that, if some mishap is associated with them, persons who took the actions are held responsible for what they did. But these are perfectly free actions when they are not forced on them by others. For Preston, however, they would be unfree actions since they did not involve deliberation, the self-conscious, self-monitored mental process which is characteristic of intellectual activities such as theorizing about freedom.

Furthermore, if persons are metaphysically free — possess free will or the power of self-determination — they might not elect to inform themselves about the facts that may make a choice a wise one and thus they may be regarded as unfree. Yet they *are* free, since they *might* have gained more information. No one prevented them. Therefore they are essentially free.

What sense of the term 'freedom' is then primary? On the one hand, if we are focussing on progress toward human flourishing, human freedom may well mean what the tradition from Plato, through Rousseau, Hegel, Marx, T. H. Green, and many contemporary intellectuals has argued. This tradition sees the libertarian conception of human freedom as narrow and incomplete. To pretend to be concerned with human freedom when one is really interested only in freedom from the aggressive intrusion of other people — so well expressed in that American war cry: 'Don't tread on me!' — is seen as distorting an important value in human existence. (Even some neoclassical economists prefer to understand by 'freedom' the maximizing of our options, creating a broad range of possibilities. Our freedom, they say, is enhanced with an increase of our wealth.)

On the other hand, the view that human 'freedom', in the anti-libertarian sense, is a political concern, which ought to be regulated by political processes, can also be disputed. The reason is that it assumes a conception of human nature which is contrary to fact. Plato, Hegel, and Marx — to name just the main proponents — did not credit human individuals with a basic kind of freedom, namely, freedom of the will or the power of self-determination. Nor does Preston. He notes that "Capitalist exchanges have become coercive because participants can recognize an alternative situation which would provide them with substantially greater freedom, a situation that the capitalist market prevents them from having."[63] In short, people are not acting freely under capitalism because they are forgoing options that they might enjoy and it would be beneficial for them to enjoy. The "freedom" Preston thinks people might enjoy involves what people could benefit from in their relationship to others: greater access to information, better conditions for deliberation, and so on. For example, they might have been better educated, they might have possessed more wealth. This is, of course, not so much any kind of freedom but rather a better standard of living.

This outlook sees persons as we do trees or flowers that grow not from their own determination but spurred on by the natural environment. And if there are deficiencies in that environment, there will be impediments standing in the way of growth.

As Preston puts the point, "We now realize that the exchanges of capitalism generally do not represent agreements in which both (or all) participants are better off if 'better off' is viewed as gaining access to the resources needed to exercise freedom."[64] Once Preston has recast "free choice" as making "the best possible choice one could make", it is no wonder that capitalist exchanges are not free. Preston, as others in this tradition, identify human freedom with human success.

In this perspective the primary task of good government — of those who understand and have the power to upgrade the species — is to free them from such impediments to growth. This is clearly not accomplished simply by protecting people against the aggressive intrusion of other human beings. No, they need total 'liberation' — the prevention of all intrusions such as poverty, disease, ignorance, illness, and even sin. Thus Preston holds that "Physical force need not always be either morally objectionable or a denial of freedom. Efforts physically to restrain drug addicts from gaining access to drugs may be done for moral reasons and in the interest of freedom — to enhance the addicts' ability to make deliberate choices."[65] It is but a short distance from here to the view that forcing people not to advocate revolutionary policies, or the wrong religion, or censoring trashy movies and bad literature is morally proper because it enhances people's ability to live properly.

Natural rights:
STABLE POLITICAL PRINCIPLES

Natural human rights are not the unstable rules of thumb that they are taken to be in utilitarian theory, wherein what determines whether they apply is the consequences their application will produce. Instead, natural human rights belong to that sphere of rights determined by the fact that one is a human being who has chosen, with moral propriety—in pursuit of a good, happy, human, life—to embark on social-political life. This life is at the disposal of others only when one gives permission, except in extraordinary situations (such as when one is crucially incapacitated). As can be seen from the foregoing chapter and passage, my version of the doctrine of natural rights rests on ethical egoism. Can we defend natural rights, a proposed set of standards for political justice, on the basis of ethical egoism? To use Leonard Choptiany's words, is it true that "being agreeable to egoists . . . could make . . . an institution just"?[66]

To establish the justice of a legal framework, it would have to be shown that this framework agreed with basic principles of morality. In the present case it would have to be shown that classical ethical egoism supported certain political, legal, or constitutional standards in terms of which it could be claimed that justice among members of a human community would be best secured. Justice in the context of politics refers to circumstances in which everyone relates to others suitably. If everyone is treated in a fashion that he or she deserves under the circumstances, it can be said that justice prevails. The political principles and legal framework of a human community are aimed at the maintenance of justice, so that various elements of such a system must provide the standards of justice.

The standards at issue are the natural rights each member of the community possesses. A system that embodies these rights in its constitution, its judicial and penal code, its administrative methods (due process of law), and functions satisfactorily (without widespread systematic abuse and corruption), provides the community with *political justice.*

All this rests on the view that human beings ought to pursue their happiness, their rational self-interest. Inasmuch as this pursuit must occur by choice each member of the community must be treated in such a way as to retain personal authority within a certain sphere of reality. (A slave would not be bound to obey, but this is because others would have violated his rights as a rational, social, morally responsible human being.)

These rights are not instruments for keeping people apart, as Marxists hold, but for making it possible for them to come together willingly, of their own choice, not as slaves, or serfs, or conscripts. Human rights free men and women of ties that may be imposed on them by other persons. They do not free them from hardship, difficulty, even catastrophe.

The concrete manifestation of the capacity of human rights to secure justice may be illustrated by considering the cardinal virtues of ethical egoism: rationality and productivity, and how their practice could be protected and preserved in a human community by reference to the legal system and instruments that rest on such rights. The justification for such protection and preservation would then be properly regarded as the natural rights each individual possessed. The administration of the system and the conduct of citizens in terms of the standards these rights provided would secure political justice.

The term 'justice' is often used to mean something much broader than what I am concerned with here. One can do an injustice by misrepresenting another's argument, by betraying a friend, by failing to heed the requirements of one's promises. One can be unjust by overburdening a friendship, by failing to fulfill the expectations of one's colleagues, or by not according to one's employees the rewards their performance warrants. But here we are using the concept of justice in the ancient, Platonic sense, meaning 'fully virtuous'. Society may have ample need for justice in that sense, but what concerns political philosophy is the conditions of *political* justice or virtue, which would guide the conduct of citizens *qua* citizens and governors *qua* governors.

As for the moral virtues of rationality and productivity, the former, of course, is the primary, and the second a corollary, virtue. Rationality is a basic virtue, the exercise of which is required by one's nature as a human being and the value to each person of living the life of such a being. Productivity, though narrower in scope, is a virtue related to our dependence for securing a good human life from various instruments of sustenance and wellbeing: food, shelter, specialized knowledge, pleasures, and so forth. In complex societies productivity can, of course, take a wide variety of forms, as do other virtues. Nevertheless, ethical egoism implies that some form of productivity, determined by one's individual attributes and circumstances or opportunities, is a moral imperative.

Each of these virtues requires a sphere of implementation. To guide one's actions reasonably, one needs a place in which these actions can occur. To be a rational parent or student or conference organizer or political campaigner or newspaper editor, one requires a sphere of authority. Room for children, a study area, a conference hall, or offices will be needed, depending on one's tasks. A poet must have the chance to obtain paper and pencil and a place to work. The choice to live and the commitment that this implies to rational conduct give rise to the requirement of a sphere of individual authority.

Ethical egoism requires, then, that the appropriate way to treat human beings involves respecting their right to acquire and hold some sphere of personal authority for them to utilize, govern, exercise judgment about, and act within. Full rational conduct itself would not be possible without this sphere, which means that the prime egoistic virtue of choosing to live rationally could not be fully exemplified without the optimum respect for the human rights that provide individuals with their own spheres of authority and jurisdiction. This seems to me the significance of the point made in the following lines from William Pitt the Elder:

> The poorest man may in his cottage bid defiance to all the forces of the Crown. It may be frail; its roof may shake; the wind may blow through it; the storm may enter; the rain may enter; — but the King of England cannot enter; all his force dares not cross the threshold of the ruined tenement![67]

The standard of justice pertaining to such cases is the right to property, the concrete expression of the right to life and liberty. This right is not some independently existing right to freedom of trade that one is entitled to or should enjoy by virtue of certain purely economic considerations such as an enhanced flow of commerce or higher social output. Granted, respect for and protection of this right will enhance prosperity. People will be better off materially. The main moral reason in support of this right, though, is that without it, a person could not embark on the fullest possible moral life in society and would have his freedom of choice obstructed by uninvited others.

It is crucial, from a moral point of view, to secure a workable, systematic means by which one's life and works can be distinguished from the lives and works of others. This will facilitate the distinction between the often extremely valuable co-operation of individuals and the often intrusive and even debilitating interference of those whom one does not choose for associates. An individual's pursuit of a rational, self-interested life is made manifest, in part, by the associations he or she elects. If the significance of these choices is not to be lost, it must be possible to avoid and resist those not so chosen.

We can say, then, that what establishes the presence of human rights is the moral necessity of principles of justice in our communities, principles that secure for us the domain of individual moral responsibility — whether on a humble or a massive scale of influence. What we can now consider is why these rights are of the Lockean, negative, rather than the more recently-favored, positive, sort.

As we have seen, some critics of the libertarian society have rested their position on the denial of a distinction between positive and negative rights. By this denial they reach the conclusion that the moral-political foundations for such a free society, those Lockean natural or basic rights, are ultimately untenable. As well as those with egalitarian or socialist leanings, some conservatives have welcomed the argument against the negative/positive rights distinction.[68] They think this helps to prove that the fully free society lacks adequate moral grounding, that individualism is a bankrupt political idea, and that a more paternalistic state ought to be established in which statecraft merges into soulcraft.

Basic rights to life, liberty, and property are negative rights in that they require only that people do not murder, assault, kidnap, or steal from one another. Respect for these rights does not require any positive action such as being neighborly or supplying others with food, education, money, medicine, or enlightenment. There may be many other moral principles binding on persons, but as far as basic rights are concerned, only negative ones exist within the Lockean tradition.

PROPERTY RIGHTS AND THE GOOD SOCIETY

THE NATURE OF
PRIVATE PROPERTY

In this chapter I will explain why one element of individualism, the right to private property, is a vital part of a good human community. I will discuss and defend the political idea of the right to private property. I will also argue that the assignment of property rights in a legal system ought to follow principles of production, acquisition, and trade that preclude arbitrariness and demonstrate respect for the relationship between items of property and the individuals who have acquired them.

Under Marxism's influence the idea of the right to private property has suffered relegation, not just by Marxists but by many others, to the field of intellectual archaeology. Marxism is the guiding — albeit not often explicit — perspective for many intellectuals, at least in the sense that the terms of political debate are often chosen from within that frame of reference ('exploitation', 'liberation', 'emancipation', 'alienation', and so forth). Thus the principle of private-property rights, which Marxism accepts only provisionally for human communities and seeks to abolish, is largely in doubt for most intellectuals concerned with political matters.

Yet the principle of private-property rights is indispensable for a just society. Before I explain why, let me note that property — any rightful and exchangeable belonging — cannot include human beings. (Incidentally, when I say 'cannot' and 'must', I emphatically do not mean these in the sense of 'it is logically impossible' and 'it is logically necessary', respectively, as the earlier segments of this work tried to make clear.)

Nor can one own oneself, as some libertarians (such as Murray N. Rothbard) maintain: A person is not two beings, one the self who owns, the other the self who is owned. I *am* myself and cannot at once also *own* myself. It may at times be convenient to talk of owning oneself or, rather, owning one's life. This seems to be the sense in which John Locke spoke of the property one has in one's person, meaning that the individual, not others, must be the final authority directing his or her life, for guiding and governing what he or she will do. 'Property', the relationship of rightful possession, means that some items or skills or other valuables may belong to someone.

Property can be land, or 'estate', to use Locke's term, as well as furniture, paper, machinery, or other physical items. Property can also include poetry, computer programs, musical arrangements, paintings, works of fiction, reports, designs, roles, and so forth. To put the matter in the form of a definition, *property is anything tradable or exchangeable that may be of value to persons*. But it is not itself a person, since property, as a belonging, is a distinct relation in which 'person' is one of the pair of related items. To regard a person, therefore, as property is a metaphysical and categorical mistake, as well as an injustice toward the person involved.

Let us turn now to privacy. The term, from the Latin, meaning 'separate, not public or belonging to the state', designates *a state of independence, of sovereignty* — as in private sector, private firm, private room, private elevator. 'Private' and 'public' are polar concepts, each presupposing the meaningfulness of the other. Much of the debate in political thought concerns where the private ends and the public begins. On this depends the issue of the scope of legitimate state or governmental power. Private property is proposed to serve, in part, to check the state's or government's morally proper reach and power.

Because throughout much of human history human beings had been considered by prominent thinkers as part of the whole — for example, part of the Greek *polis* — personal privacy did not receive paramount attention and treatment, although some exaggerate this point and draw unwarranted conclusions from it. (They claim that the individual and his moral sovereignty are *inventions* rather than conceptual *discoveries* based on a better understanding of human life reached at some point in history.)[1] Finally the individual human being came into sharp enough focus to be paid heed to by philosophers. At first a rather extreme characterization of individuality came to dominate. Marx was right to object to this lopsided conception of the human being as "the limited individual who is limited to himself."[2] It is arguable that this extremism about individuality was a reaction to

its substantial suppression for so much of the preceding segment of
human history. In some cultures and worldviews even today the individual is treated as fundamentally non-existent or at least not
distinctly identifiable but rather as part of a larger individual or
whole.

There is no warrant for the doctrine that everyone is wholly
private or individual — entirely unique and separate from everyone
else, capable of isolated self-sufficiency. We can more realistically
conceive of human beings as members of a definite enough species
but nevertheless with an indefinite range of manifestations. Human
beings are multifaceted, with some characteristics that are indeed
fundamentally private, and with others that are familial, fraternal,
social, and political. What matters here is that the concept of privacy
indicates that aspect of a person which *is* separate from others,
capable of being, for better or for worse, autonomous, and on which
self-direction or self-governance in life depends. As such, one's private self may carry ultimate responsibility for one's life, provided
one is not subjected to unjustified outside dominance.

'Private property', then, refers to any valuable item or service
which may be separated off from the public or state, for individuals
to manage or control. The concept of a right to private property
presupposes a moral standpoint that suggests a justification for the
individual's authority, within a social context, to decide on the
disposition of a certain range of valued items that qualify as 'private'.
It presupposes an account of human life that fixes resonsibility for
some basic human goal(s) and accomplishments resting with the individual.

If the task of every person is self-development, the right to
private property is a moral prerequisite for the realization of that
task within a social context. In such a context borders between individuals are needed to make self-governance possible. And how
these borders ought to be drawn is then a crucial question.

An early suggestion of this view can be found in William of
Ockham, writing in the twelfth century. Heinrich A. Rommen has
characterized Ockham's idea of the right to private property as "a dictate of right reason."[3] Ockham believed that "natural right is nothing
other than a power to conform to right reason."[4] That, in turn, may
be best interpreted to refer to the requisite sphere of personal
(private) jurisdiction and authority presupposed for purposes of
making effective moral judgments.

I argue below that the right to private property is justifiable on grounds that (a) a sphere of jurisdiction, consisting of such items, is indispensable for the moral life of human beings and (b) one (not others) ought to be the authority over items or processes one has recognized and made valuable or received from someone, or from a series of persons who have done the same. To the extent that the right to private property — which, however, is not the most basic natural human right — is eroded, the prospect for a moral life will also erode.

OUR MORAL TASK AND OUR SPHERE OF AUTHORITY

As we saw before, a central tenet of any morality is that we are responsible to choose[5] our course of conduct correctly. We ought to choose what we will do in a way that accords with the moral standards applicable to human life.

Concretely this means that we ought to guide ourselves properly with respect to the reality that we encounter. Such a minimum idea is implied by all genuine moral systems and by our commonsense understanding of what it is to blame and praise persons for how they conduct themselves. All the details of morality must ultimately presuppose this element of personal responsibility, whether in modern or in ancient times. There are normative stances which do not presuppose it, but, as I have argued earlier, these really are value-theories, not specifically moral or ethical viewpoints, since they affirm the justifiability of the process of evaluation but deny self-responsibility for all human conduct that may or may not accord with favorable versus unfavorable evaluation.

We are committed, by choosing our human life, to the exercise of rationality which will enable us to identify our moral responsibilities. I have in mind 'rationality' in the sense of thinking clearly, being perceptive and aware of how we should act. We are committed to being thoughtful, to applying ourselves to concrete tasks in a basically principled fashion. Work, communication, integration of goals, choice of friends and country, concern for long-range tasks, and so on, are all part of the concrete and varied moral task of every individual capable of rationality.

The brief outline of the general position discussed in Chapter 2 can help us to understand the vital role of the right to private property in human community life. One characteristic of rational living is the conscientious consideration of available alternatives. A person should choose the right course of conduct, and this means that he or she must know what alternatives are open to choice. For example, the questions might be: Should I attend church or go to the golf course? Should I purchase a car or an encyclopedia? Should I allocate my earnings to stocks or Care packages? Should I spend my time with my children or doing extra work at the office? Should I move from my present quarters to new ones? In each case the availability of the alternative is presupposed: going to church or to the golf course both have to be available for the question to arise. Frequently, numerous options are available. Should I take swimming lessons, send my child to dancing school, purchase a new tire for the family car, contribute to the homeless children's welfare fund, write a philosophy paper, or send a gift to my parents? Given my limited resources, I have specific options.

In any case, if, as any conception of human moral life supposes, persons are responsible for the decisions or choices they make from among alternatives, these alternatives have to be clearly available to them. To put it another way, jurisdiction over the alternatives is required to make a determinate choice among them. In the absence of such jurisdiction, the moral situation is systematically ambiguous, and just what a person ought to or ought not to do is impossible to clearly specify. While approximation may be possible, the possibility of clear assignment of blame or praise will be rare.

We can put it another way: Without a clear idea of what is ours, what belongs to someone else, and so forth, we must remain morally confused and ultimately lose confidence in our ability to live a moral life. That in turn can produce a demoralized society.

All this should begin to indicate one reason for the moral significance of private-property rights. Suppose that my available options are unclear. I do not hold membership in the church and the golf club. Whether I am authorized to select either as an alternative is indeterminate, membership is largely at the discretion of the congregation and the city athletic association respectively. Then whether I will go to one or the other is not something I *can* decide. 'Ought' implies 'can'. If it is not up to me whether I will be going to one or the other place, I cannot be responsible for where I shall go, and so on down the line with every option involving two or more alternatives. (Of course I may still be responsible for asking permission to go, although one can easily imagine that even that would be something democratically governed — certain hours having been designated for receiving requests, and so forth. Eventually, in a fully totalitarian regime my behavior could be so precisely circumscribed by the public via the 'authorities' that virtually none of it would be up to me. With full control over all property — all of nature surrounding me — this would be the case except for those times when I am able to escape notice.)

One way of interpreting the famous doctrine of 'the tragedy of the commons' is to realize that when common ownership *and* authority attach to some valuable option, individuals who are responsible for making morally right choices cannot make them. They are unable to determine what they *should* do because they lack jurisdiction over the various alternatives that face them. As a result, one of their alternatives is to not consider externalities their use of the commons imposes on others. Indeed, it is not even possible to know what are externalities and what are not. 'External' and 'internal' presuppose borders spelled out by property rights and property law. With this goes the problem that when no individual authority is recognized with respect to some alternative — for example, the choice of going to the club does not impose responsibilities of doing this carefully, prudently, and so forth — the ramifications, consequences, implications, and so on, will be ignored.

Suppose I may personally select some portion of land with no obligation to admit others to share it, at least for a given time period. Now it is also clearly my responsibility whether I take good care of or neglect this land while using it. But if 'we all' or some other indeterminate group has this authority, it becomes inherently ambiguous whose responsibility it is to take care. As Aristotle observes,

> For that which is common to the greatest number has the least care bestowed upon it. Every one thinks chiefly of his own, hardly at all of the common interest; and only when he is himself concerned as an individual. For besides other considerations, everybody is more inclined to neglect the duty which he expects another to fulfill; as in families many attendants are often less useful than a few.[6]

Yet even Aristotle misses the full story. What is ultimately tragic in 'the tragedy of the commons' is that even if one were determined not to neglect any of one's responsibilities *it cannot be clear what one's responsibilities are.*

One might suppose there is a way out of this problem. By finding an overriding common interest, so that when no personal sphere of authority is evident, one would know to aim at this common concrete goal. But no such alternative is possible. The common or public interest, though capable of being specified, takes care of only a minimum of the concerns human beings have in life. The common interest or good is limited to values people in fact share, based on their nature as human beings. But all alternatives must be linked to actual or actually possible outcomes, only a few of which can affect the common good.

When considering the public interest apart from the protection of the rights of everyone—for example, the upkeep of public parks or beaches—it might be thought that it is clear enough what our duties are. The public areas must be used with proper care. They should be kept clean. In discussions of 'public education', it often sounds as if there is a very clear purpose at hand. Appearances to the contrary notwithstanding, attempting to deal with societies along these lines poses insurmountable difficulties.

In anyone's life, sound decisions are required pertaining to what will be attended to, what will be cared for considerably, and what will be neglected. No one has infinite time and resources. For example, during any timespan a parent may have to choose between attending fully to a baby, to work, or to other responsibilities. Because of the fully dependent status of the baby, its care will normally rate most attention, with other matters having to be relegated to lesser significance.

When, however, we do not have full authority over our sphere of activity and a choice presents itself, we cannot determine what we should do about the common sphere. Say we are suddenly called away from a public beach because our child needs us, and we do not clean up after ourselves. We might, of course, spend time cleaning up before we rush away, but that could turn out to be irresponsible in light of the parental obligation we would thus neglect. If we behave likewise in our own bathroom, there we have jurisdiction and impose our decision only on those within its sphere—for instance, our family. The beach is left for others, unrelated to us, to care for. But they too have pressing matters calling on them, and eventually collective spheres become neglected, not because people fail to do their duty but because in public places exact duties become indeterminable.

Such cases have also been called 'uninternalizable negative externalities', meaning that apparently legitimate activities taking place in or adjacent to the commons have negative impact on others who have not agreed to suffer them. All this may appear to be quite mangeable if we elect politicians and appoint bureaucrats to take care of collective affairs. Yet they administer these matters with the resources of others — some of whom sincerely, and possibly rightly, judge the allegedly collective purpose to be morally or otherwise objectionable and thus resist it. Accordingly, unresolvable discord is inherent in the management of virtually all but the most specific and delimited sorts of collective affairs.[7]

Even the most conscientious individuals will find it impossible to avoid 'the tragedy of the commons'. Few individuals will be morally excellent and consistently responsible, and exacerbation of the problem is unavoidable without establishing a sphere of individual dominion and the corresponding legal machinery to keep track of it for purposes of making self-responsible conduct possible, as well as for resolving disputes among human beings.

The right to private property is indispensable for a decent human community, one in which the moral life of individuals can flourish. Individuals cannot conduct themselves morally without a determinate sphere of authority.

None of this is touched by such red-herring assertions as that 'the right to private property is not absolute'—meaning, one may suppose, that we are not omniscient about its full extent and implications and would need constantly to be vigilant about its clear, practical determination, its implementation, and its protection. What is evident is that by any reasonable conception of the moral nature of human life, the right to private property is a necessary—though by no means sufficient—condition of morality within human communities.

It might be asked, then, just how much of what is valued in the society should be part of the private sector. My answer is: As much as satisfies the requirement of creating the fullest possible realm of personal authority for all persons, yet enabling the government to administer a system of justice. Private-property rights must prevail to the maximum extent compatible with a secure realm of public administration of justice. Public resources are needed to uphold the law, including provision for defense against domestic and foreign aggression, and the necessary bureaucracy. The rest of what could be privately owned should be privately owned.

Assigning Private Property Rights

While it may be true that property rights are a prerequisite of a just society, their assignment might be made *ad hoc*. But more can be said on this point.

Property rights are not only necessary for the practice of the moral life. There is a way to ascertain how they ought to be assigned without resorting to mere arbitrary edicts, majority rule, or some other method independent of moral considerations. The right to property in some particular item should be assigned on the basis of who it is that first made a judgment, and acted on it to secure the benefits of that item of nature, including producing goods and services, with the aid of such items, for consumption, or sale, or investment. The crucial element is not 'mixing one's labor' with nature, but doing this as a result of prudent judgment, wisdom, clear assessment of the prospects one might anticipate from such 'mixing of one's labor'. The right to property ought to be assigned in line with the entrepreneurial judgment and activity of members of a human community, including the subsequent unimpeded trading of the valued items.

Of course, not all cases of trading or bestowing the rewards of such entrepreneurial activity will be meritorious, which is why so many people find the private property system unwelcome, even unfair. But once again what is at issue is whether a system where such assignations ought to be made on the basis of entrepreneurial judgment and action is more just than others.

For example, to consider bequests first, Harry, who is George's father, may have invented a new coffee cup which efficiently keeps coffee hot, and he has earned a 'fortune' from its effective marketing and sale to willing purchasers. Before he dies Harry bequeaths this fortune to his son George, who is, however, an undeserving, ungrateful, reckless bum. George now owns the fortune, if the right to private property is indeed a just principle of political economy. Yet it could hardly be argued that George has done anything to earn it. But the prior issue is Harry's right to private property and how he may exercise it. Harry did earn the fortune. He owned it. And he chose to give it to George. George chose to accept it. Now it is George's asset without his having earned it.

But how is this any different from some other possible asset that George might not have earned—his good health, his 20/20 vision, his fine features, his good head of hair? What of his having been born in a place where he is free to accept the gift his father bequeaths to him? What of having wise and diligent parents?

In short, George will, of course, have assets he has inherited, those he did not create by his own good judgment and prudent conduct. But this is unvoidable without grave injustice to Harry. Some find this unfair, as Rawls evidently does. But the concept of 'fairness' presupposes some prior commitment made to treat people as members of a team or club or pursuers of some common objectives, with some common obligations. If Harry failed to give any of his wealth to George's more deserving brother Pete, Harry would have acted unfairly, given his presumed obligations to his two sons (although this presumption is open to dispute — perhaps by the time Pete grows up there cannot be any sensible reference to unfairness here, only to lack of generosity and decency). It seems evident that no one would have the moral and political authority to enforce such fairness. First, it would be arbitrary for other persons to usurp Harry's responsibility to manage properly whatever is his. Someone forcing fairness upon Harry here would be undermining his moral life. Harry owns the fortune and to dictate to him what he ought to do with it is unjustified. Nor is there any reason to suspect *a priori* that those who might be empowered to administer justice would make better judgments in these matters, although exceptions can easily be imagined, contrary to what some neo-classical economic defenders of the free society would probably claim. Yet even if the interference evinced some wisdom, it would be wiser still not to interfere. Interference is generally demoralizing; to usurp another's moral realm aside from very rare, emergency cases is acutely demeaning.

Yet, most importantly, the government simply does not have the moral and political authority to run people's lives beyond what bears directly on protecting and preserving individual rights. Individual sovereignty does not always guarantee satisfactory, desirable or even morally proper solutions, but this does not justify the usurpation of that sovereignty by anyone, least of all some remote agency that is supposed to be concerned with administering justice, preventing crime, and protecting the integrity of the society from foreign aggression or threats.

The Right to Do Wrong

Judy earns her fortune by creating a machine that more efficiently produces orange juice than other machines available. She then invests part of her capital in the manufacture of pornographic books aimed at gullible, sexually desperate people who pay for them willingly. Judy gains even greater wealth by this entrepreneurial endeavor than from her admittedly more valuable machine.

Why ought Judy's fortune from manufacturing and selling pornography to be treated as her private property and thus why ought taking it from her be regarded as legally impermissible?

The reason is that her kind of conduct was not in violation of anyone's rights and is thus politically unobjectionable. It is the kind of activity that might be proper under some circumstances and violates no one's human rights. It is not a categorical political wrong to have engaged in this conduct. As a moral wrong it must be tolerated, lest those who would block it usurp the jurisdictional sovereignty of the parties whose commercial conduct is (possibly quite rightly) deemed immoral.

The issue is not whether entrepreneurs or capitalists or workers producing and selling deserve what they receive. Some do and some don't. What is at issue is whether those who 'reward' or benefit them have the right to engage in voluntary, albeit possibly unwise, wasteful, yet more often very useful and creative, exchange with these persons. It is not very different from the privacy right which so many people who are otherwise critical of capitalism uphold in relation to sexual interactions between consenting adults. The issue is *not* good sex, or wise sex, or proper sex, but whether those involved have the right to engage in it. Generally, the natural right to private property rests on the greater probability of mutually harmonious self-enhancing conduct within a system in which it is protected. But this does not commit its defenders to the claim that each instance of the exercise of the right to private property — for example, each instance of free trade — will be morally unobjectionable. We do have the right, on occasion, to do wrong — this is merely another way of saying that the sphere of rights is narrower than that of ethics.

Nor is it the case that, when immorality contaminates conduct involving valued items, nothing good can eventually come from the situation. Judy may take her fortune from pornography and invest it in support of a major symphony orchestra, or in research in Austrian economics. She may leave her fortune to her talented daughter who is going to spend it in her pursuit of artistic excellence. While such considerations are by no means decisive, they should somewhat diminish the fierce indignation of those who indulge in intuition-mongering when discussing these issues. How dare someone benefit from such trade? Well, indeed, because there is much to be said, in intuitive moral terms—by reference to familiar moral ideals—for not intruding on it, and for the possible desirable consequences of such non-intrusion.

The immense array of non-rights-violating actions tends to be of mixed moral merit. We have, however, at least one method of assigning economically valued items that does respect moral principles, namely, rewarding one who has judged and acted prudently vis-à-vis some possibly valued item. From then on the process goes on its admittedly morally risky way. And while there is a general justification for assigning property rights on the basis of the initial judgment of the value of some item and the action taken as a follow-up to that judgment, much remains to be said about the details of such assignments in a complex society. Questions may arise as to whether one owns the air above one's home; whether one who speculates that the Moon could be a valuable piece of real estate, builds rockets to get there and develops parts of it then owns the entire Moon or only portions of it; how one might come to own untouched water in a lake, or rivers and river-beds, or wildlife.

Property law can develop only in a society that first acknowledges the right to private property and affirms the basic principles of how, initially, to assign property rights. After that, case law, resulting from the disputations and explorations that are carried on in courts of (property) law would set the standards. Property is a very wide concept and its application, like that of liberty or happiness, has to be tried out in concrete situations. There are enough cases of the clear application of the concept before us now that we can spell out what it is to own company stock, a horse, a piece of land, copyright in a novel, an arrangement for a musical composition, or an invention. We are not starting on this journey in a vacuum. So while there are unanswered questions of great interest, there are also some sufficiently clear answers. Simply because there is no guarantee of a smooth, effortless process of handling such matters, it doesn't follow that there is justification for insisting that one group of people in the society, the government, ought to be empowered to manage things. The incessant calls for regulations covering all manner of detailed issues and problems testify less to the existence of good grounds for empowering the government to attempt remedies in these areas than to inertia or indolence. Anyone who appreciates how long it can take for members of a society to overcome prejudice, bigotry, and other bad habits, will not be surprised that in a culture subjected to varieties of slavery, feudalism, or absolutism for most of its recorded history (and in which even now the welfare state still beckons as an ideal) the practice of self-governance is not widely embraced and is deemed largely aberrant, incongruous.

Yet is there any better, more just general approach? We are talking not about whether now and then one may find moral justification for disregarding property rights (though even in such cases, it is arguable that we should not turn first to the government, which risks misusing its tremendous coercive power, properly designed for defense and crime-fighting). In such emergencies as earthquakes or tidal waves life-saving may take precedence over property-saving. The issue is, rather, whether the system of principles governing a human community ought to be fundamentally altered to remedy market failures—that is, bad judgments people make on the market in voluntary co-operation with others. In short, we are talking about integrated systems and conceptions of justice in the context of political economy. That is what the key debates are about with socialists, welfare statists, syndicalists, solidarists, communists, fascists, social and economic democrats, and other opponents of capitalism.

CAPITALISM, FREE TRADE, AND ECONOMICS

FREEDOM REVISITED

I will now discuss a fundamental conflict between the critic's idea of what freedom involves and the idea of freedom he disparages in capitalism. This will help us to see why a normative analysis of free trade would be more suitable for purposes of contrasting capitalism with, for example, socialism, than the value-free approach used by economists. If the concept of freedom, in its socially relevant sense, means the condition of individuals not being aggressed against by others, then the right to freedom found in the American political tradition seems vindicated. This view of the right to freedom does not rest mainly on the virtue of market processes as such but on the recognition of every individual's equal moral nature as a self-determined and self-responsible agent, regardless of admittedly enormous circumstantial differences, self-induced or inherited.

What is the relationship between the right to liberty and capitalism proper? Capitalism follows from the right to free trade, in the classical liberal tradition of political economy. To understand the nature of trade or exchange in the economic sense, one must recognize that it logically depends on the truth of and respect for the principle of the right to private property. One cannot trade if one does not own anything. Ironically, Karl Marx poignantly identified the function of property rights:

> the right of man to property is the right to enjoy his possessions and dispose of the same arbitrarily, without regard for other men, independently from society, the right of selfishness.[1]

But Marx focussed on the worst case. The right to private property makes (free) trade possible — it is right for one (in contrast to its being right for someone else) to dispose of one's possessions, for example, arbitrarily. But private property authorizes one also to act and trade in accordance with the best judgments one can form — something Marx doesn't mention here. Private-property rights also secure the authority to dispose of one's belongings responsibly, so that the act yields worthy results. That part of the story must, however, be left to morality — a person of generosity, liberality, moderation, prudence, fellow-feeling, and self-respect will use his or her just authority over valued items responsibly, productively, creatively, benignly. Unless one takes a particularly malevolent view of persons, surely Marx's emphasis is one-sided.

There is little doubt that the most prominent and articulate champions of capitalism are economists. But this reliance on economic defenses has caused problems for capitalism. The reason is that economists are always concerned to retain for themselves the mantle of science. They insist that economics is not committed to any particular values. Yet it is transparently false to claim that an economic system isn't tied to moral and political views that may or may not be correct, sound, or well-founded. Maintaining a purportedly value-free stance plays into the hands of the opponents of both capitalism and sound economics. Noting the economist's slight subterfuge, opponents can more easily discredit the best economic system and the discipline that studies it.

Economists who favor the free market on grounds of its efficiency both presuppose a vital normative point and commit themselves to furthering a controversial conception of the good. Effective trade or exchange presupposes private property rights. If no such rights exist, then there is no need for or possibility of trade. Individuals could just take from others what they wanted and would not need to wait for agreement on terms. Setting terms is something that presupposes the authority to decide about what one possesses. It is a moral condition, not a purely 'descriptive' one, as positivist economics asserts (even though it does not need to do so, since nothing would be taken from its analytic character by admitting that market economics contains a moral component). If I own something, that means that others *ought to* refrain from blocking my choice of what to do with it. I am authorized to set terms, not others. This is a moral issue.

One might object by noting that whether or not certain rules prevail in a community can be described without commitment to the obligatoriness of adhering to these rules. Yet, insofar as the economic defenders of capitalism maintain that such a system is more efficient than others, they do commit themselves to the preferability of the rules governing the system. When they uphold the merits of capitalism, they uphold the merits of the private property system that it presupposes. This is true even if they ascribe no more merit to the system than its superior facility for producing what people want.

Not surprisingly, critics of mainstream economics are often aware of this. They capitalize on the fact that economists are so eager to deny it, noting, dryly, that something must be amiss in their theory, otherwise they would not hide this fact. Yet despite the value — indeed, moral — component in economic theory, much of what mainstream economists say about capitalism is correct. What is wrong is their profession of the purely value-free status of the market, a point that is not really a part of economic theory but which rather belongs to the philosophy of the social sciences.

Should some federal wealth distribution Agency intervene at various points in the innumerable transfers and exchanges of the market process? Such a body certainly has no basis for initial acquisition. That body's claim to the property seems to be confined to the fact that now and then its judgment as to what course the property ought to take — what the rightful owner ought to do with it — may be correct. But that does not justify taking the decision out of the hands of the owner — any more than one ought to take away from the editors of *The New York Times* decisions about what they ought (what's fit) to print because they sometimes print what they ought not (what's not fit) to print, and often fail to print what they ought to print. The arbitrariness of the power exercised in these kinds of cases should be obvious. The issue is not whether sound judgment is involved in the criticism but whether sound judgment is involved in taking the action that would enforce that criticism. That is where the arbitrariness enters, since from the former the latter does not follow. (In the last analysis, of course, whether the present approach or another, such as Rawls's, Gewirth's, Dworkin's, or the Marxists', is successful in general — which is what is at issue for political economy — must be evaluated comparatively. In this work I am concerned with making out a case for the natural-rights libertarian approach, taking occasional potshots at the others.)

Some economists point out that, while it may be true that a capitalist market cannot exist without a system of individual property rights, describing what sort of system is needed for capitalism to work and making the judgment that the system of rights ought to be instituted are two different things. But most of the economists who favor the capitalist system do not simply focus on describing what is required for it to work but rather claim superiority for the capitalist system over alternatives. Yet they insist they are carrying out a value-free analysis. They argue that capitalism realizes wealth more efficiently, and leads to prosperity. Thus they endorse prosperity, although when pushed, they claim that they merely tell us how to obtain what we want. But if we ask, Do not many of us in fact not share in this objective?, they deny it. They take every want or desire as aiming for income, for utility — even if it aims at suicide. Thus 'income maximizer' is either a necessary description of all of us, and reduces to a tautology, or it presupposes the superior value of material prosperity, something that is by no means necessarily true.

In practical terms, terms that matter directly for political discourse, economists also endorse the private-property rights system that is presupposed by the market's operations. But that, too, is a value commitment, namely, to the right to private property, in so far as they find capitalism more efficient, useful, workable, and so on. All of these notions presuppose some objective, and if we admit that capitalism serves our prosperity better than alternative institutions, then we need to show why prosperity is such a fine and overriding thing.

If economists who defend the marketplace admitted that at its base we find certain assumptions about how individuals ought to act and what governments should uphold, they could still carry on with their analysis of how such a system works and why it produces more efficiently than all others. This would leave open the question of whether the moral assumptions on which capitalist market analysis rests are sound. Even if they turned out to be unsound, economists could insist that the business of economics is to study market processes, and others should take on the task of figuring out whether alternatives to a market economy might be preferable for other than economic reasons.

The principle of property rights underlies the market. Such rights are necessary preconditions of genuine trade and thus of a free market, specifying one's area of jurisdiction in nature.

When it comes to defending the morality of the free market most economists claim their hands are tied, consequently capitalism has been under fire. Both the Right and the Left attack the system.

COLLECTIVISM AND RATIONALITY

In the discussion thus far I have responded to criticisms levelled at the

right to private property. All the objections to natural-rights libertarianism in Chapter 4 are, in effect, objections to the right to private
property. The main significance of the role of the right to private property for politic theory, is that it serves ultimately to ground or justify
objections to all kinds of collectivism, systems that organize the entire society as a team, organism, club, or enterprise.

Despite the popularity of collectivism both on the political and
philosophical Left and Right,[2] it has a serious problem. Even if individuals who comprise government were not fallible, collectivist
planning would be inherently flawed. The reason becomes evident
from one socialist argument given in support of extensive state
powers:

> The idea of social planning seemed to socialists to be inherent in their
> definition of rationality, indeed, in their definition of man. To be
> human was to be rational, and rationality consisted in planning one's
> conduct and environment in a way that helped realize one's consciously
> formulated purpose. The bourgeois view of man also defined him as a
> rational being, and rationality as a capacity for planning, but for
> socialists there was a contradiction. They thought it odd that men
> should plan their lives individually but not collectively, that they
> should live as men individually but as 'animals' collectively, and
> wondered if it was ever possible for an individual to act rationally in a
> society that was not itself rational.[3]

The essence of this argument is that if individuals can rationally plan
their lives, so can societies, and it is as vital to do this in the case of
societies as it is in the case of individuals. Socialism, in turn, is the rational organization of the society.

This general line of argumentation has thereafter led some
defenders of capitalism to argue against the value of rationality. F. A.
Hayek, for example, developed an elaborate attack on constructivist
rationalism, the idea of "reason . . . conceived as . . . a capacity of the
mind to arrive at the truth by a deductive process from a few obvious and undoubtable premises."[4] This modern idea of reason,
made prominent under the very strong influence of René Descartes,
has dominated both individualist and collectivist thinking. The difference between individualists and collectivists seems here to amount
to the difference between planning and *laissez-faire*. Individualists
think that only individuals should carry out plans, in voluntary co-
operation if need be, while socialists believe society, too, ought to try

to implement efficient means for its goals, namely, rational central economic plans.

Yet there is far more to reason than mere efficiency. The narrow idea of reason derives from an unproven and unscientific assumption, namely, that human motivation follows the principles of mechanical motion. Going by that Enlightenment idea, the difference between persons and other things is a matter of mere complexity, not of kind. Therefore the principle of motion of all things applies to persons, only in a somewhat more complicated fashion, and could be extended to societies as well.

Since the time of this scientistic optimism much scientific change has occurred. We have discovered the inadequacy of the mechanical model, even for the sphere of nature where it had been thought to be most successful in the first place, namely, physics. But more to the point, human nature gives clear evidence of being crucially different from the rest of nature. Furthermore, there is ample difference within the various spheres below human nature. A monkey is vastly different from a bee, a shark from an ant, an oak tree from a tulip, a pebble from a mountain, a planet from a star, and so on. One reason the familiar and pervasive extrapolation is unjustified is that nature contains vastly different kinds of entities. A pluralism, permitting great diversity in the types and kinds of beings, as well as their principles of motion, is most likely true.[5]

If the pluralistic metaphysics sketched in Chapter 1 is sound, and if the evidence for a distinctive human nature is sufficient, then the possibility of principles of motion or motivation applicable to human beings could be fundamentally different from the principles of motion to be applied to rocks and machines. In that case the prevailing conception of rationality is flawed, and both individualism and collectivism must be rethought in that light. The antecedents of these conditional statements seem true. I have already indicated that classical individualism embraces a different view of rationality from Hobbesian individualism.

Reason Reconsidered

In *Essays on the Laws of Nature* John Locke, who himself made powerful use of the concept of 'reason' within political thought, states,

> By reason . . . I do not think is meant . . . here that faculty of the understanding which forms trains of thought and deduces proofs, but

certain definite principles of action from which spring all virtues and whatever is necessary for the proper molding of morals.[6]

Hayek, who mentions Locke's observation, notes that "to the medieval thinkers reason had meant mainly a capacity to recognize truth, especially moral truth, when they met it, rather than a capacity of deductive reason from explicit premises."[7] And he notes that it is against this older 'natural law' theory of reason that the modern instrumentalist or positivist conception — proposed by Francis Bacon, Thomas Hobbes, and René Descartes — had been advanced. The older conception, in contrast to the modern, did "recognize that much of the institution of civilization was not the product of deliberate human design."[8]

Just what Hayek himself concludes about all this is not of great importance here, although I have discussed the matter elsewhere.[9] Despite his awareness of the broader conception of reason in ancient and medieval culture, Hayek still tends to denigrate reason and insists that the bulk of society relies on spontaneous action and the order resulting there from, rather than on rational thought and what might flow from it, that is, well-thought-out human behavior and institutions. This makes it appear that collectivists have confidence in human reason, while individualists embrace a conception of political life that is in some sense arationalist or even anti-rationalist.

Human reason involves not simply the capacity for calculation. It is more broadly to be seen as involving our conceptual capacity for recognizing truth — for integrating and differentiating the evidence of the senses, for guiding action in the light of such truth, and thus for guiding moral conduct. If this is right, the complaint of collectivists against individualists concerning the alleged rejection of reason (when it comes to analyzing society) turns out to be unjustified.

Is the planning of societies comparable to the planning of individual lives? Only individuals possess the faculty of reason. To choose to use it most effectively, one would need specific information to guide one's conduct. (But even then it may not be so used, if the agent fails to sustain the effort also needed to use it efficiently.) The mind of one person, however, is not in a position to substitute as the guide for the life of another, not without serious conflicts arising when the particulars about the two individuals offer conflicting direction as to what each ought to do.

This, in turn, translates into the general point that plans for the whole of society are not at all like individual plans. Socialists "thought it odd that men should plan their lives individually but not collectively". So long as rationality is viewed instrumentally, there might be something to this complaint. Surely, given certain goals, efficient means may be found for pursuing them whether the goals are those of individuals or those of the entire society. Collectivists think that these set goals *for society* exist; they are designated by such notions as the public purpose, the public interest, the public good, the full emancipation of humanity, and so on. So long as some such goal for society *as a whole* exists — so long as there is some 'end state' for humankind, to use Robert Nozick's phrase[10] — there is no good reason to refrain from planning for its achievement from above, by central direction. But when we acknowledge that an individual mind, the concrete manifestation of reason, must engage in the discovery of individual or social goals, the collectivist complaint is defused.

Discovering what principles we must adhere to and what our individual goals are or should be, is something that can only be done through the use of the individual human faculty of reason, something collectives do not possess. This does not deny general principles of human conduct, of course. Identifying such general principles and choosing to live by them is, however, necessarily a private task, albeit possibly facilitated by co-operative effort. This is Hayek's and the Austrian economists' main point, although they put it in economic or 'praxeological' terms:

> The most significant fact about this [price] system is the economy of knowledge with which it operates, or how little the individual participants need know in order to be able to take the right action. In abbreviated form, by a kind of symbol, only the most essential information is passed on and passed on only to those concerned. It is more than a metaphor to describe the price system as a kind of machinery for registering change, or a system of telecommunications which enables individual producers to watch merely the movements of a few pointers, as an engineer might watch the hands of a few dials, in order to adjust their activities to changes of which they may never know more than is reflected in the price movement.[11]

But we need to add to what Hayek teaches us something his argument seems to presuppose. This is that an economy *ought to* function so as to satisfy individual preferences. Yet that is hotly debated in political economy and philosophy, certainly not to be taken for granted as it is by many economists.

If ethical egoism or individualism is true, so that each person has the moral responsibility to be individually successful in life, then each must have a determinate sphere of sovereignty or authority for action. If so, then collective planning is not only inefficient for allocating resources where they are most wanted and needed, but morally reprehensible.

Collectivists are not entirely oblivious to the 'calculation problem', as it is called, but they can resist it by noting that much of the allocational efficiency of the free market presupposes the value of meeting all kinds of individual demand. Yet much of that demand is frivolous, irresponsible, wrong, trivial, and so forth, so we can do without the market's efficiency, after all. Collectivists usually continue to maintain, perhaps inconsistently, that the needs and wants of individuals should be largely satisfied, that people's standard of life should be improved.

But there is more to it than that. We ought to be concerned not merely with the utilitarian goal of satisfying higher expectations. There is nothing frivolous about the freedom that makes frivolity possible. The objective of recognizing political and moral sovereignty is at stake. Thus collectivist planning undermines the moral nature of human beings.

How to Design the Polis

Humans are not able to escape their humanity—they are *human* individuals. Treating them as isolated monads or atoms—an idea often seized upon and rightly denounced by socialists—has to be rejected. And with this we must reject the impossibility of any degree of political-economic collective 'planning', the notion from Hayek that gives anarchists so much intellectual fuel. With respect to their equality as moral agents, individuals must be understood to share certain features which require a human social order to be constituted in certain ways; that is, it must rest on natural, individual, human rights to life, liberty, and property, and be protected in an integrated, principled manner.

Based on our human nature, certain natural rights may be identified and a political order *can* be planned or designed. But the collective planning must be confined to the genuine concerns of the public at large, that is, to everyone's few identical concerns.

For example, the Constitution of the United States is a possibly suitable general plan or design. What is different in such a plan from those spoken of in connection with socialist planning is this: Socialists model their planning on the business firm or social club; they treat all property and persons as if they had an (agreed-to) common purpose and were available for use in the realization of this purpose. A constitution only spells out certain prohibitions and procedural rules, not goals. It does not specify the goals for society but makes goal-seeking possible to all members of society. If we can consider a constitution as a design, its purpose is to serve the innumerably varied purposes of individuals with equal respect for everyone's task of pursuing the best possible purpose that he or she has come to identify. And the rules in terms of which a constitution aims for this purpose is to make possible for everyone to follow through on his or her moral task.

Here we return to our main topic: the role of the right to private property in a good human community.

Individuality, Morality and Liberty

The function of a good society is to enhance the moral life of its members. This is best achieved if individuals are understood to require, and are in fact secure in, their proper sphere of authority to govern themselves. The best way to achieve this end is to identify and protect individuals' right to private property.

The law of property of such a society could, of course, be very complicated. From real estate to copyright law, fences to patents, the justice departments of various levels of government to the police departments and the military — all these must keep a constant vigilance about the task of identifying and protecting the individual right to private property. The central purpose of such a system of law — not its sole end — is to make it possible for individuals to carry out their moral tasks in life.

The moral task of every individual is to succeed in his or her individual life. This places no priority on equal attainment in terms of prosperity, education, artistic endeavors, and so on, so fairness in such a society, contrary to widespread impression, is not the main feature of justice. Instead it is individual liberty — the negative freedom whereby individuals may not be interfered with by other individuals. And this condition is most directly enhanced by the clear identification and protection of the right to private property, each person's sphere of personal authority.

It may be objected that I am defending here a reactionary and obsolete framework. But a progressivist bias is just another case of extrapolating from science and technology to all human concerns. Some aspects of human life progress quite smoothly, some, such as art and literature, do not; and there may be actual regression, for example in the conduct of governments, which clearly belies the doctrine of historical progress in political matters. Trends may change.

Pluralism of Good Living *via* the Right to Private Property

Individualism is not an apology for the exploitation of some by others, as Marxists have held. It is, rather, the soundest conception of social life yet rationally formulated by the minds of human beings. Collectivism distorts the kind of rationality involved in human planning. Bona fide rationality can only be exercised by individuals. The values identified by human reason relate to human individuals. Only individuals can have determinate goals or purposes, such as getting to play at Carnegie Hall, or running in the Olympic Games, or curing AIDS, cancer, or malaria. Societies cannot have these sorts of plans. Constructing societies as if they could plan must lead to disaster. Thus the collective or public domain is a very limited, specific realm of concern, properly restricted, by a sound constitution, to the administration of justice.

The free market, resting on the basic human right of every person to private property, will help, in turn, to preserve among human beings one *necessary* condition of civility, decency, and morality, provided that they attend to the maintenance of those legal principles which do help to identify private-property rights. (Ultimately the task of a moral life for human beings includes their political mission.)

The right to private property, and the free marketplace that is implied by the protection and preservation of that right, is, then, a necessary and indispensable — though by no means sufficient — condition for a good human community.

The right to private property is not the most fundamental right. The right to life and the right to liberty are conceptually prior, thus more fundamental. But for practical policy purposes the right to private property — concerned as it is with concrete features of our lives, the particular, actual, specifiable dimensions of living — is central: Through its protection we can secure those more fundamental rights, as well as the conditions for a decent human life within human communities. Certainly there are numerous societies in which something resembling a structure of property rights is evident — we might call it a structure of property *privileges*. In these societies persons are *permitted* to hold and trade goods and services, although the government, the local Coastal Commission, the Federal Communications Commission, the king or some other powerful group or person can legally revoke the privilege. This is true even of such communal assemblies as that of Plato's leaders in the ideal polity of the *Republic* and of the Israeli kibbutz. In such societies there is no genuine free market. Yet they have what resemble free markets, somewhat in the way a sophisticated zoo can resemble the actual wilds or just as in some families children are given limited personal responsibility. And, of course, the more such privileges become entrenched and relied upon, the more the quasi-market will exhibit the tendencies we expect in a free marketplace, including moral autonomy and self-responsibility.

INDIVIDUALISM AND POLITICAL AUTHORITY

WHEN IS GOVERNMENT PROPER?

The problem of political authority is whether the institutions, practices, and activities commonly comprising governments have sound moral foundations. The question is whether even the best of human communities, with their myriad official elements, possess moral underpinnings so that what they require of all their members may be enforced by some of them. Political authority is expected to lend moral support to giving orders or issuing commands or handing down directives to people, which they may be *made* to follow by officials in the name of the public interest or as requirements of good community life.[1]

One problem often associated with political authority is *how* some people acquire the power connected with it. Whether there is bona fide political authority or mere political power—and whether the former is even possible—it is of distinct interest what it takes to obtain it in different societies. But this problem won't concern us here.[2]

The problem of political authority we will be addressing is whether it is possible to acquire and possess it at all, that is, whether such a category of authority can even be found and what would comprise it. Although we have some general notion of what political authority is, my objective here is to give one line of argument in its support, as well as to clarify its nature. In effect I hope to provide the right conception of political authority, insofar as the individualist political framework is the correct one regarding human community life.

INDIVIDUALISM AGAIN

Individualists hold, as Nozick puts it, that "Individuals have rights, and there are things no person or group may do to them (without violating their rights)," adding, again with Nozick, that "So strong and far-reaching are these rights that they raise the question of what, if anything, the state and its officials may do."[3] Nonindividualists have little trouble defending the moral propriety of all manner of state activity with which members of a human community have to contend.[4] They don't need to worry much about thwarting the will of other individuals; but this is not the position of the individualist who argues for the primary political value of individual autonomy and liberty. Indeed, many, perhaps most individualists reject the idea of political authority altogether. My purpose, however, is to show that political authority, once it is properly understood, is justified within an individualist moral framework. I have argued that persons should strive to live an excellent human life, and since doing this is virtually impossible outside the context of a good human community (conceived along individualist lines), they should, morally speaking, establish such a community. And they should empower some of the members of the community to protect and preserve the principles of such community life.[5]

As evident from what has gone before, I do not rely on either state-of-nature or hypothetical-contract approaches for establishing any political principle. Neither would I depend on such approaches for establishing political authority.[6] Instead I invoke an ethical-individualist approach. I expect to find moral reasons for the propriety and possible emergence of political authority in human communities. Given that human beings are both free to seek certain ends of their own (the free-will assumption) and capable of identifying standards in accordance with which they ought to make their choices (the objectivist assumpton), then whether political authority can exist needs to be answered by reference to whether people should seek what it entails and whether they can attain it in accordance with moral standards. Without these assumptions, captured in the slogan 'ought implies can', it is a sheer mystery how any binding principles, whether in ethics or in politics, could apply to human conduct and the development of human social institutions and practices.[7]

CHAIN OF COMMAND

Normally, certain people in human communities enforce edicts, prohibitions, rules, and so on. The police enforce the rule against trespass. They have legal authority to do so. In turn, those who issue the orders or commands which are being enforced also claim authority, and in this they lay claim to political authority. They maintain, implicitly at least, that in their official roles they should issue, and other members of the community should accept, such orders.

Whenever some 'officer of the law' enforces an edict or command—forcing someone to act in certain ways or to desist from so doing, as in 'Open up in the name of the law'—a chain of command extends far beyond the conspicuous uniformed individual. Usually the officer could refer to some source of the *legal* authority being exercised, in an attempt to legally justify the enforcement involved. However, not just anyone, at any time, is justified in forcing another individual or group to do something in the context of a system of laws, whether in a democracy, a republic, a monarchy, under socialism or capitalism. For instance, not just anyone is justified in forcing another, or threatening to force another if no compliance is forthcoming, to go along to police headquarters. One's next-door neighbor usually has no recourse to such measures, mainly because no legal justification exists for any putative authority to bring someone in (except in cases of 'citizen's arrests' in which proper procedures are followed).

Nor could just anyone appoint police officers, spell out the rules they must follow as they carry out their police work, and instruct police officers as to their duties and their jurisdiction. And those who appoint the police also have to come by their role through specific procedures. In a democracy, for example, such people are usually elected by some appropriately held electoral process. In such a system the authority of the police to make arrests and so forth would ultimately derive, through elected officials, from decisions by a majority of members of the politically active population. In short, the authority to enforce public policy is obtained from the bulk of the people, in the last analysis, based in part on the alleged propriety of the democratic process. This may or may not amount to a proper method of acquiring political authority, but it exemplifies one familiar contender.

CHALLENGING THE LINKS

Claims to authority may be challenged in many ways. In the arena of politics and law one who resists compliance might simply wish to refuse so as to do something else. But it is also possible to resist for other reasons. One might believe that the officers have made a mistake. One might also deny that they have proper jurisdiction over oneself, and thus challenge political authority directly.

Civil rights protesters refused to accept that officers of the law acted properly by removing protesters as they carried out their 'sit-ins' at segregated facilities. Whether the resistance is peaceful or violent, a challenge to legal authority is very possibly its basis, but it could go considerably further, of course. When American Indians reject the authority of the Bureau of Indian Affairs of the U.S. Department of the Interior, they do not protest some specific edict, nor the claims of the officials to be bona fide officials, nor again the legal authority of the agency. Instead they maintain that the institutions of that authority are themselves unfounded, morally illegitimate. When the Black Panthers fought the police in the late 1960s, they or their leaders often argued that they wholeheartedly disputed the moral authority of the officers of 'white America's law', regardless of the wisdom or lack thereof of the particular issue during a confrontation. It is when these sorts of challenges or protests are levelled that we are faced with what comes closest to a genuine questioning of political authority. The point of such challenges is that those who level them refuse to accept as justified the implicit or explicit claim of others to be acting rightly in enforcing on them any public policy.

The crux of political authority, the point where an individualist would balk most readily at granting its moral legitimacy, is that physical force and its threat may be used by those who possess it against those who do not, to secure the public interest. Those who possess political authority may order behavior and force the public to obey their orders. A system of laws which carries political authority within itself is, in turn, morally binding on members of a community and may be enforced by those who are in possession of political authority. The orders or laws involved must uniquely pertain to matters that are of concern to the members of the community in their role as such members and not as parents, students, plumbers, or baseball stars. We are concerned with political authority, and politics concerns persons as members of organized human communities, that is, as citizens.[8] Perhaps politics, as in totalitarian social systems, encompasses all aspects of human life; perhaps, as in an individualist system, it would encompass either very few or none. But whatever its scope, politics bears on people as members of human communities. Political authority, in turn, involves morally justified delegated powers and their use vis-à-vis members of communities in their role as such members.

One way to approach the question of whether anyone can ever rightfully possess political authority would be to ask first whether there are any principles or rules which could justifiably be imposed by force, and then how (or whether) it might be possible for a particular person to be in a position to employ such force with moral justification.

THE PRIVATE USE OF FORCE

One situation which seems to most of us (except pacifists) to justify using force on unwilling others is self-defense. The principles one enforces in self-defense concern the definition of one's exclusive sphere of (private) authority — one's 'moral space'. This enforcement seems morally justified at least for the person who is first and foremost responsible for securing the safety and wellbeing of the target of aggression, namely, oneself. In self-defense, then, it appears[9] a person may, from the moral point of view, use force against another.

But what is the proper relationship between the defensive use of force and some moral framework or system? Let me put the question differently. Although most people appreciate the difference between the force applied by a boxer against his opponent in the ring and the same by some thug, why, if at all, should we, at least as individualists, regard the former as justifiable and the latter as morally wrong? I will here merely suggest the answer within the general field of ethics I wish to draw upon.

The right answer to the question 'How should I conduct myself?' is the initial step needed for discovering whether the use of force on others might sometimes be morally justified.[10] *Classical* egoism is, as I have argued, the best answer to the question raised in ethics. Classical egoism as an ethical position takes self-interest (or benefiting oneself) to be objective and necessarily connnected with the nature of the self involved, that is, with human nature. As will be recalled, the classical egoist holds that the primary ethical task for each person is the fullest development of himself or herself as a living human being *and* as the individual that he or she is. This view ties values to life and moral values to human life. The valuation of human life for every individual amounts, in turn, to the valuation of the particular human life over which the person has direct responsibility, namely, oneself. Since a person's pursuit of values, and first and foremost of his or her life as a human being, is a matter of choice, this pursuit is a moral task. Ultimately, it comes down to the fulfillment of the chosen responsibility to enhance oneself to the fullest, as dictated by human nature and one's own individual identity.[11] What bearing does all this have on politics?

Many individualists attempt to establish the limits of political authority by defending the Lockean natural rights position, which upholds exclusive personal authority over one's life. Thus they hope to lay the groundwork for self-defense and a limited conception of politics. This approach, however, misses the fact that natural rights themselves require a moral or ethical foundation. The doctrine of self-ownership, espoused by some libertarians, raises the question why a person and not other persons, or society, or the majority, should have authority over that person's life?

One answer that may be given is that morality involves choice, so whatever moral position is true, one needs personal authority over one's life so as to have a chance at being a good human being, to have a chance at moral excellence, whether in terms of hedonism, altruism, or whatever other moral system one holds to be true. While there is much significance in this insight, it does not completely solve the problem as it is now understood. What are the boundaries of self-responsibility? What is the self that must be under the person's own jurisdiction for him or her to enjoy moral dignity?

To establish what scope personal authority ought to have, one needs to know what a person is and what the moral task of every person as a person is.[12] And here it is crucial to know whether egoism, altruism, utilitarianism or some other ethical system is right. If ethical egoism is correct — and if the human ego is to be understood as we have maintained within the framework of classical egoism (as a rational animal with the capacity to choose to act as he or she will), then political individualism rests on more than quicksand and there is little difficulty in concluding that self-defense is very often not only unobjectionable morally but indeed required.[13] Moreover, ethical egoism would best explain the commonsense understanding about self-defense. When someone protects himself or herself and uses force in the process, the person is, within specified limits, acting in the capacity of self-enhancement, doing what every human being ought, morally, to do. It would be cowardly and negligent to do otherwise.

The private use of force is, then, morally proper for each person in the retaliatory task of protecting himself or herself. Pacifism, the only serious negation of the moral propriety of self-defensive force, would have to be rejected to the extent ethical egoism is true.

PRINCIPLED SOCIAL LIFE IDENTIFIED

There is no doubt about the innumerable values to be attained from interacting with others. So it would seem to be morally proper for everyone, in terms of classical egoism, to embark on social life, as long as provision is made to overcome the serious dangers also inherent in this task. Because human beings all possess the capacity to be evil, and because some of the evil they can do is of direct impact upon one's life, a morally responsible involvement in social life requires taking full account of that fact and making preparations for coping with it. Furthermore, the division of labor makes it possible in human communities to secure valuable services in especially competent ways. So from an egoistic standpoint one ought to seek the help of a heart specialist when suffering heart disease, not merely try some home-brewed medicine or go to some amateur for help, and one ought to establish a system of organized self-defense within the context of community life, not try to fend for oneself. Human beings should, because it is good for them as human beings, make provisions for coping justly and competently with the general fact of interpersonal evil, that is, for coping with basic and complex rights violations.[14]

This is the point at which the sphere of politics emerges in human life. Socially organized self-defense requires the promulgation of the principles of good community life, the selection of experts specially prepared in methods for protectng and preserving these principles, and what can be called due process in law enforcement. We will consider in a moment the principle involved. We can now see that it is morally proper for human beings not just to embark upon social life. It is crucial, also, to establish the appropriate type of organized self-defense — namely, proper principles of politics and law, including the proper methods of law enforcement and of selecting those law makers and enforcers.

For individualists there are two factors which constitute the basis for the suitable conditions of good human community life: (1) One's moral task of governing one's life properly and successfully (leading a happy life), and (2) the need for a determination of wherein each person's sphere of authority (regarding the former task) lies within a community of other human beings (also expected to be facing such a task).[15] These factors, pertaining to the moral nature of human life, ground the theory of natural rights referred to by Nozick at the outset of this discussion. Freedom and independence, as Locke observed, characterize the moral nature of a human being and accordingly certain social conditions are morally right or required for persons as they live in human communities. As Rand puts it,

> 'Rights' are a moral concept – the concept that provides the logical transition from the principles guiding an individual's actions to the principles guiding his relationship with others – the concept that preserves and protects individual morality in a social context – the link between the moral code of a man and the legal code of a society, between ethics and politics.[16]

These basic rights to life, liberty, and property are natural rights because they "are conditions of existence required by man's *nature* for his *proper* survival."[17]

The sort of natural rights we find in John Locke's political theory and in theories which have built upon and refined it rest on a conception of the individual as free and independent and on ethics which require persons to pursue their self-interests as they make use of this freedom and independence. Marx was not mistaken when he associated the doctrine of the rights of man with egoism,[18] but he was mistaken in construing the separation of man from man embedded in the Lockean approach to presuppose a view whereby "a man [must be] treated as an isolated monad."[19] The only respect in which the classical egoist and the Lockean natural-rights positions require man to be separated from man is in respect of each person's moral life, that is, in that each person must take responsibility for his or her actions within some range of possible behavior he or she might engage in.[20]

As I argued earlier, the individualist political framework amounts to the view that each person has the natural right to life, liberty, and property, which one ought to make provisions to protect and preserve. Without authority over one's life, one's conduct would be thwarted at its roots. Without authority over the particular actions one will or will not embark upon, this same moral task is virtually frustrated from the start. And without the authority to interact fruitfully, productively, creatively with nature – including other willing human beings — the moral task one has becomes divorced from one's *actual* values, needs, and prospects.

AUTHORIZING LAW ENFORCEMENT

How is the connection between the morally required task of protecting and preserving one's basic rights and political authority to be established? The institutionalized social process of government, carried out by select people for the sake of the public at large, needs to be grounded in morally acceptable considerations. Only when the authority to govern — to engage in politics — has been obtained in a morally appropriate fashion, can it be justified. Such authority must stand for a proper purpose. And to obtain the authority to govern in support of the maintenance of the individualist principles of community life, the appropriate manner is consent, that is, the choice to be involved in politics. In obtaining such authority it is necessary to respect fully everyone's basic human rights, even as the purpose of having this authority is the protection and preservation of such rights. ("Consent" means not merely agreement with an idea or plan but the *justified authorization* to act in certain ways.)

The morally proper procedure to be followed may first be appreciated from the following simple cases of authorizing either the use of permissible (self-defense) force or, in connection which such authorization, the use of force against oneself: First, if George chooses to have himself defended by Susan and Susan chooses to defend George, and they agree to this mutual relationship, then if George is attacked (unjustifiably), Susan is authorized to carry out the suitable defensive actions. Note, however, that if George unjustifiably attacks (uses non-defensive force against) a third person or group, Susan is not authorized to assist him in light of their agreement, since George never possessed the authority to use force on such third parties or groups. George is at liberty,[21] from the moral point of view, to enter into an agreement or contract with Susan for a service George himself has a right to and should produce, in this case self-defense. Second, George and Harry are at liberty, morally, to enter into an agreement with each other and with Fred for the purpose of having Fred adjudicate some possible future dispute between George and Harry as well as to enforce the verdict by force, according to standards of justice (so that in the adjudication and enforcement processes no one's rights will be violated).

I have already noted the worth of these sorts of arrangements within the egoistic-individualist moral framework. The single case of hiring a bodyguard or security guard shows the value of the sort of agreement entered into by George and Susan. We can also point to the ordinary circumstances of athletic competitions to highlight the value of such agreements as that between George, Harry, and Fred. In their reflective, dispassionate moments, when they are presumably focussed on long-range and overriding values, athletes clearly appreciate such factors as impartial judgment, accuracy, and consistency concerning matters of rule violation. They know that they themselves are less likely to be focussed on these factors than would be an independent, impartial referee hired for that purpose. To facilitate competition, it is prudent to elect persons with special training for such tasks as watching whether anyone is violating the rules of the game. All this should motivate them, as athletes, to designate referees to exercise full authority during competitions as regard observance of the rules, even though the athletes know very well, also, that when a referee makes a particular judgment regarding who has violated some rule, the implicated party might protest bitterly. (John McEnroe comes to mind here, for anyone who is familiar with contemporary tennis. And the Olympics are replete with protests.) The initial consent based on prudent sportsmanship, to carry on within the framework at hand commits the athletes to live with the arrangements, despite objecting to and violating them now and then.

The athletic competition analogy is inadequate, however, since in such cases the consent given is usually explicit and players can always withdraw in protest. Nor is there authorization of the use of physical force in implementing the rules; in cases of violent protest the law is called upon, not the referee. The situation with human political life is different. As the individualist anarchist will readily remind us, many who are subject to the governing principles of human community life, even when these are indeed the just principles, have not given their consent. Nor have they given their consent to having the rules enforced by the persons who would be enforcing them. These considerations appear to speak most forcefully against the possibility of ever justifying political authority within the framework of an individualist ethical-political theory.

It is true that, strictly speaking, individualism does not sanction just any form of enforcement of rules or laws against a person, when no consent by that person has been given to such enforcement. In the state of nature one has the authority to defend one's rights when they are being directly violated. But if there is only a suspicion of someone's guilt and a process of discovery needs to be initiated, authorization for subjecting to questioning persons not proven guilty of any violation of rights needs to be secured from such persons. In other words, the bulk of political and legal authority must, for an individualist, rest on the consent of those on whom it may be exercised. Yet, consent may be given in a variety of ways. The choice to submit to a just government may be made in different, sometimes subtle ways. This is a tricky matter and anarchists are correct to concern themselves with the introduction of such notions as tacit consent or implicit consent. Such ideas carry with them a hint of underhandedness and threaten to introduce that very subjugation of one person's will to others that the individualist demands be excluded.

So far it can be seen that the authorization of law enforcement, in case the laws are just — or, less restrictively, in case the system of laws is essentially just — could very possibly be based on individualist premises. Yet, for the present all we can accept is that such authorization would have to be explicit and sporadic. Politics, unlike such short-term endeavors as tennis tournaments, is a very long-range project. Human communities rely on a set of stable well-coordinated principles and numerous derived rules, as well as on the effective and just enforcement of these, in order to embark on all that constitutes human life. Political authority requires longevity. Without durability, fruitful and morally decent human community life would be impossible and attempts to secure it, via the institution of political authority, would be in constant violation of the very principles which are to protect and preserve it. Is there a way to have community life and political authority without this tragic result?

CONSENTING TO JUST GOVERNMENT

Would the idea of implicit consent thwart or help the task of defending an individualist conception of political authority? The most prominent contemporary advocate of individualist anarchism, Murray N. Rothbard, finds no great problem with the idea of implicit consent however, at least when it comes to one aspect of community life. In one of his discussions of the moral superiority of anarchism, Rothbard says that "the hallmark of an anarchist society is one where no man may legally compel someone who is not a convicted criminal to do anything . . . . "[22] But within this idea, as well as throughout discussions of criminal justice, we find embedded in individualist thought the sanction of implicit consent. Clearly criminals cannot be said to have consented to their own conviction other than implicitly.

From an individualist, natural-rights viewpoint, a convicted criminal gives implicit consent to (become familiar with) the system of laws (and what flows from them) in terms of which he has been convicted, provided those laws are objectively just. From this perspective, interacting with others rationally and morally commits all persons to observing that they possess basic rights and are morally free and even responsible to defend these rights. The following points from Eric Mack help to clarify this:

> Let us suppose that Smith is acting, pursuing certain goals. In the course of these actions, Jones is used [Jones is made a victim of Smith's actions]. That is, as a result of the actions performed by Smith (not necessarily actions that are in Smith's interest) some portion of Jones' life is consumed. Smith acts in a way that would be justified only if that portion of Jones' life were at his disposal, in the same sense that an unclaimed natural resource might be at Smith's disposal. It is this sort of action, action wherein Jones is used, treated as a natural resource at the actor's disposal, that I claim are actions done as if it is not the case that Jones ought to act in his own interest. These are the actions that cannot be justified with the egoistic principle.[23]

Interactions with persons entail moral as well as other conditions. For example, if someone attacks another, that act carries with it, as a matter of the logic of aggression, the implication that from a rational moral standpoint the victim may, and often should, retaliate. And if that victim is a citizen of a legal system, such aggressive action also carries with it the implication that the just response of those administering the system should be accepted by the aggressor. (This is why, contrary even to some natural rights theorists, punishment need not, and just punishment does not, involve any rights-violation.)

In order to see whether this analysis is convincing, we should examine whether less drastic cases of implicit consent are at least plausible. Suppose a person takes a teaching job but will not administer tests, correct papers, or read up on recent findings in the field. When questioned he tells us that all that had been agreed to was that he would do some teaching. Suppose, again, that one is put up at a friend's home but when about to use the bathroom is told that, well, the agreement was to provide a place to stay but no mention was made of using the bathroom. These and related cases show that one can implicitly consent to something which one has not explicitly agreed to, given the rational implications of what has been agreed to explicitly.

If to embark upon a task it is contextually necessary also to perform some other tasks or accept some other responsibilities, then one who has agreed to do the former in explicit terms is committed to the latter implicitly. For living among other human beings this implies that in the process of interacting with others one is morally unjustified in treating them as if they were natural resources, available for use without permission. It is also implied that if one breaches this moral obligation one may be acted against in certain ways either by one's victim or by properly designated third parties.

Consent, then, is possible both implicitly and explicitly. Yet there are discernible standards governing the scope of consent in all sorts of cases, including politics. Clearly, there are things one should not consent to do such as embark upon bad business ventures, marry on pretext, participate in deadly sports, and so forth. From the egoistic viewpoint one cannot, morally, consent to do such things. From the point of view of law it may still be appropriate to tolerate and even uphold, for example, contracts, which should not have been entered into. This principle must hold if the law is not to intrude on just any form of improper human interaction, as it surely should not, by most accounts.

But there are also courses of conduct and institutional arrangements to which it would always be improper to consent. Even the attempt would pervert the very idea of consent. This was suggested earlier in connection with George's authorization of Susan to act in George's defense. Such authorization could not extend to acting aggressively in George's behalf. One cannot legitimately consent to something one has no basic right to do, nor to institutions which are in violation of basic rights. The expression 'government by the consent of the governed' therefore cannot be interpreted to mean, 'any type of government by consent of the governed, including tyranny'. Although it might be thought that one can consent to anything, it is clear from the case of George and Susan that that is a mistake. And insofar as consenting to fascism or socialism or even to the welfare state amounts to agreeing that something be done to others who have not themselves agreed to being so treated, it is impossible rationally to construe such decisions as any kind of consent. (This is something to keep in mind whenever one hears discussions about the importance of democracy in making social decisions or whenever one hears the phrase 'we have agreed' or 'the people have agreed'.)

One upshot of this line of analysis is that only those who accept the lifestyle of a hermit manage to accomplish what some take to be the necessary outcome of the individualist stance on political authority. Yes, not everyone may be subject to political authority, but the price of this is that those electing not to be subject must live in total solitude, in isolation from human community life, or in a social situation where everyone has consented to fend only for himself in such matters as self-defense, retaliation in the face of aggression, and punishment. Furthermore, the consent to be governed need not be made explicitly but can be implied, even in ignorance by the consenting party. Anyone may undertake to do something but fail to think of what is implied by that undertaking, and this is possible to do as a member of society. But there are also strict limits on what may be consented to, and from the individualist standpoint it is impossible to consent to something one has no right to decide upon, for example, the disposal of another person's life, liberty, or property.

Another point that follows from the above discussion is that one cannot consent to the authorization of enforcing principles of community organization which are in violation of the rights to life, liberty, and property. That would mean 'consenting' on behalf of others without having gained the authority to do so.

To argue that one can consent to the violation of one's own rights is, as far as I am able to discern, confused. At best it is merely a bad way of asserting that occasionally people have indeed exercised their right to liberty by agreeing *not* to do certain things, for example, not to behave in a way that would otherwise be construed as self-defense or protecting one's property. (This indeed is what may be agreed to when a motion picture company purchases the 'right' to destroy someone's house or farmland.) Granting others permission, within limits, to dispose of one's life, order one's actions, or use one's belongings is just one of the ways one may exercise one's rights. But this does not include granting others permission to violate one's rights — something that is implicit in the talk of absolute democrats who say that 'we have authorized the government to tax us'.

Some Critical Rebuttals

To the charge that the notion of implicit consent within the individualist framework gives away the very principle that individualism wishes to uphold, the answer is that consent, whether explicit or implicit, has its limits. 'One may by consent establish a just government. One cannot establish by consent unjust governments, for one has no right to act unjustly, no authority to delegate unjust powers.

But in the case of consenting to be governed, the implicit consent carries so much weight that no one could possibly appreciate all he is consenting to when he is said (by this analysis) to offer that consent. The entire weight of even a perfectly just political system cannot be said to be accepted by the mere agreement to interact with human beings in an organized community.

While there are limits on what may be consented to, there are also requirements to be met so as to earn the consent of others. A legal system needs to be publicized. Its basic (and perhaps some of its less obvious) features need to be promulgated so that those who have consented to live by such a system can learn its provisions without great difficulty — or can learn how to find out what they need to know when they need to know it. A legal system must also possess the authoritativeness worth giving consent to. It must embody a system of political principles (for example, in its constitution) that can earn willing consent from those who will be governed by authorities who will protect and be guided by those principles.

What one gives consent to in interacting with others in an organized human community is not so much the actual full system of laws and its myriad implications, but one's willingness to find out what the system requires of one as the need arises. Ignorance of the law then would be no excuse. In complex social life it is laws that guide interpersonal conduct, and as one chooses to interact with those party to such life, one accepts the responsibility to learn the laws which make this life possible. (This lends support to the view that education should include civic studies.)

Given an individualist conception of social life, one may pose certain challenges in light of the above discussion. Can political authority extend as far as such compulsory institutions as conscription, taxation, subpoenas, and so on? I won't answer these questions in detail but I will suggest what I take to be the correct approach to handling them.

Conscription and taxation do not qualify as measures implicitly consented to by the governed. At first blush it may appear that consenting to be governed must surely imply a consent to submit to the demand to defend the community in which one lives by one's own choice, just as such consent may seem to imply a consent to submit to taxation for governmental services. However, defending a country is possible by *hiring* people from home or abroad. Financing a country is also possible by *charging* for services provided by the legal system—via a system of contract fees, *post facto* charges for police services, and so on.[24]

Subpoenas, in cases in which a citizen is the sole source of indispensable information needed to implement justice, would seem to be justified on grounds of implicit consent. To choose to be part of a system of justice but refuse to aid it when one is the only possible source of securing that justice would appear to involve a breach of a commitment.

One of the thorniest topics facing an individualist analysis of political authority is whether government can claim exclusive political authority, and how defections or secessions should be dealt with. This is the topic with which Nozick began his discussion of the justice of the minimal state and it has occupied the attention of numerous individualist theorists, before and since.

As to defections or secessions, my remarks on who can escape political authority already suggest that although it is possible to withdraw or secede from a just human community, it is *very* difficult, indeed virtually impossible, to do so without forgoing the task of living a fulfilling, flourishing life.

As to the challenge concerning exclusivity, it needs to be noted first that the objective of political authority is, in large part, to ensure that members of a community possess the opportunity to have conflicting claims (alleging rights violations) properly resolved. Unless some kind of court of *final* authority exists, this is in principle impossible in some cases, for example, when different (systems of) courts end in conflicting resolutions of the same dispute (when one party is subject to one court's, the other to the other's jurisdiction). Under such circumstances the potential for physical conflict is always present, just as it is in international relations (without goodwill and suitable treaties). In international relations there is no such final authority, and while many instances of mutual trust are evident and of voluntary acceptance of arbitration of disputes, for instance at the World Court, there is no way to bring to justice those who simply refuse it, without extended violence, namely, war.

Embedded in the conception of political authority developed here is the requirement that however many different avenues toward the resolution of disputes concerning claims to rights violation may exist, a just human community can have only one final authority. That authority must enjoy jurisdiction over a homogeneous sphere of human occupancy and command an enforcement agency with loyalty to no other final authority. (This matter would, of course, be one of the provisions in need of promulgation within a good human community.)

A system of justice that cannot be implemented for ordinary cases of human disputation cannot claim political authority over anyone. It would be fraudulent to claim that such a system even aims at justice if it cannot in principle reach it. It is a necessary feature of a good human community that its political authority be undivided. (This in no way denigrates such prudent measures as checks and balances between legislative, executive, and judicial branches of government.)

I have elsewhere confronted explicitly the arguments for so-called anarcho-libertarianism or individualist anarchism.[25] I must, however, mention here something about second- or third-best circumstances and how the present theory applies to them.

It would be far-fetched to claim that the real-life communities with which we are familiar exhibit bona fide political authority in their regimes and systems of law. How, then, do we apply the natural-rights arguments defended in the present discussion? The most sensible way to think about this is to distinguish between acting from obligation and acting in compliance. Those parts of the system to which we would have given consent had we had the opportunity to do so explicitly may be regarded as those parts to which we implicitly consent by our continued presence and various activities.[26] These parts we have an *obligation* to respect and if we fail to do so we are rightfully punished.

On the other hand we may also find it prudent to comply with numerous features of existing systems because failure to do so would land us in jail, however unjustly. Not all cases of injustice can and should be fought directly. Sometimes pamphleteering, as practised, for example, by revolutionary Americans or dissident Chinese, South Africans, or Russians, is all that can be done in the way of resistance. At other times outright rebellion is the best choice of conduct. But one does not buy into a whole system merely by virtue of buying into parts of it, even if one tolerates or does not openly challenge some highly objectionable parts.

INDIVIDUALISM ISN'T ANTI-POLITICAL

I have tried to show that it is possible to provide individualist, (classical) ethical-egoistically-based moral justification for the existence and exercise of political authority. I have maintained that the motivation to live a morally good human life makes the choice to live among others in an organized community a sound one. I have argued that once that choice is made, it implies (because of the requirements and opportunities associated with such community life) consent to adhere to certain principles and to obey certain powers established to protect and preserve those principles. I have also indicated how the limits of those powers are best understood. Finally, I have tried to indicate some of the ways in which the present perspective on political authority preserves the values of individualism, for example, in rejecting taxation, expropriation, conscription and other forms of forced labor as unjust, and that it requires a homogeneous jurisdiction for the implementation of that just system of laws by which a community ought to be organized.

THE UNAVOIDABILITY
OF NATURAL LAW AND NATURAL RIGHTS

SOME RIGHTIST BACKLASH
AT NATURAL RIGHTS

Thus far many of the criticisms I have considered of natural-rights theory have issued from thinkers who may appropriately be regarded as advocates of the 'leftist' expansion of the scope of the state. But there are also many conservatives and anti-socialists who wish to grant the state extensive powers beyond those justified within a natural-rights, libertarian framework. Among academic political philosophers there are few who fit this description — the profession is mostly hospitable to those with the Left's moral and political agenda. But there are those, outside of professional philosophy proper, who nevertheless advance interesting and worthy arguments.

In a recent paper entitled 'Against Natural Rights' — published in a journal that is frequently friendly toward the kind of free society that the Lockean natural-rights theory is often taken to support — Professor Ernest van den Haag attacks natural rights.[1] Van den Haag is well known for his championing of anti-libertarian causes — the death penalty, community censorship of pornography, and the narrow interpretation of the Bill of Rights. He attacks not so much the Lockean or more recent developments of that tradition, but rather the welfare-statist or socialist-revisionist school of rights theorists. Although van den Haag often attacks theses connected with the Lockean position, he aims his criticism at non-Lockean usurpers rather than genuine Lockean natural-rights theorists.

Here is the gist of van den Haag's argument. While various necessary conditions may be required for human existence and excellence, just as natural-law rights theorists suggest, it does not follow that from knowing these it is possible to infer norms or virtues or moral principles. (Here van den Haag restates the Humean 'is-ought gap' thesis that no judgment of what one ought (not) to do is deducible, with strict logical necessity, from any (true) judgment of what is the case.)[2] Not only are we unable to establish that there are basic individual rights, van den Haag believes, but it is not really desirable to do this by invoking any firm idea of human nature or excellence — whatever school of philosophical politics advances this idea. Assuming the desirability of negative liberty — freedom from the forcible intrusions of others in one's life — there is, van den Haag contends, reason to believe that any natural-law approach to politics would jeopardize such liberty. He here reiterates what Karl Popper maintained in *The Open Society and its Enemies*. Most thinkers who have supposed that we can derive 'ought' judgments from 'is' judgments about human nature have promulgated views hostile to negative liberty. Plato, Hegel, and Marx all fall into this category with their holistic or totalist moral and political philosophies.[3] While van den Haag does not claim that this proves the invalidity of the natural-law/natural-rights approach, he wishes us to consider the suggestiveness of the intellectual-historical record. He wishes to warn those of us fond of liberty against the temptations of the naturalist schools.

Finally, van den Haag also discusses difficulties concerning the sort of ethical and political doctrine we may expect from a consequentialist or utilitarian approach. This is the approach he favors and considers the main alternative to the natural law, natural rights tradition, especially in connection with the justification of the more conservative versions of the classical liberal political order. Van den Haag does not deny that there are problems with his favored view, but he argues that we must bite the bullet: admit that consequentialism is not clean, that one might be able to use it to justify some *prima facie* abhorrent practices, but that, despite this, there is nowhere else to turn for a sensible moral and political framework since the natural-law, natural-rights approach fares even worse with such hard cases. These difficulties with consequentialism-utilitarianism may have moved John Rawls, Robert Nozick, and Ronald Dworkin to look for different answers, but van den Haag is not himself so moved.[4] He denies that the horrid results are really implicit in the consequentialist-utilitarian school, at least when we consider matters in detail. The pursuit of the greatest happiness of the greatest number, even without some clear idea of happiness, will not lead to policies trampling the lives of the minority, at least no more so than any other viable option. It is not necessary, for example, to favor the random killing of some to ensure the environmentally safe survival of the majority; nor the giving of healthy body organs from the less socially useful to the more socially useful who suffer from disease.

Difficulties with Anti-Naturalism

First, van den Haag's criticism of the natural-rights school falls prey to the error of the epistemological positivists. The Humean argument was aimed at epistemological rationalists who believed that we could know moral truths the way we supposedly know basic principles of logic or metaphysics. Hume showed that if this was what knowledge required, we could not have some very precious kinds of knowledge indeed, including moral and scientific knowledge. But Hume seems to have been making this point as a *reductio ad absurdum* of the rationalist view of what knowledge must be. Once this view is rejected, there is no reason to claim, even in Hume's own terms, that moral knowledge is impossible.

True enough, as I have already allowed, 'ought' cannot be derived from 'is', if by 'derived' one means that it cannot be deduced as a necessary conclusion from true premises. But this does not imply that we cannot rationally establish the truth of certain judgments concerning what is best for human beings to do, how they ought to behave in life and in politics.

The 'is-ought' gap, made into a powerful skeptical intellectual weapon by David Hume, was an offshoot of Hume's strict model of knowledge that governed his strict empiricism. To know something, within that model, meant to have as firm a grasp of what one knows as one would have if one were the thing itself. 'Knowing it' means 'becoming it', and, barring this, one ends doubting that one knows at all. Of course this ideal is impossible, utopian, and implies solipsism.

An important way to appreciate that the Humean 'is-ought' argument is not decisive against the possibility of moral knowledge is to see that empiricism begs the question of what there can be in reality. It holds that only whatever is capable of being sensed can be known to exist. This rules out any type of existence that does not consist solely in the manifestation of sensible properties. Moral judgments aim to identify principles of conduct, relationships between some consciously acting agent and various aspects of reality vis-à-vis that agent. They thus cannot be reduced to statements of fact as understood in empiricism, nor can they, thus, be derived from such statements of fact without remainder. Moral facts — that lying is evil or that everyone possesses the natural right to life, liberty, and property — are embedded in a broader conception of the nature of 'fact'.

The empiricist stance is highly dubious — certainly it does not any longer accurately characterize the epistemology of the natural sciences. Why we should use it as a basis for evaluating the possibility of moral knowledge is a mystery.[5] To the extent that the 'is-ought' gap rests on such a philosophical background, we need not accept it. It is arguable that a different tradition warrants a new look — the neo-Aristotelian teleological conception of human nature, which seems to be perfectly compatible with modern science, deserves more attention from those who wish to flatly assert the is-ought dichotomy in our time.[6]

There are some who deny that the 'is-ought' gap rests on empiricism, although the only argument to this effect that I am aware of comes from Kai Nielsen, whose view I discussed earlier. It is claimed that the 'is-ought' gap gains support from G. E. Moore's open-question argument against naturalism. Yet that argument, as I have shown, misconstrues the role open questions have in our investigations. They can usefully function as initial queries about the soundness of a theory, only to be abandoned once the theory has been vindicated. In ongoing debates, however, the questions persist and are given standing despite the possibility that they no longer raise a valid point.

The Popperian idea that naturalist views pose a threat to classical liberalism because they encourage holism, totalism, or authoritarianism, misses its target. It should be directed at the frequent error committed by naturalists, namely, attempting to force human beings to do or not do what they ought or ought not to do. Aristotle understood very well the connection between volition and the moral virtues. He taught that "The virtues are modes of choice or involve choice," and "it is in our power to be virtuous or vicious."[7] The moral (as distinct from intellectual) virtues are, in Aristotle's view, a matter of volition or free choice. If, then, the natural rights tradition embraces some ethical doctrine based on an understanding of human nature, and this understanding recognizes that to be morally good a person must choose to act rightly, this is a wholly adequate basis on which to defend negative freedom as a necessary condition in society for the very existence of the possibility of morality. The natural rights school attempts to develop this idea in full. The reason the idea was mistakenly omitted from some naturalist moral philosophies is that they focussed exclusively on the good state of affairs that actions and institutions ought to aim at, and failed adequately to emphasize that the goodness of attaining those goals depended on the choices of individual persons.[8]

As to the trouble with hard cases, van den Haag discusses them not in light of the works of defenders of the Lockean tradition but vis-à-vis the work of such welfare-state 'human-rights' advocates as John Rawls, Ronald Dworkin, and Alan Gewirth. He never comes to terms with the extensive literature on just this topic produced by libertarian philosophers. This is significant because the welfare-state advocates tend to avoid ethics — theirs are only political philosophies and it is doubtful that with their proposals for extensive regimentation of society they would have much room for ethics independent from politics. In Rawls we do not find any discussion of personal ethics, of those virtues that a good human being would live by. Similarly, in Dworkin and Gewirth, all the apparatus of their philosophizing is focussed on forging public policy.

Hard cases are just the kind that depart from the arena in which politics is possible. Hard cases are exceptions to the political situation and not the norm. The laws of a good human community are not supposed to be geared primarily to handling emergencies. They are, so to speak, the social navigational principles for ordinary human beings who have the opportunity, in the main, to aspire to excellence in one another's company if these principles are respected and protected.

Yet, the reality and significance of hard cases cannot be ignored. The answer to how to cope with them, however, must come from a more basic system of action-guiding principles than law, namely, ethics. And the neo-Aristotelians, such as Mack, Miller, Rasmussen, Den Uyl, and others, have prepared themselves to deal with them. Thus Mack has argued that when we are in an emergency situation, where no mutually advantageous or beneficial resolution of a problem is possible — the standard life-boat or desert-island kinds of cases — the matter must be handled independently of political principles.[9] No such resolution is possible for the politicized 'moral' philosophers van den Haag chose to attack as defenders of natural rights. For them, any solution to the theoretical problems posed by hard cases must come from within their political framework. The natural-rights theorists who have developed the neo-Aristotelian ethical foundations (natural laws) for their Lockean political principles (natural rights) can approach hard cases by leaving politics and law and drawing on the more fundamental reservoir of ethical standards.

Thus, it is possible to see how one might handle emergencies for which the political legal system is not prepared by consulting ethics in, say, the life-boat situation. Here persons occupy a boat that will sink unless some leave it, but who is to leave the boat? By referring merely to a doctrine of human rights, there seems to be no answer to this question. Utilitarianism seems inadequate to the problem since there is no objective criterion, even in principle, as to what is the greatest happiness of the greatest number. It won't suffice simply to save the majority and let the minority, randomly selected, drown. Utilitarianism offers no principled resolution. But some other ethics might — for example by reference to the idea that individual human happiness must be supported and by invoking a conception of human nature in terms of which such support can be clearly understood and a criterion of selection arrived at. Thus perhaps the very old *should* offer to die, given that theirs will be a full and dignified life by doing so, whereas the more immature would have to cut short a possibly flourishing life. Or those with more creative talent might be preferred to those with less. Exactly what the standard of choice should be is perhaps difficult to decide when one is so remote from the situation, but we all know of good novels in which just these kinds of choices are made, as well as some famous cases in law where actual persons have come to grips with them. The point here is that with a sound ethical system at one's disposal, it is not inherently impossible to conceive of dealing with hard cases.

More generally, the nature-rights position links up with a more substantial ethical tradition than those van den Haag picks for attack.[10] Even Locke suggests how hard cases must be approached when he advises us to distinguish between situations "where peace is possible" and those where it is not. Once rights have been widely violated, or where their observance is not even possible, some other approach needs to be taken. At times it may even be morally proper to flip a coin to reach a solution — but even this has to be understood as arising from the implementation of standards, not as a matter of arbitrary decision.

The basic thrust of the natural rights approach in handling hard cases may be summarized as follows: The purpose of ethics or a moral system is to provide for the guidance of human living; political ethics and law are branches which provide for the guidance of human life in the company of other (unrelated) persons. To the extent that an ethical or political system helps achieve the purpose it naturally has — the purpose assumed in asking the question that gives rise to it as one of the many competing answers — it is a sound system, it is naturally justified. But even a sound system of ethics or politics can face difficulties, so the question is whether one or another faces them more successfully — more comprehensively, and with greater integrity. What about the relationship between the ethical system and the political — the principles of which would form a constitution or set of common laws on which positive law would most appropriately rest in human communities aimed at justice? It is best seen in light of the fact that each person, as an adult, faces questions of living concerning himself before facing questions of living with others. This is a matter of the ontology of the situation; that is, because one is one's own behavioral motivator in need of guidance in one's conduct, one needs to have the answer to what one should do *per se* before adding the more specialized political question of what one should do vis-à-vis others. (Although there are many who claim that Aristotle saw this the other way around, regarding politics as prior to ethics, there is also some scholarship that argues that he, too, understood ethics to be prior to politics.)[11] The ethical dimension of one's life has priority and the political is subsidiary to it since one must guide oneself, first and foremost, not others. Therefore, when a conflict arises the ethical framework is decisive; one's moral obligations dominate, and however statists might like to deny it, a person must answer to morality before he answers to law.

Official representatives of the political dimension may not stress this publicly, of course. And as far as their own conduct is concerned, given their personal commitments or oaths of office, the issue of priority may not even arise. Indeed, in a free society, where men and women are governed by virtue of having given their consent, it may be assumed that, with a decent citizenry, the bulk of what politics requires of citizens will also be what morality demands of them. (The difficulties with the highly mixed situations we face in our actual world are well illustrated by such stories as Melville's *Billy Budd*. Political principles alone cannot serve as a sufficient guide to right conduct.)

The natural law is prior, so the natural rights each person has vis-à-vis others (whose actions serve to express either a chosen respect for or violation of their personhood) may on occasion be disregarded (not violated) in the face of one's ethical responsibiliies.

CONSEQUENTIALISM IS NOT ENOUGH

Of course, the above sketch immediately suggests some congruence with certain elements of van den Haag's consequentialist position. But this is due to van den Haag's badly chosen representatives of naturalism. Had he focussed on the neo-Aristotelian defense of natural law and natural rights, a defense much more hospitable to liberty than the human-rights theories he discusses, he would have seen that the teleological approach incorporates many elements of consequentialism, notably a concern with the facts bearing on how the future will turn out for us.

Yet, whereas van den Haag is entirely uncommitted to any definitive conception of the human good or *summum bonum*, the neo-Aristotelians are. They claim that human happiness is indeed the proper goal of the moral life, and that although this happiness may manifest itself in various ways, depending on whom we are talking about, the fact that we are talking about *human* happiness circumscribes how it can be manifest.

With van den Haag's human good left essentially subjective — which is the central flaw of all utilitarian ethics and politics — questions of moral right and political rights are also undecidable. While he does claim that some kind of escape is possible — "stipulated along the lines of Ulpian's maxims, or along Roman or Common law lines"[12] — he just cannot make sense, in his own theoretical terms, of the assertion that there is "right or even a moral duty to be unjust to individuals in certain circumstances."[13] Utilitarianism isn't able to provide guidance in the area of personal morality where such circumstances arise. With a subjective theory of the good — where good ends or consequences are just those that satisfy what persons desire — utilitarianism fails to offer us a guide to how we ought to choose. This theory of the good already presupposes that we have made a choice in order for it to be able to specify what is a good thing to do.

There is one other difficulty in giving a subjectivist account of values, including the value of liberty. It is self-defeating to maintain that, although one values liberty, liberty as a value is rationally indefensible. Many have made this charge, including some conservative friends of liberty.[14] Any action-guiding theory that rests on principles that permit one to be indifferent to the truth of that theory, is theoretically flawed. If one cannot apply one's principles to giving one's actions a rational justification, such that this justification defeats other possible justifications, one's system cannot be claimed to be superior to alternatives. (Perhaps this is the thrust of Solzhenitsyn's contention that the West lacks the will to defend itself.)

I do not deny that difficulties can arise in attempts to reconcile principles of morality with principles of politics and law. But there is reason to doubt that *any* moral system would handle these equally badly. There is, I believe, no good reason to abandon the idea of the inalienability or absoluteness of natural rights — e.g., by characterizing them as merely 'prima facie'[15] — even if some instances can be found when such rights need to be disregarded.[16] But whenever such difficulties seem to face us, the course to follow would be to attend very carefully to the intricacies of the situation. The positive law itself follows this course in cases of alleged wrong-doing in exceptional circumstances, such as shipwreck, famine, or earthquakes. Such cases call for the fullest possible knowledge of details since only then can we learn whether those involved made full use of their moral faculties. Sketching such cases will not suffice, however tempting that may be for argumentative and illustrative purposes.

The naturalist framework is not fully satisfying for those who wish for mechanical solutions to complex moral and political problems. No doubt, also, many efforts to develop such a framework have been failures. But the main reason for their theoretical shortcomings has been foundational — the frequent weakness of the philosophical theories underlying these views. Yet these are not incapable of remedy.[17] If we heed Gilbert Harman's advice to "take care not to adopt a very skeptical attitude nor become too lenient about what is to count as knowledge",[18] especially in how we conceive of moral and political knowledge and what tests we expect claims to such knowledge to meet, the task of developing the naturalist position seems promising. Nature, which while not purely geometrical is still quite coherent, should be our guide in formulating principles to cope with our human lives. The subjectivism involved in the consequentialism-utilitarianism that is often advanced as a viable alternative in political theorizing, does not seem to be able to overcome some of the problems that any promising theory must tackle.

MORE CHALLENGES FROM
WELFARE-STATE PHILOSOPHERS

At this point I wish only to add a brief discussion of why, contrary to prominent mainstream opinion in contemporary moral and political philosophy, defenses of the welfare state, that compete with the libertarian theory, do not fare very well. I have already examined some of these views and will touch on one such position, Alan Gewirth's, once more, but this time with a somewhat wider focus. Political viewpoints must be evaluated comparatively, and while this work is not primarily a comparative analysis of contemporary political perspectives, some comparative analysis will be useful.

THE WELFARE STATE
VERSUS THE NATURAL-RIGHTS DOCTRINE

From its earliest days, the American legal system developed under the influence of conflicting political philosophies. The Constitution stressed individual rights — though not consistently enough, when we judge it by the Declaration of Independence and its doctrine of the equal rights of all persons. Even the Bill of Rights does not pay equal attention to the three fundamental rights listed in the Declaration — to life, liberty, and the pursuit of happiness — and singles out the right to a free press for special protection, leaving the right to the variety of pursuits of happiness less stringently protected. For example, the Fifth Amendment obliquely affirms the right to private property. Yet with sufficient political support and a certain amount of sophistry, courts can justify state intervention in all manner of economic affairs despite that reference.[1]

Furthermore, the common law left ample room for a paternalistic theory of the supremacy of government. Many jurists and justices embraced elements of both these viewpoints, which in part accounts for the conflicting tendencies within our legal institutions and, indeed, for the ease with which a country of individualism could be turned, without revolution, into a country of substantial collectivism and statism.

The natural-rights individualism of Locke contained certain features which many found difficult to reconcile with conventional morality. Perhaps the most telling criticism of the natural-rights thesis, which stressed private-property rights and therefore free-market capitalism, is that it lacks compassion. As John Maynard Keynes noted, capitalism

> implies that there must be no mercy or protection for those who embark their capital or their labor in the wrong direction. It is a method of bringing the most successful profit-makers to the top by a ruthless struggle for survival, which selects the most efficient by the bankruptcy of the less efficient. It does not count the cost of the struggle, but looks only to the benefits of the final result which are assumed to be lasting and permanent, once it has been attained. The object of life being to crop the leaves off the branches up to the greatest possible height, the likeliest way of achieving this end is to leave the giraffes with the longest necks to starve out those whose necks are shorter.[2]

It was this sort of heartless capitalism that the welfare state was (re)introduced to tame. Proponents of the welfare state take government regulation — such as OSHA (the Occupational Safety and Health Administration) — to be necessary means for ameliorating the hardship and callousness allegedly inherent in a capitalist system.

The Moral Theory of the Welfare State

The welfare state rests largely on the view that while individual liberty, including the freedom to earn and even amass wealth, needs to be respected by the legal system, so must be the special needs of those, to use Keynes's phrase, "whose necks are shorter". Such expressions of moral concern for those who failed, for whatever reason, to flourish under capitalism resulted in a moderation of confidence in the merits of the capitalist system and the gradual emergence of the welfare state as a more humane alternative.

Alongside all the avowedly anti-capitalist schools of thought, there emerged one that did not entirely dismiss capitalism and its moral-political foundations, upholding as they do negative liberty as the supreme political value.[3] Rather, this school intended to combine some of the fundamental values of capitalism with certain additional and even alien values, such as the notion of the right to welfare (or wellbeing or happiness).

A major consequence of this idea has been the abandonment in the law of commerce of the doctrine of *caveat emptor*, 'let the buyer beware'. This doctrine held that whenever a transaction occurs, both parties are legally obligated merely to act in a nonviolent and non-fraudulent manner; that is all.[4] No special assistance was owed, in law, to those with whom one is engaged in trade. One might not perpetrate outright fraud or *misrepresent* one's wares or services. But in trade all parties were held to be concerned mainly with what served their own purposes. No one by law owed any help to a partner in trade.

The implications of this for the labor market, for example, should not be difficult to imagine. Capitalism implies that when workers take jobs, it is their responsibility to choose, for instance, whether they will work with the risk of health and safety hazards, or work elsewhere, or perhaps not work at all. This idea is still embedded in pure capitalist economic theory.[5]

Let us now look at some recent efforts to make the moral case in favor of the welfare state (and, thus, of government intervention in the marketplace and government regulations such as OSHA). We will examine three central contemporary ideas, namely, the doctrine of *prima-facie rights*; the doctrine of *equal rights to freedom and wellbeing*, and the doctrine of *justice as equal resources*. The first of these states that there are no absolute human rights to liberty and that there are competing rights, for example, to happiness, which sometimes may override the prima-facie right to liberty. The second holds that individuals actually have basic human rights to both freedom and wellbeing. The last states that a society must implement a policy of equality concerning the acquisition of resources (income, material goods), provided certain conditions obtain. The three positions are advanced by the philosophers Gregory Vlastos, Alan Gewirth, and John Rawls, respectively.

VLASTOS: PRIMA-FACIE RIGHTS

Gregory Vlastos advances a widely-studied argument in support of the modification of the idea of natural rights. He holds that although it is true enough that we all possess certain basic rights as human beings, these are not absolute or do not really deserve full or consistent protection in the legal system.[6]

Here is what Vlastos's point amounts to: As expressed in the Declaration of Independence and in Locke's theory, each of us is said to have *inalienable* rights. This means these rights — to life, liberty, and the pursuit of happiness — may not be separated from the individuals who hold them. And governments are established for the purpose of protecting these rights, of resisting any effort to try to prohibit or forcibly thwart these pursuits. So understood, these rights are absolute.[7] They may not be alienated, not even by the individual who has them (one may not 'sell' oneself into slavery).

Vlastos argues against such an absolutist conception of human rights. He holds that "We would . . . improve the consistency of Locke's theory if we understood him to mean that natural rights are subject to justified exceptions."[8] He proposes to speak of human rights as "prima-facie" rights meaning that "the claims of any of them may be over-ruled in special circumstances . . . ."[9] Vlastos does not mean to deny the existence of rights — "prima facie" is not used to mean 'on its face' or 'apparent'.

Vlastos claims that, real as these rights may be, "*any* of them may be over-ruled in special circumstances."[10] The reason is simple: Clearly we can imagine circumstances when rights must be over-ridden, as a matter of moral decency. Locke's claim that "government . . . can *never* have a power to take . . . the whole, or any part of the subjects' property, without their consent"[11] seems plainly wrong. Vlastos claims that Locke himself appears to have accepted this in his actual political conduct.

Vlastos outlines a position in favor of a doctrine of "equal welfare-rights and freedom rights" for all.[12] Welfare rights would entitle all persons to being provided with what is required for their wellbeing, while freedom rights entitle them to being left alone to live and act as they choose. Thus, if either welfare rights or freedom rights were absolute, they would cancel each other out in virtually all circumstances. An absolute right is a condition that must be fully and invariably respected. If one has the absolute right to be free, then no one may ever curb one's freedom. The welfare of someone is often secured only through another person's productive support — to gain shelter and food, those who do not have it can get it only if others provide it. If others have an absolute freedom right, it would not be morally justified to obtain such shelter and food without these others' consent. However, if those without shelter and food (welfare) have an absolute right to it, then others, both morally and legally, would have to provide this. One person's absolute right to liberty trumps or cancels out another's absolute right to welfare, and vice versa.

A doctrine of prima-facie rights appears to solve the problem. Only it does not really. What it does is to leave things pretty much 'deuces wild'. It becomes entirely arbitrary whether the 'prima-facie' right to liberty or the 'prima-facie' right to welfare will be protected.

GEWIRTH: HUMAN RIGHTS TO FREEDOM AND WELLBEING

Alan Gewirth, as we have already noted, defends what he calls the "supportive state" on the basis that each of us possesses the human rights to freedom *and* to wellbeing. He holds that we are all equal in possessing *generic rights*. As he puts it,

> What is of central importance here is not that wealth or property itself is to be equalized but rather that, beyond the minimum required for basic goods, persons have as nearly as possible equal chances for developing and utilizing their own capabilities for successful agency [that is, human action].[13]

Earlier I looked at Gewirth's attempt to reconcile both a right to liberty and a right to wellbeing. But how does Gewirth defend the position that we have these rights?

He holds, basically, that anyone with good sense who does anything whatever must believe that that thing is a good thing to do, otherwise he would not freely choose to do it. And then, Gewirth argues, he must view every other person in the same light. So whatever he demands for himself—for instance the freedom and the basic ability to do what he wants—he implicitly demands for others as well.[14] That, in turn, implies that none may rob us of our freedom and that we must be provided, at least when we lack it, with the materials required for action.

But Gewirth has not demonstrated that each of us has a *right* both to freedom and wellbeing, only that both freedom and wellbeing (the ability to act) are necessary for the pursuit of our goals. He has not shown that wellbeing is something others must provide us with, only that it is vital for our lives. The right to freedom or liberty, understood not as opportunity to do something but as the absence of intrusion by others, is different, since if others do not 'provide it for us' we won't have it. Without others' refraining from assaulting, killing, or stealing from us, we cannot be free. But wellbeing, though also necessary to pursue our goals, is yet something we can secure for ourselves, is something we ought to produce for ourselves. The only exceptions to this may be in the case of some drastic emergency, or in the case of children, who depend on adults and are owed care from those who brought them into the world.

Gewirth's argument for a welfare or supportive state fails because he does not fully appreciate the importance of the distinction between values *only* others can produce for us—such as (negative) freedom—and values that almost all adult persons could produce for themselves, even if sometimes with very great difficulty and, on rare occasions, only with the help of others. Contrary to his insistence, it does make sense that there should only be the basic (negative) human right to freedom from others' invasion of our lives. A right is just the sort of moral condition which must be secured through the cooperation of other people and it is the only moral condition which may be secured by force if other people don't respect it. We have a *right* to freedom because autonomy or sovereignty is something that one would always possess were it not for others' taking it away. Freedom cannot be given, only taken and then regained. The point of the concept of a basic human or natural right is to identify a value we rightly or justly possess but which could be taken from us *by the actions of others.* Wellbeing is a different kind of value. We may lack wellbeing *quite apart from what others do or don't do to or for us.*

People *can* unjustly, wrongfully hurt us. If they do unjustly hurt us, then they are liable to us for the harm caused. Theft, assault, and murder all wrongfully take values from us. We know this because we know we have the right to life, liberty, and property. That also means others may be thwarted in their efforts to take these values from us. If we had no right to our lives—if it were not for us to decide whether to live or not to live; to our liberty—if it were not up to us what we would do; and to our property—if it were not up to us what to do with what we have produced or created—then it would not be possible to tell that actions invading these rights were categorically wrong. If our lives did not belong to us, if we were not the rightful agents of our actions, if we did not own what we produced, then murder, assault, and theft would not be generally wrong and prohibitable actions. In contrast, if we lack some value which others were not responsible for taking from us, we could not have a right to that value.

If I have a right to something, and another takes it, I may take it back or send the police to recover it (via the court system). If someone kidnaps me, I may regain my freedom, even by force. But when nothing has been taken from me, no one has assaulted me, no one has kidnapped me or threatened to kill me—my basic and derivative rights have not been violated or abridged—I am not morally entitled to *forcibly deprive* anyone of anything who hasn't taken from me what is mine. Plainly, any laws which authorized such conduct would substitute *need* for *justice* as the ground of legitimacy.

The value of wellbeing is undeniable. Sickness, insecurity, worry, and so on can all undermine it. Obtaining relief against these is, then, also immensely valuable. But to regard such relief as a right is a mistake. It imposes on innocent parties legally enforceable duties which they do not have.

So we do not have a human right to wellbeing. If something is ours by right, it can be compelled from others. Freedom is something we have by right, so it may be compelled from others who would invade it. Any political system which authorizes the initiation of force for any other purpose is most probably wrong.

Rawls: Justice as Equality of Resources

John Rawls has defended the welfare state without extensive reliance on any doctrine of rights. He argues that unless we are going to contribute to the needy in some exceptional way, we should not be permitted to enjoy greater welfare than others. Inequalities are morally and legally justified if they raise the people who are the worst off to a better station in life. As Rawls himself makes the point:

> Those who have been favored by nature, whoever they are, may gain from their good fortune only on terms that improve the situation of those who have lost out . . . .[15]

But why should this be so? Rawls is very clear about that matter as well:

The assertion that a man deserves [that it is *just* for a man exclusively to possess and to benefit from] the superior character that enables him to make the effort to cultivate his abilities is . . . problematic; for his character depends in large part upon fortunate family and social circumstances for which he can claim no credit.[16]

Therefore, of course, as Rawls points out, "No one deserves his greater natural capacity nor merits a more favorable starting place in society",[17] which is why we must have a system that guarantees equality of resources for everyone in life, unless inequality can be expected to yield welfare improvements for those "who have lost out".

The gist of Rawls's view, then, is that we are all products of forces over which we have no individual control; so when some of us are better off than others, it cannot be just, not at least as Rawls understands that concept, to mean *fair*.[18] When we view human life in this light, it indeed seems unfair that some are better off than others.

In Rawls's view we are really back to what Keynes told us: it is unjust or unfair to leave a society to be governed on the basis of winners and losers. The welfare state is the remedy for this. It does not fully destroy liberty, so with regard to some matters in their lives people are justified in acting autonomously, independently. But they have a right to anything of great value only if by getting it they also improve the lot of the needy.

Rawls's position is problematic for several reasons. First, there is a paradox in the theory that our moral character is something we largely obtain by accident. Essentially, our character is what explains our better- or worse-chosen deeds. A person does the right thing often because of his or her character — his or her self-developed ability for moral discernment. Character is something we ourselves cultivate. If it is simply acquired by us from our circumstances, then our good and bad deeds are not really something for which we are responsible.

Rawls's view, in short, precludes, at least implicitly, any merit to individual effort and accomplishment, and thus denies the possibility of differential welfare status which might have been earned through such difference of merit. Yet Rawls *morally* exalts the merits of his system and rests with all of us the task of implementing its tenets.

So, all of us are substantially unfree to choose and thus to gain moral credit. On the other hand we ought to choose (and thus might be credited with) being on the side of justice as Rawls understands it.

Although Rawls does not say that people are unfree, his view of character and the attendant moral and political implications of what he says leave no room for free will and, thus, for a prerequisite of moral choice. Since Rawls believes that there is no need for any metaphysical and epistemological grounding of moral theories, perhaps we should not discuss these neglected features of his theory, but in fact they cannot be left out of a reasonably complete account of the moral and political situation human beings encounter in their lives.

Second, are we really unfree to choose to make something of our lives? As we have already seen, there are reasons to think that we are quite free: The very effort to seek answers to questions rests on our freedom to seek and find such answers. It presupposes that we aren't prisoners of our prejudices, preconceptions, and simple opinions. The diversity of human life, the uncanny recurrence of the notion of good and evil throughout it, is explained most successfully by accepting that individuals have substantial control over how they conduct themselves. There is scientific evidence, as I mentioned in Chapter 1, for the view that human beings have the kind of brain that makes self-generated, self-initiated conduct possible, and self-understanding or introspection gives evidence of personal freedom.

HUMAN RIGHTS
VERSUS THE WELFARE STATE

Now that we have considered the most recent prominent arguments for the welfare state, it will be useful to reconsider the ground of moral opposition to even the more accommodating alternative of the welfare state, with its institution of government regulation of commerce. Let us take a last look at the updated version of John Locke's doctrine of natural human rights developed in the earlier sections of this work.[19]

Human beings are rational animals, with the moral responsibility to excel as such. A good society requires standards for guiding human beings in their conduct toward one another, showing where the proper jurisdiction of one begins and another ends. This is because living in human dignity requires, at least for adults, that persons govern *themselves*, guide their *own lives*. This requirement of freedom from the willful invasion of others ('negative freedom') is promulgated with a framework of basic human rights in relatively large human communities. This means, roughly, that we need ask no one's permission to live, to take action, and to acquire, hold, or use as we see fit the results of our productivity or creativity. These rights are absolute, inalienable, and universal. Within their scope, that is, in our legal systems, no excuse legitimatizes their violation or infringement. No one can lose these rights, although some actions a person might take can lead to placing that person in circumstances in which he or she must exercise them in very restricted ways (for example, in jail). Every human being has these rights, even when they are not respected by others. And finally, having these rights entitles us to resist, with reasonable force if necessary, attempts by others to violate or infringe them.

As we have seen, many people believe in another kind of human 'right to freedom', different from that which is at the heart of the above viewpoint. They wish the government to protect so-called 'positive rights' or 'positive freedoms', meaning, the *ability* (rather than the right to freedom from others) to flourish as a human being. In plain terms, many people want government to protect not just our right to freedom from other people's violence against us, but also our alleged right to have help provided by others as we face life's hardships, sometimes as innocent casualities of acts of nature, sometimes because of our own misdeeds or negligence.

Yet in my judgement such positive 'freedoms' can be secured only by assuring the full protection of negative rights. Only when negative rights are fully secured, will human beings be willing and able to provide both for themselves and for others, including the specially needy. The so-called positive freedoms, opportunities to overcome hardship and make headway toward a reasonably successful life, can be secured only when each person is secure in his or her rights to act productively, helpfully, creatively.

The condition of freedom that characterizes a society that affirms in its basic law that everyone ought to be respected as a self-developing, responsible human being is best secured by the identification and implementation of the standards outlined in this book. It is the primary requirement of human social life that each person's moral nature be protected and everyone be left free by others, and thus morally responsible, to govern his or her life. (Capital punishment, if there is independent justification for it, does not necessarily contradict this line of analysis. Criminals tacitly consent to their punishment. In a just system, when someone commits a crime — and in such a system only those actions would be classified as crimes which infringed other people's rights—he or she ought to know that others will resist by banishing the offender from their midst or by some other agreed-upon response. If someone proceeds with the criminal deed, what he or she faces is something he or she has invited. There is in fact no right-violation going on in punishing criminals, just as no theft is going on when a creditor collects from an unwilling debtor. The logic of their actions calls for it, as I argued in Chapter 6. As it happens, I oppose capital punishment for different reasons.)

Thus, the welfare state promotes a series of 'entitlements' and government interventions based on the notion that individuals within a capitalist system need some equalizing forces to soften the hardship of that social system. On the other hand, a doctrine of natural rights, such as that sketched by Locke and developed here and elsewhere by libertarians, identifies a more limited set of individual rights, those to life, liberty, and property. These rights are identifed by an understanding of human nature as possessing a moral dimension; that is, each individual has moral responsibilities and others may not interfere with the efforts (or lack of them) of individuals to face up to them. Here the task of overcoming life's hardships is left to voluntarily co-operating individuals and groups, not to efforts of a coercive state. The reasonable expectation is that a society with such rights adequately protected will be decent and prosperous as well as just.

Workers' Rights

Essentially, workers are individuals who intend to hire out their skills for whatever they will fetch in the marketplace. Workers have the right to offer their skills in return for what others will offer in return for those skills. The framework of human rights sketched here implies free trade in the labor market.

Defenders of special 'workers' rights' believe that employees possess special rights as employees, for example, rights to occupational health and safety. In general, proponents of such special 'workers' rights' hold that, aside from negative rights, workers are owed a positive right to be treated with care and considerateness on the job.[20]

'Workers' rights' in this sense is, however, a morally flawed idea. Those who fail to treat workers with care and respect can be open to moral criticism. When values such as safety and health are neglected by employers, some crucially important features of the work situation are missing. (Ordinarily, but not in every case, such skimpings occur when other values take priority, for example, lowering costs to stay in business.) Whatever the moral criticisms in a given case, they are categorically different from holding that workers have legally enforceable basic positive rights. Adults have no basic, noncontractual rights to have benefits provided for them by unwilling others, including their employers. These others are free agents whose conduct should be guided by their own judgments unless they encroach upon someone's natural rights.[21] The positive-rights approach reintroduces a type of involuntary servitude into the economic sphere of human social life. While this is evidently not the intention behind the forging of the basic positive-rights doctrine, it is its result.

Of course, in response, many positive-rights advocates claim that a free labor market can lead to the horrors of child labor, hazardous and health-impairing working conditions, and so on.

However, it is far from true that a free labor-market leads to child labor and rampant neglect of safety and health at the workplace. Children are, after all, dependents. Hence parents owe enforceable duties to children. To subject children to hazardous, exploitative work, to deprive them of normal education and health care, can be construed as a violation of their individual rights as young dependent human beings. Similarly, knowingly or negligently subjecting workers to hazards at the workplace may constitute a form of fraud and assault and comes under the prohibition of the violation of the right to liberty and even of the right to life. Such conduct is actionable in a court of just law—based on the natural rights framework—and workers, individually or organized into unions, would be morally justified, indeed well advised, to challenge it. In short, even as we note that the positive rights doctrine is defective, it is also useful to keep in mind that some of the values motivating it are obtainable within the natural-rights libertarian capitalist system developed here. But a different route may be necessary for securing these values.

It is futile to attempt to engineer human goodness. There is no political solution to the problem of human folly and evil. Making others good by force is impossible, and the attempt is both wasteful and insulting. It will be resisted with black markets, mobs, tax-evasion, draft-dodging, and the like. That is why the welfare state, with all of the benign—though sometimes, perhaps, only apparently benign—motivations supporting it, is ultimately a morally and politically flawed system of human community life.

NOTES

Introduction

1. Karl Marx, 'On the Jewish Question', David McLellan, ed., *Selected Writings* (Oxford: Oxford University Press, 1977), pp. 51–53.

2. See, especially, Brian Barry's review in *Political Theory*, vol. 3 (1975), pp. 331–36, in which we are told that Nozick's conclusions "articulate the prejudices of the average owner of a filling station in a small town in the Midwest who enjoys grousing about paying taxes and having to contribute to 'welfare scroungers' and who regards as wicked any attempt to interfere with contracts, in the interest, for example, of equal opportunity or anti-discrimination." Never mind that all of Marx's conclusions could be given just as nasty an interpretation, as indeed they have been by those who claim that they simply articulate the envy and resentment of the lazy and inept observing the success of the diligent and able. See, also, some essays in the *Arizona Law Review*, vol. 19 (1977) (a special issue devoted to Nozick's book), e.g., Scaff, 'How Not to Do Political Theory: Nozick's Apology for the Minimal State', 193–219.

3. Karl Marx, *Selected Writings*, p. 171.

4. Ibid., p. 351.

5. Ibid., p. 360. Marx repeats this kind of terminology when he refers to "the childhood of human society", "its most beautiful development", and "immature social conditions" (ibid.). Nor was this the young Marx writing, but Marx in the years 1857–67.

6. Ibid., p. 126.

7. Thomas Hobbes, *Leviathan*, pt. II, ch. XXV.

8. Margaret Jane Radin, 'Residential Rent Control', *Philosophy and Public Affairs*, vol. 15 (Fall 1986), 352.

9. John Rawls, 'The Independence of Moral Theory', *Proceedings and Addresses of the American Philosophical Association vol. XLVII* (Newark, DE: American Philosophical Association, 1975), 21. Another defense of intuitionism, put more simply and thus more powerfully than Rawls's, may be found in William H. Davis, 'The Morally Obvious', *The Journal of Value Inquiry*, vol. 19 (1985), pp. 263–277. "It is better to say that some things are known to us to be evil and leave it at that, than to make unsatisfactory and controversial attempts to explain the moral imperative, which explanations, even if they were successful and uncontroversial, would then require further justification of precisely the same sort, and often of the same feebleness, as they themselves originally provided" (ibid., 276). Two points in reply to this: First, since the 'morally obvious' is never as obvious as some people claim, we do not reduce controversy by forgoing justification. We simply leave matters in disarray at the outset. Second, of course there cannot be an infinite regress of

justification, but what should count as the ground of justification is itself reasonably debatable (so that some claims could be shown to be axiomatic, some could be shown not to be axiomatic, perhaps even in morality).

10. Samuel Scheffler, 'Natural Rights, Equality and the Minimal State', *The Canadian Journal of Philosophy*, vol. 6 (March 1976), 62.

11. Ibid.

12. Sidney Hook, *Pragmatism and the Tragic Sense of Life* (New York: Basic Books, 1976), pp. 83–84.

13. John Gray, *Liberalism* (Minneapolis, MN: University of Minnesota Press, 1986), p. 49.

14. Ibid., p. 50. Some of this will be discussed in chs. 2 and 3.

15. Stuart Hampshire, *Freedom of Mind* (Princeton, NJ: Princeton University Press, 1971), p. 79.

16. David L. Norton, 'Review of John Gray, *Liberalism*', *Reason Papers*, no. 12 (Spring 1987), 81. See, also, David L. Norton, *Personal Destinies: A Philosophy of Ethical Individualism* (Princeton, NJ: Princeton University Press, 1976) pp. 131ff. But see Kurt Baier, *The Moral Point of View* (Ithaca, NY: Cornell University Press, 1958). "If the point of view of morality were that of self-interest, then there could *never* be moral solutions of conflicts of interest" (p. 190). Yet what is really at issue isn't A's self-interest versus B's self-interest but, rather, what A desires versus what B desires. Seen this way, a different question may also be asked, namely, By what standard ought one to decide how to resolve the conflict? It should not be ruled out that such a standard could consist of principles that might guide one toward realizing one's happiness as a human being, nor that acting on such standards by both A and B might not ever, barring extraordinary or extreme cases, lead to conflict. Perhaps the rational choices of all persons, barring prior errors or evils, are in harmony. Indeed, judging by the kinds of cases invoked to show that such conflicts could (indeed, *must*) arise, the prospect does not seem very bad at all for the compossibility of the individual-goods thesis. Baier's famous case is two persons vying for the presidency. Yet must it be bad for one to lose, the other to win, even if the result rests on considerations of competence and suitability? We must also remember that any theory, since it must be developed without the benefit of omniscience, will involve some conceivably unmanageable cases—for example, runaway trolleys, life-boat dramas, Donner-party situations, and so on.

Chapter 1. Rights Theory at a Glance

1. Joseph Raz, 'On the Nature of Rights', *Mind*, vol. XCIII (1984), 195. Raz is a suitable support for the task of giving a reasonably neutral characterization of rights since he tries to scrupulously avoid "infecting an account of the nature of rights with an illegitimate bias" (p. 194).

2. Aristotle, *Politics*, bk. III, ch. 9, 1280b10. See Fred D. Miller, Jr., 'The State and the Community and Aristotle's *Politics*, *Reason Papers*, no. 1 (1974), 61–69.

3. William of Ockham, *Opus Nonaginta Dierum* (quoted in M. P. Golding, 'The Concept of Rights: A Historical Sketch', in E. B. Bandman, ed., *Bioethics and Human Rights* (Boston: Little, Brown, 1978), p. 48).

4. Alasdair MacIntyre, *After Virtue* (Notre Dame, IN: University of Notre Dame Press, 1981), p. 69.

5. Stuart Hampshire, *Thought and Action* (London: Chatto and Windus, 1959), pp. 12, 13. Cf. John Kekes, 'Is Our Morality Disintegrating?' *Public Affairs Quarterly*, vol. 1 (1987), 79–94. Although Kekes's conception of human nature is not identical with mine, the point of citing him is that he does not entertain any great difficulty about referring to human nature. When he states that "I have to discuss human nature," he adds, "In doing so, I shall only repeat what everybody knows anyway, but the repetition has a point, because the significance of these commonplaces tends to be overlooked" (p. 85). Kekes is ignoring the large body of skeptical opinion concerning just the task he undertakes, something we cannot afford to do here.

6. This assumes that the free-will thesis can be established and shown to be wholly consistent with the findings of modern science, otherwise the idea of attending to reality as a matter of choice, and thus the possibility of doing so irresponsibly, wrongly, not just mistakenly, cannot make sense.

7. Aristotle, *Metaphysics* 3. 1006b 18–24.

8. Keith Lehrer, *Knowledge* (Oxford: Oxford University Press, 1974), p. 6.

9. This is my characterization, following Wittgenstein who distinguishes, in *On Certainty* (New York: J. & J. Harper, 1969) between reasonable and unreasonable doubt. Here the eminently apt distinction applicable in courts of law—namely, between certainty 'beyond a reasonable' and 'beyond a shadow' of doubt—would appear to be warranted.

10. For a statement of this see John Tienson, 'On Analyzing Knowledge,' *Philosophical Studies*, vol. 25 (1974).

11. B. F. Skinner, *Beyond Freedom and Dignity* (New York: Bantam Books, 1972), p. 23. Or, "The mistake . . . is to put the responsibility anywhere, to suppose that somewhere a causal sequence is initiated" (p. 72); "The hypothesis that man is not free is essential to the application of scientific method to the study of human behavior. The free inner man who is held responsible for the behavior of the external biological organism is only a prescientific substitute for the kinds of causes which are discovered in the course of a scientific analysis." *Science and Human Behavior* (New York: Macmillan, 1953), p. 47. Whereas earlier the reduc-

tionist program rested on a Newtonian perspective, today's reductionists tend to rely on the computer model, as exemplified by the more imperialistic members of the artificial-intelligence community. See, e.g., Gerald Feinberg, *Solid Clues: Quantum Physics, Molecular Biology, and the Future of Science* (New York: Simon & Schuster, 1985). Cf., M. F. Perutz, 'Brave New World', *The New York Review of Books*, September 26, 1985, pp. 14–18. Perutz examines, step by step, the reductionist predictions of Feinberg and finds them largely wanting, especially where molecular biology's prospect for reduction to subatomic physics is concerned. This, of course, directly affects the plausibility of analyzing mind based on the computer model. See, also, R. C. Haddon and A. A. Lamola, 'The Molecular Electronic Device and the Biochip Computer: Present Status,' *Proceedings of the National Academy of Sciences of the U.S.A.*, vol. 82 (April 1985), 1874–878. But see, also, Richard D. Alexander, *The Biology of Moral Systems* (Hawthorne, NY: Aldine de Gruyter, 1987). The work argues the reductionist view that morality is a biproduct of the ultimate interest of human beings in reproduction. But this line of analysis rejects the distinctive nature of morality and treats the sphere as simply another value realm, akin to any other we find in plant or animal life.

12. John Gray, *Liberalism* (Minneapolis, MN: University of Minnesota Press, 1986), p. 46. There are those who offer the false alternative of either reductionism or dualism, e.g., Paul M. Churchland, *Matter and Consciousness* (Cambridge, MA: MIT Press, 1984), pp. 15ff. But there are other alternatives, including pluralism, which does not require the acceptance of the oddity that nature simply departs from its norms when we come to human nature. See, also, Etienne Gilson, *From Aristotle to Darwin and Back Again: A Journey in Final Causality, Species, and Evolution* (Notre Dame, IN: University of Notre Dame Press, 1987).

13. Ibid.

14. Roger W. Sperry, *Science and Moral Priority: Merging Mind, Brain, and Human Values* (New York: Columbia University Press, 1983), p. 21.

15. Ibid.

16. Ibid., p. 32.

17. Ibid., pp. 33–34.

18. Ibid., p. 39. For Sperry's more detailed exposition, see 'Mental Phenomena as causal determinants in brain function', in G. C. Globus, G. Maxwell, and I. Savodnik, eds., *Consciousness and the Brain: a Scientific and Philosophical Inquiry* (New York: Plenum Press, 1974), pp. 163–177.

19. James N. Jordan, 'Determinism's Dilemma', *The Review of Metaphysics*, vol. 23 (September 1969), pp. 48–66.

20. Joseph Boyle, et al. *Free Choice* (Notre Dame, IN: University of Notre Dame Press, 1976).

21. Ayn Rand, 'The Objectivist Ethics', in *The Virtue of Selfishness* (New York: New American Library, 1964), pp. 13-35. Rand here defends a naturalistic account of the place of ethics in human life, asking first of all, "Does man need values at all — and why?" (p. 13) Elsewhere I have spelled out the epistemological and metaphysical framework which would be presupposed by a theory of ethics that is wholly compatible with a sensible conception of the requirements of science. See Tibor R. Machan, *The Pseudo-Science of B. F. Skinner* (New Rochelle, NY: Arlington House, 1974); 'Epistemology and Moral Knowledge', *The Review of Metaphysics*, vol. 36 (September 1982), 23-49; 'Naturalism, Values and the Social Sciences', *Wittgenstein, The Vienna Circle and Critical Rationalism* (Kirchberg am Wechsel, Austria: International Wittgenstein Symposium, 1978), pp. 451-55; 'Education and the Philosophy of Knowledge', *Educational Theory*, vol. 6 (Summer 1970), pp. 253-268. Rand gives the following explanation of values:

> Metaphysically, life is the only phenomenon that is an end in itself: a value gained and kept by a constant process of action. Epistemologially, the concept of "value" is genetically dependent upon and derived from the antecedent concept of "life." To speak of "value" as apart from "life" is worse than a contradiction in terms. It is only the concept of 'Life' that makes the concept of 'Value' possible. . . . In answer to those philosophers who claim that no relation can be established between ultimate ends or values and the facts of reality [i.e., who pose the "is/ought" gap problem], let me stress that the fact that living entities exist and function necessitates the existence of values and of an ultimate value which for any given living entity is its own life . . . . The fact that a living entity *is* determines what it *ought* to do. (pp. 15-17)

22. Karl Popper, *Unended Quest* (La Salle: Open Court, 1982), p. 194.

23. I will touch on this in ch. 2. See, however, David Lowenthal, "The Case for Teleology," *The Independent Journal of Philosophy*, vol. 2 (1978), 95-105. Here we must keep in mind that the mechanistic-empiricist position on these matters is not tenable, despite the many social philosophers and scientists who still cling to it. That alone, of course, will not show that causes different from efficient causes do obtain, only that they are not precluded from obtaining on metaphysical grounds alone. See Tibor R. Machan, 'Naturalism, Values and the Social Sciences', *Wittgenstein, the Vienna Circle and Critical Rationalism* (Kirchberg am Wechsel, Austria: International Wittgenstein Symposium, 1978), pp. 451-55, and 'Some Ontological Considerations of Skinnerism', *Cogito*, vol. 3 (1985), pp. 49-72.

24. Emerson Buchanan, *Aristotle's Theory of Being* (Cambridge, MA: Greek, Roman, and Byzantine Monographs, 1962), p. 2.

25. If causality is the relationship between the actions of various kinds of entities in reality, and if these are not reducible to one kind of being, there is no reason why the causes exhibited by them should have to be reduced to one kind of cause. Indeed, the function of science, again, would be to identify the various kinds of causes that the various kinds of beings exhibit. The idea that reality can be basically diverse in its on-

tology but must be uniform in the sorts of causes that are found within it seems entirely incongruous. See, for an extensive discussion of this issue, H. W. B. Joseph, *An Introduction to Logic* (London: Oxford University Press, 1916). See, also, John Herman Randall, Jr., *Aristotle* (New York: Columbia University Press, 1961).

26. Karl Marx, *Selected Writings*, ed., David McLellan (London: Oxford University Press, 1977), p. 126.

27. This is the remnant of Socratic humanism in which Plato's influence has been very strong regarding the superior status of the concrete universal "human being" to the mere particular individual persons who actually constitute that universal and whose distinctive nature the concept aims to identify. Sperry himself is inclined toward a kind of one-world government and ecological ethics. Both of these view individual human lives as part of the larger collective rather than as the only concrete manifestation of humanity as such.

28. John Hospers, 'Justice versus "Social Justice" ', *The Freeman*, vol. 35 (January 1985), 9.

Chapter 2. From Classical Egoism to Natural Rights

1. Karl Marx, *Selected Writings*, ed., David McLellan (London: Oxford University Press, 1977), pp. 39–62. "Far from the rights of man conceiving of man as a species-being, species-life itself, society, appears as a framework exterior to individuals, a limitation of their original self-sufficiency. The only bond that holds them together is natural necessity, need and private interest, the conservation of their property and egoistic person." (p. 54).

2. Milton Friedman, 'The Line We Dare Not Cross', *Encounter* (November 1976), p. 11.

3. Ayn Rand, *The Virtue of Selfishness* (New York: New American Library, 1964) and *Capitalism: The Unknown Ideal* (New York: New American Library, 1967).

4. Quoted in Richard Higgins, 'British Philosopher Says Self-interest Corrupts Western Liberty', *Boston Sunday Globe* (October 28, 1984). Similar sentiments have been expressed about the predicament of the free society by Irving Kristol, Daniel Bell, Leo Strauss, George Will, and many others. See Irving Kristol, *Two Cheers for Capitalism* (New York: Basic Books, 1978).

5. See, Tibor R. Machan, 'Ethics vs. Coercion: Morality or Just Values?' in L. H. Rockwell, Jr. et al., ed., *Man, Economy and Liberty: Essays in Honor of Murray N. Rothbard* (Auburn, AL: Ludwig von Mises Institute, 1988).

6. James Buchanan, *The Limits of Liberty: Between Anarchy and Leviathan* (Chicago: University of Chicago Press, 1975). See, also, his 'Boundaries of Social Contract', *Reason Papers*, no. 2 (1975), pp. 15–28.

NOTES TO PAGES 29-36

7. John Rawls, 'The Independence of Moral Theory', *Proceedings and Addresses of the American Philosophical Association vol. xlvii* (Newark, DE: American Philosophical Association, 1975), p. 21.

8. Leland B. Yeager, 'Rights, Contracts, and Utility in Policy Espousals', *Cato Journal*, vol. 5 (1985), pp. 259–294. But see Tibor R. Machan, 'Are Teleological Rights Theories Utilitarian?' *Cato Journal*, vol. 7 (1987), pp. 255–258.

9. George Stigler, *Lecture III*, Tanner Lectures, Harvard University, April 1980, quoted in G. Brennan and J. Buchanan, 'The Normative Purpose of Economic "Science": Rediscovery of an Eighteenth Century Method', *International Review of Law and Economics* (Winter 1981), p. 158.

10. James Rachels, 'Two Arguments Against Egoism', *Philosophia*, vol. 4 (April/July 1974), 297–314.

11. Ibid. This resembles the argument earlier cited from Quentin Skinner, Irving Kristol, et al. All these and many others fault Hobbesian egoism for implying that human beings ought to do what they prefer, what they desire, or what will please them in terms they themselves set by reference to no objective criteria. Strictly speaking, Hobbes's egoism says nothing about what we ought to do but any ethical egoism that draws on Hobbes rejects the determinist but retains the subjectivist element.

12. John Rawls, *A Theory of Justice* (Cambridge, MA: Harvard University Press, 1971), p. 488. See also Kim-Chong Chong, 'Egoism, Desires, and Friendship', *American Philosophical Quarterly*, vol. 21 (October 1984), pp. 355–56.

13. Derek Parfit, *Reasons and Persons* (Oxford: Oxford University Press, 1984). For a defense of the more fundamental metaphysical idea of individuality, see Jorge Garcia, *Individuality* (Albany: State University of New York Press, 1988).

14. Tibor R. Machan, 'Recent Work in Ethical Egoism', in Kenneth G. Lucey and Tibor R. Machan, eds., *Recent Work in Philosophy* (Totowa, NJ: Rowman and Allanheld, 1983), pp. 185–202.

15. See, e.g., David L. Norton, *Personal Destinies: A Philosophy of Ethical Individualism* (Princeton, NJ: Princeton University Press, 1976). Norton's work effectively responds to claims such as that "properly speaking, there is no such thing as individualism — for the very simple reason that there is no such thing as an individual. It's part of our vocabulary; I can't speak at any length without speaking of 'individuals' myself. But the word 'individual' is an adjective. And an adjective ain't nothin' 'til there's a noun to which it is attached. It's an attribute without a substance." Harry V. Jaffa, 'A Conversation with Harry V. Jaffa at Rosary College', *Claremont Review of Books*, vol. 1 (December 1981), p. 8. Shirley Robin Letwin also remarks that "there is no more room for individuality in Aristotle's *philia* than in Plato's *eros*" ('Romantic Love and

Christianity', *Philosophy*, vol. 52 (April 1977), p. 134). Letwin claims that "because for Aristotle, as for Plato, rationality is the power to recognize a universal order, Aristotle cannot account for rational consciousness that is ultimately unique" (p. 135). In contrast to this, see Walter Leszl, 'Knowledge of the Universal and Knowledge of the Particular in Aristotle', *Review of Metaphysics*, vol. 26 (1972), pp. 278–313. Others, too, have argued that Aristotle's metaphysics identifies the fundamental being of things as their individual existence. This makes ample room for the actual, individual being of entities. See Emerson Buchanan, *Aristotle's Theory of Being* (Cambridge, MA: Greek, Roman, and Byzantine Monographs, 1962). If Buchanan is right, the 'what it is for a thing to be' of human beings would have to indicate individuality in view of every person's self-determination, something that is distinctive of human beings. (For more on this, see Gracia, *Individuality*, op. cit.) See, also, Alasdair MacIntyre, *After Virtue* (Notre Dame, IN: University of Notre Dame Press, 1981), for a sustained critique of the idea that individual rights could have had any place in pre-modern, i.e., pre-Hobbesian, philosophy and culture. While there is some merit in this claim, we have already seen that so long as human nature involves, by natural necessity, the individuality and volitional conduct of each human being, the foundation for individual rights is present. These points are discussed at length by Fred D. Miller Jr. in his forthcoming book on the topic of natural rights and ancient Greek philosophy.

16. Aristotle, *Nicomachean Ethics*, bk. *ix*, ch. 8, 1168b33. For a thorough discussion of the sense in which Aristotle can be regarded as a kind of ethical egoist, see W. F. R. Hardie, 'The Final Good in Aristotle's Ethics', *Philosophy*, vol. 40 (1965), pp. 277–295, and Jack Wheeler, 'Rand and Aristotle: A Comparison of Objectivist and Aristotelian Ethics', in Douglas J. Den Uyl and Douglas Rasmussen, eds., *The Philosophical Thought of Ayn Rand* (Urbana and Chicago: University of Illinois Press, 1984), pp. 81–101. For another discussion, which is addressed directly to those contemporary moral philosophers who regard matters of prudence as irrelevant to morality, see W. D. Falk, 'Morality, Self, and Others', in H. N. Castañeda and G. Nakhnikian, eds., *Morality and the Language of Conduct* (Detroit: Wayne State University Press, 1965), pp. 25–67. Wheeler writes: "In a certain real sense, no Greek can be labeled an egoist any more than an altruist. The whole issue of egoism and altruism is modern. Indeed, the entire project of attempting to reconcile one's own interests with benevolence or the interest of society as a whole seems clearly to start with Hobbes and the Hobbesian view of man" (p. 97). For a rather rare explicit statement of altruism see W. G. Maclagan, 'Self and Others: A Defense of Altruism', *The Philosophical Quarterly*, vol. 4 (1954), pp. 109–127.

17. See the discussion in ch. 1, especially drawing on R. W. Sperry, 'Changing Concepts of Consciousness and Free Will', *Perspectives in Biology & Medicine*, vol. 20 (1976), pp. 9–19. For more on this, see

T. R. Machan, *The Pseudo-Science of B. F. Skinner* (New Rochelle, NY: Arlington, 1974), ch. 6.

18. In a recent discussion of my views by Mark Francis, 'Human Rights and Libertarians', *Australian Journal of Politics and History*, vol. 29 (1983), 469ff, the natural-rights position discussed here is charged with being confused on the grounds that the natural is confused with the moral. There is no confusion here except for someone who regards the moral domain as inherently non-natural rather than a dimension or asepct of the natural. In the view I am discussing, having human rights is indeed something along the lines of having a good figure or an interesting personal history, as distinct from having a car or a nice house. Human rights are relational attributes, but because they involve an element of choice by other persons to uphold a certain relationship, they are open to being violated. Francis's claim that human rights can "be given up" is mistaken. One can violate human rights, abridge them, and so forth, but basic rights are inalienable and thus cannot be given up. Of course, there are differences among natural laws as proper, suitable, right procedures for a thing, vis-à-vis, say, inanimate matter, plants, animals, and human beings, Nonetheless, all these can be natural, in so far as they pertain to something in virtue of its nature as the kind of thing it is. Francis claims that Machan "uses moral and natural in harness, or as if they meant the same thing." Rather I use moral as if it were a species of natural.

19. Natural ends are to be distinguished from ends which are matters of convention and have no connection with the way we discover something in nature—e.g., the end or objective of a ping-pong game or TV-channel selector. In contrast, consider the end served by the heart in the human biological organism, or the objective of the porcupine's stiff, sharp spines mingled with its hair. Contrary to some notions in the history of ideas, it isn't necessary to impute natural ends to inanimate beings if one imputes them to some beings, nor need Aristotle be read as someone who makes that imputation to all of nature. For a discussion of how Aristotelian ideas on teleology are compatible with modern conceptions of biological teleology, see Allan Gotthelf, 'Aristotle's Conception of Final Causality', *The Review of Metaphysics*, vol. 30 (October 1976), pp. 226–254. But see, for some emendations, Fred D. Miller, Jr. and Michael Bradie, 'Teleology & Natural Necessity in Aristotle', *History of Philosophy Quarterly*, vol. 1 (1986), pp. 133–146. See also Etienne Gilson, *From Aristotle to Darwin and Back Again: A Journey in Final Causality, Species, and Evolution* (Notre Dame, IN: University of Notre Dame Press, 1987).

20. Marx speaks of "humanity" as an "organic body" or "organic whole". Karl Marx, *Grundrisse*, abridged ed'n, trans., David McLellan (New York: Harper Torchbook, 1971), p. 33. For a discussion of the philosophical approach that will secure a basis for abstraction that yields knowledge of human nature, see David Kelley, 'A Theory of

Abstraction', *Cognition and Brain Theory*, vol. 7 (Summer/Fall, 1984), pp. 329-357. See, also, Tibor R. Machan, 'Epistemology and Moral Knowledge', *Review of Metaphysics*, vol. 36 (September 1982), pp. 23-49. The theory of human nature involved rejects the realism of universals, thus the presence of metaphysical essences or natures; yet it secures the objective basis for classification as a result of human concept-formation, differentiation and integration. These views draw considerably on Ayn Rand, *Introduction to Objectivist Epistemology* (New York: New American Library, 1979).

21. Gilbert Harman, 'Human Flourishing, Ethics, and Liberty', *Philosophy and Public Affairs*, vol. 12 (Fall, 1983), p. 312.

22. Ibid., p. 313.

23. Tibor R. Machan, 'Harman's "Refutation" of Flourishing Ethics', *Thomist*, vol. 49 (July 1985), pp. 387-391.

24. Op. cit., Harman, p. 315.

25. See Tibor R. Machan, 'Social Contract as a Basis of Norms: A Critique', *Journal of Libertarian Studies*, vol. 7 (Spring 1983), pp. 141-45. I am unaware of any recent contract theorist, from John Rawls and James Buchanan to David Gauthier, who has addressed this issue. Why does it not appear clear to them that moral judgments come into play even in the determination of whether one ought to join in a contract or compact?

26. For a discussion of how this kind of conceptual evolution clears up some of the misconceptions which have supported moral (historical) relativism, see Hanna F. Pitkin, *Wittgenstein and Justice* (Berkeley, CA: University of California Press, 1972).

27. I develop some of these same points in ch. 3, earlier sketched in my paper, 'Toward a Theory of Natural Individual Human Rights', *The New Scholasticism*, vol. 61 (Winter, 1987), pp. 33-78.

28. A. John Simmons, 'Inalienable Rights and Locke's *Treatises*', *Philosophy and Public Affairs*, vol. 12 (Summer 1983), 175-204. For some elaborations, see Tibor R. Machan, 'Human Rights: Some Points of Clarification', *Journal of Critical Analysis*, vol. 5 (July/October 1973), 30-38.

29. Adam Smith, *The Theory of Moral Sentiments* (Indianapolis, IN: Liberty Classics, 1769, 1976), pt. III, ch. 3, p. 235. It is interesting to note here that Smith echoes exactly—almost verbatim—Aristotle's view (*Nicomachean Ethics*, 1168b28-33) that "such a man [who 'at all events assigns to himself the things that are noblest and best, and gratifies the most authoritative element in himself and in all things obeys this'] . . . is most of all a lover of self." So much for an unbridgeable gap between ancients and moderns, as proposed by some students of Leo Strauss.

30. Here is the crucial moral distinction between the socialist idea, according to which, "The human essence is the true collectivity of man"

(op. cit., Marx, *Selected Writings*, p. 126) and classical individualism that sees individuality as an essential part of the nature of man. I discuss these points further in my 'Rational Choice and Public Affairs', *Theory and Decision*, vol. 12 (1980), 229–258.

31. Peter Winch, *Ethics and Action* (London: Routledge, 1972), p. 75. Hazel Barnes, *An Existentialist Ethics* (New York: Vintage Books, 1971), also criticizes the naturalist or objectivist approach, with direct reference to Rand's ethical views. Barnes's view, like Sartre's, is influenced by the post-Kantian conception of why metaphysical knowledge is impossible.

32. When one attempts to define the concept 'human being' by reference to human needs, one probably cannot avoid relativism. This is because a need arises in connection with a value one aims for. We need water in the context of seeking to continue to be alive. If, however, our goal of being alive is itself groundless, unjustified, then the need for water will also be, and if the goal of being alive may be fulfilled without obtaining water but by some other means, it is these other means that will become needed for us. This leaves needs too flexible to serve as a basis for defining ongoing human nature.

33. John Gray, *Liberalism* (Minneapolis, MN: University of Minnesota Press, 1987), p. 34.

34. Tibor R. Machan, 'A Reconsideration of Natural Rights Theory', *American Philosophical Quarterly*, vol. 19 (January 1982), 61–72, and 'Individualism and the Problem of Political Authority', *The Monist*, vol. 66 (October 1983), pp. 500–516. The former is an initial, brief version of ch. 4, the latter of ch. 7, of the present work.

The argument advanced in John Searle, *Speech Acts* (Cambridge: Cambridge University Press, 1969), pp. 177ff, has the following in common with the present derivation of 'ought': Searle thinks, rightly, that making a promise obligates one to keep it. He says that his proof "rests on an appeal to the constitutive rule that to make a promise is to undertake an obligation, and this rule is a meaning rule of the 'descriptive' word 'promise' " (p. 185). But Searle does not show how much beyond that promising commits one to fulfilling the promise. In life we might do without promising. (This is the problem with Kant's defense of promising.)

In the present argument, however, the initial (tacit, implicit) choice — and act — to carry on with living commits one to the pursuit of one's success at this task, one's happiness. For a human being to choose to live is to make a very long-range promise, as it were, to carry forth with life in a successful way that is appropriate to the kind of thing one is (within one's own possibilities). The commitment is not, however, the same as a contract or compact with others, thus it is not enforceable. That is why moral conduct that does not involve a prior (implicit or explicit) compact that it may be enforced may not be forcibly induced. It must be freely chosen, lest its *moral* value vanish.

35. Adam Smith, *The Wealth of Nations* (New York: Modern Library, 1936), p. 726.

36. See, Douglas Den Uyl and Tibor R. Machan, 'Recent Work on the Concept of Happiness', *American Philosophical Quarterly*, vol. 20 (1983), 115–134. A criticism of classical egoism is offered by S. L. Newman, *Liberalism at Wit's End* (Ithaca, NY: Cornell University Press, 1984), pp. 99–114. He claims that in identifying the moral life as the rational life, I rely "on a rather muddled distinction between instrumental rationality and some vaguely presented notion of a higher rationality associated with membership in the human species. (p. 114)" I do not believe that the distinction is vaguely presented, and certainly it is clear enough in the literature on rationality—e.g., Aristotle is credited with defining human reason as a faculty, while, for instance, Hobbes and Descartes are credited with defining human reason as an instrument.

Newman also complains that no determination is possible as to "what is rational for the individual *as an individual* opposed to what is rational for the same individual *as a human being* . . . ." The main point to be made is that there is no "opposed to" involved here since a human being is always an individual person. What is important to note is that each individual human being has certain characteristics by virtue of which he or she is human. These are not opposed to his or her being the individual person in question, only there are *additional* characteristics present which are not those that render someone a member of the human species but which are relevant to how that individual ought to conduct himself or herself in life. Thus those individual attributes are morally significant, especially within the ethical egoist framework.

37. Quentin Lauer, 'Why Be Good?' *Proceedings and Addresses of The American Philosophical Association* (Newark, DE: The American Philosophical Association, 1986), p. 14.

38. Ayn Rand, 'Value and Rights', in John Hospers, ed., *Readings in Introductory Philosophical Analysis* (Englewood Cliffs, NJ: Prentice-Hall, 1968), p. 382.

39. Ibid.

40. Robert Nozick, *Anarchy, State, and Utopia* (New York: Basic Books, 1974), p. 57.

Chapter 3. Grounding 'Lockean' Rights

1. Nozick implicitly assumes that people in the state of nature do what is in their self-interest. How else would he be able to argue that the best explanation of the emergence of the state is that people will gravitate toward the monopolization of state-like powers? If they were free to act against their own interest, one would have to grant that they might choose to neglect the benefits to be gained from such monopolization. Nozick might then have to invoke the 'explanation' put forth in ch. 7, namely, that morally we ought to establish government.

2. Russell Hardin, 'The Utilitarian Logic of Liberalism', *Ethics*, vol. 97 (1986), 49. Let me again note the one-sidedness of Hardin's application of utilitarian analysis, namely, to property-rights issues. Why not to assault, kidnapping, or rape? To believe that somehow the utilitarian can escape these implications is to be selective about the criteria of adequacy of moral theories.

3. Ibid., p. 67.

4. Tibor R. Machan, 'Some Recent Work in Human Rights Theory', K. G. Lucey and T. R. Machan, eds., *Recent Work in Philosophy* (Totowa, NJ: Rowman and Allanheld, 1983), pp. 227-246. For a more recent argument for human rights, based on a type of social-contract theory, one that gains its motivational force from a theory of the vitality of human projects, see Loren Lomasky, *Persons, Rights, and the Moral Community* (Oxford: Oxford University Press, 1987). See, also, his 'Personal Projects as the Foundation for Basic Rights', *Social Philosophy & Policy*, vol. 1 (1983), 33-55.

5. Hardin, op, cit., pp. 73-74. In early 1987, *Time* magazine reported on the phenomenon of date-rape (March 23, p. 77). Kent State University psychologist Mary Koss is reported to have found that 15% of 6,200 female students related "experiences that met legal definitions of forcible rape". Yet "[t]he number of forcible rapes reported each year — 87,340 in 1985 — is believed to be about half the total actually committed. Experts say the victim knows the assailant in at least a third of all rapes." Yet the conclusion drawn is not that these rapes are justified, since it at least appears that they are accepted by the person having been raped ('victim' in nonutilitarian, natural-rights language). No one suggests that we consider the interpersonal utility of rapist versus victim to decide whether the rapes had moral merit. Rather it seems that the principled approach to rape is accepted — forcing sex on the victim without her consent, is morally wrong and should, indeed, be illegal. One may wonder how it would strike Hardin if someone were to substitute for "unvarnished right of contract" the phrase "unvarnished right of sexual autonomy or of romantic engagement". Clearly, on purely utilitarian grounds, it is possible rape is not always wrong, i.e., wrong *in principle*. Perhaps (following a line of thought analogous to Hardin's) each case of rape needs to be considered on its own merits, as each case of theft or trespass should be. Should the choices of two persons to become lovers or married, when another — say an unrequited lover — wants to undermine it by separating them, be assessed on the utilitarian merits of each separate case? For the connection between body rights and property rights, see Samuel C. Wheeler III, 'Natural Property Rights as Body Rights', in Tibor R. Machan, (ed.), *The Main Debate* (New York: Random House, 1987), pp. 272-289.

6. Max Stirner, *The Ego and His Own* (New York: Harper and Row, 1971 [original German version published in 1845]).

7. Samuel Scheffler, 'Natural Rights, Equality, and the Minimal

State', *Canadian Journal of Philosophy*, vol. 6 (March 1976), 62.

8. Henry David Aiken, 'Rights, Human and Otherwise', *The Monist*, vol. 52 (October 1978), 519. Aiken's fear is justified. Ultimately attention must be paid by natural-rights theorists to the character of moral facts, if you will, although I see no reason why there should be fewer problems with general facts or principles of morality than with those, say, in chemistry. The problem with normative and especially moral principles is different, of course, but on a certain level the same difficulties face scientific and moral principles, as Hume realized.

9. Kai Nielsen, 'Skepticism and Human Rights', *The Monist*, vol. 52 (October 1968), 573-594.

10. Kai Nielsen, 'The Myth of Natural Law', in Sidney Hook (ed.), *Law and Philosophy* (New York: New York University Press, 1964), p. 124.

11. M. P. Golding, 'Towards a Theory of Human Rights', *The Monist*, vol. 52 (October 1968), pp. 521-549.

12. Ibid., p. 549.

13. Thomas S. Kuhn, *The Structure of Scientific Revolutions* (Chicago: University of Chicago Press, 1962).

14. Tibor R. Machan, 'Kuhn's Impossibility Proof and the Moral Element in Scientific Explanations', *Theory and Decision*, vol. 5 (December 1974), 355-374; 'On the Possibility of Objectivity and Moral Determinants in Scientific Change', K. Knorr, *et al.* (eds.) *Determinants and Controls of Scientific Development* (Dordrecht, Holland: Reidel, 1975), pp. 75-111.

15. Karl Popper, *The Open Society and its Enemies* (Princeton, NJ: Princeton University Press, 1950), p. 625.

16. Popper does criticize numerous non-philosophers, such as Max Weber, for employing a "method of intuitive understanding" (p. 627), and throughout Popper stresses the inadequacy, not so much of the idea that correct or true definitions can be stated but, rather, of the proposed means by which the truth of such statements is to be established. Even when he recognizes that Weber puts controls of "ordinary methods" on any intuitive understanding, Popper turns to his third and main line of criticism of the prospects for true definitions, namely, "The problem of avoiding an infinite regression of definitions".

17. Willard V. Quine, *Word and Object* (Cambridge, MA: MIT Press, 1960), p. 199. For detailed criticisms of Quine, see Robert Hollinger, 'A Defense of Essentialism', *The Personalist*, vol. 57 (1976), pp. 327-344, and Douglas B. Rasmussen, 'Quine and Aristotelian Essentialism', *The New Scholasticism*, vol. 58 (1984), pp. 316-335. For a general discussion of some of the recent antimetaphysical, antirealistic views in epistemology, see Roger Trigg, *Reality at Risk* (Totowa, NJ: Barnes & Noble Books, 1980).

18. 'Necessarily' for Quine means that it is an analytic truth that it is so and so. Quine, of course, rejects the cogency of the analytic/synthetic (necessary/contingent) dichotomy. The view I propose does not embody the distinction in its familiar form, although it admits of a significant difference between definitionally true statements, such as 'human beings are capable of reasoning', and others, like 'human beings have inhabited the earth for more than 20,000 years'. But nothing much in my argument here turns on necessity and contingency or the like. Cf., W. V. Quine, *From a Logical Point of View* (New York: Harper Torchbooks, 1963), p. 155.

19. Stuart Hampshire, *Thought and Action* (London: Chatto and Windus, 1959), p. 12. Consider, in this connection, also P. F. Strawson, *Individuals* (Garden City, NY: Anchor Books, 1963), where one of the first contemporary excursions into something akin to metaphysics offers the typical Kantian proviso: "Hence, given a certain general feature of the conceptual scheme we possess, and given the character of the available major categories, things which are, or possess, material bodies must be the basic particulars" (p. 29).

20. Alfred North Whitehead and Bertrand Russell, *Principia Mathematica to *56* (Cambridge: Cambridge University Press, 1962).

21. Ernest van den Haag, 'The Author Replies', *Intercollegiate Review*, vol. 8 (1972-73), 144. This reply is directed to letters (including one by me) in the same issue of the journal, critical of van den Haag's paper, 'Moral Rights and the Law: A Response to Dworkin', *Intercollegiate Review*, vol. 7 (1972), 33-39. I discuss van den Haag's ideas later in this work (Appendix 1).

22. Ibid.

23. Larry Briskman, 'Skinnerism and Pseudo-Science', *Philosophy of the Social Sciences*, vol. 9 (1979), 81-103.

24. Ibid., p. 100.

25. Willard V. Quine, 'Truth by Convention', in Herbert Feigl and Wilfrid Sellar (eds.), *Readings in Philosophical Analysis* (New York: Appleton-Century-Crofts, 1949), p. 250.

26. Nielsen, op. cit., 'Skepticism', pp. 579-582. Nielsen grants human rights "on the conception of morality which most of us accepted—a conception of morality that I, as a moral agent, certainly accept . . . . But I see nothing necessary in this morality; there are moral alternatives, i.e., alternative moral codes . . . ." (p. 587). My remarks concerning the role that necessity plays in many of these arguments applies to Nielsen's point as well.

27. William T. Blackstone, 'Equality and Human Rights', *Monist*, vol. 52 (1968), pp. 616-639.

28. Quine, op. cit., 'Truth by Convention', p. 252.

29. Quoted in Karl Popper, *Objective Knowledge* (London: Oxford

University Press, 1972), p. 195n. Popper adds that his "acceptance of this term should not be construed as a concession to the doctrine of 'ultimate reality', and even less as a concession to the doctrine of essentialist definitions" (ibid.).

30. In my view only Paul Feyerabend comes near to fully accepting the implications of the relativist metaphysics which many contemporary philosophers are committed to. Even Feyerabend does not go so far as Cratylus of Athens, who, if the legend has it right, fully accepted the implication of the view that meaning is indeterminate and abandoned all propositional discourse.

31. Even a fragile or tenuous connective, in need of diligent maintenance, is different from one which is regarded as quite possibly no connective at all. I will return shortly to characterize what I take to be such a genuine connective.

32. Quoted in Ayn Rand, *Introduction to Objectivist Epistemology* (New York: New American Library, 1979), p. 108. In what follows I draw much from Rand's discussion. For critical discussions of Rand's theory, see the essays by Wallace I. Matson and Robert Hollinger in Douglas J. Den Uyl and Douglas B. Rasmussen (eds.) *The Philosophic Thought of Ayn Rand* (Urbana, IL: University of Illinois Press, 1984). While known mainly for her novels and passionate defense of capitalism, Rand's philosophical essays compile a wealth of significant philosophical material, of which the above work in epistemology is the most thorough and systematic.

33. Ibid., Rand, *Introduction*, p. 109.

34. Keith Lehrer, *Knowledge* (Oxford: Clarendon Press, 1974). See, for discussions of this issue, John Tienson, 'On Analyzing Knowledge', *Philosophical Studies*, vol. 25 (1974), pp. 289-293, and Tibor R. Machan, 'Epistemology and Moral Knowledge', *The Review of Metaphysics*, vol. 36 (1982), pp. 23-49. By a 'general limitation' I mean that some requirement which some cases of *bona fide* knowledge would have to fulfill is taken as a general requirement, thus posing as a general limitation. The failure to fulfill this (unjustified) requirement, will, of course, limit our ability to know whatever could be known in terms of different, less demanding requirements.

35. Peter Unger, *Ignorance* (Oxford: Oxford University Press, 1975).

36. Hampshire, op. cit., *Thought and Action*, p. 13.

37. Renford Bambrough, *Moral Skepticism and Moral Knowledge* (New York: Humanities Press, 1979), pp. 109, 137.

38. Ibid., p. 141. Bambrough is more generous than is warranted here: the skeptic's reply or challenge would after a while turn into groundless babble. In other words, once pressed to explain why the reply or challenge should be seriously considered, the skeptic will find there is nowhere to turn without accepting the very points that have been re-

jected on skeptical grounds. (The problem that renders skepticism a non-starter, dubbed the "stolen concept fallacy" by Nathaniel Branden, involves "the act of using a concept while ignoring, contradicting or denying the validity of the concepts on which it logically and gentically depends" — for instance 'all property is theft', where theft is conceptually parasitic on property. See, Nathaniel Branden, 'The Stolen Concept', *The Objectivist Newsletter*, vol. 2 (1963), pp. 2–4. It is interesting to mention here Wittgenstein's complaint about skepticism, in *On Certainty* (New York: J. & J. Harper, 1969), whereby it is crucial that doubt itself be reasonable. Merely entertaining a shadow of doubt is not usually sufficient to call into question some well-grounded belief. The exception may be with metaphysical first principles, facts so basic that even the conceivability of their denial would be a blow against them.)

39. Tibor R. Machan, 'C. S. Peirce and Absolute Truth', *Transactions of the C. S. Peirce Society*, vol. 16 (Spring 1980), pp. 153–161.

40. C. S. Peirce, *The Philosophy of Peirce: Selected Writings* ed. Justus Buchler (New York: Harcourt, Brace & Co., 1950), p. 134.

41. R. M. Dancy, *Sense and Contradiction: A Study in Aristotle* (Dordrecht, Holland: D. Reidel, 1975), p. 142.

42. Aristotle, *Metaphysics* 3. 1006b18–24.

43. For a promising treatment, see David Kelley, *The Evidence of the Senses* (Baton Rouge, LA: Louisiana State University Press, 1986), especially, ch. 6, 'The Nature of Perceptual Justification'.

44. Although an Aristotelian, Rand notes that whereas Aristotle "regarded 'essence' as metaphysical" she "regards it as *epistemological* . . . [that is] . . . the essence of a concept is the fundamental characteristic(s) of its units on which the greatest number of other characteristics depend, and which distinguishes these units from all other existents within the field of man's knowledge . . . [so that] . . . the essence of a concept is determined contextually and may be altered with the growth of man's knowledge . . . [moreover] . . . the metaphysical referent of man's concepts is not a special, separate metaphysical essence, but the total of the facts of reality he has observed, and this total determines which characteristics of a given group of existents he designates as essential . . . ." (Rand, op. cit., *Introduction*, p. 69).

45. Robert Nozick, 'On the Randian Argument', *The Personalist*, vol. 52 (Spring 1971), pp. 282–304. But see Den Uyl and Rasmussen, 'Nozick on the Randian Argument', *The Personalist*, vol. 59 (April 1978), pp. 184–205, and Paul Vanderveen, 'Nozick's "On the Randian Argument" ', *The Occasional Review*, vol. 8/9 (Autumn 1978), pp. 183–194.

46. Matson's discussion is part of a volume edited by Den Uyl and Rasmussen. See n 32, above.

47. In D. J. Den Uyl and D. Rasmussen (eds.), *The Philosophic Thought of Ayn Rand*. One of Matson's points, raised in criticism of

Rand, suggests that there's no need for concern about concepts, only about words, using Ockham's razor. In reply it should be noted that this objection favors the idea that only propositional knowledge exists. Moreover, there is a clear counter-example in the experience of foreigners who have already forgotten the words for some concepts in one language but haven't quite learned them in another, yet 'know what they mean'. Perhaps more telling, for admirers of ordinary language, is the episode of my 18-month-old child's eagerly fingering her mother's necklace, whereupon I explain, "beads, beads", only to be told by my daughter, "I want to know what it *is*, not what it is *called*."

48. Op cit., Rand, *Introduction*, pp. 56–58. For a fuller elaboration of some crucial points about the Objectivist theory of concept formation, see David Kelley, 'A Theory of Abstraction', *Cognition and Brain Theory*, vol. 7 (1984), 329–357.

49. Barry Stroud, 'Wittgenstein and Logical Necessity', in George Pitcher (ed.) *Wittgenstein* (Garden City, NY: Anchor Books, 1966), p. 496. See, further, Friedrich Waissman, 'Verifiability', in Antony Flew (ed.), *Logic and Language* (Garden City, NJ: Anchor Books, 1965), where Waissman proposes the alternative of the open-textured concepts. This suggests what to my mind seems a fruitful approach to the issue of definitions such that they retain the realist features without succumbing to the impossible idealism or absolutism that the Platonic tradition had demanded of definitions. It is not clear to me why, if we are not able to tell everything about something for all time to come, we are therefore unable to tell anything crucial about it at all.

50. Rand, op. cit., *Introduction*, p. 52.

51. Frederick L. Will, *Induction and Justification* (Ithaca, NY: Cornell University Press, 1974), pp. 35–36. Will's book is an especially valuable source for understanding the contemporary difficulties with identifying the nature of knowledge and the requirement to be met for purposes of showing that something is known.

52. Since it is possible to know the context of knowledge available to those in past epochs, it is also possible to learn what various persons should have done. And we can distinguish such cases from ones where it would not have been possible, given the context, to arrive at certain conclusions. In this connection Stroud's remarks about responsibility and objectivity are very instructive.

53. Kuhn, op. cit., *The Structure of Scientific Revolutions*.

54. This alternative, spelled out in detail by Peirce and his followers — see, e.g., Eugene Freeman, 'Objectivity as "Intersubjective Agreement" ', *The Monist*, vol. 57 (1973), pp. 168–175 — is one amongst several aimed at overcoming post-Kantian worries. Instead of providing a grounding for our claims and definitions, this approach promises to allay our concerns with this issue by providing for a kind of socially

secure, common faith. For a view closer to mine, see Douglas Rasmussen, 'Ideology, Objectivity, and Political Theory', in J. K. Roth and R. C. Whittemore, (eds.), *Ideology and American Experience* (Washington, DC: Washington Institute Press, 1986), pp. 45-71.

55. See Tibor R. Machan, 'On the Possibility of Objectivity and Moral Determinants of Scientific Change', in K. Knorr, *et al.*, (eds.), *Determinants and Controls of Scientific Development* (Dordrecht, Holland: D. Reidel, 1975).

56. J. L. Austin, *Philosophical Papers* (Oxford: Clarendon Press, 1961), 'Other Minds', pp. 44-84. When the range of alternatives objectively available within some context of inquiry has been canvassed, a claim that is rationally warranted is true, even if subsequent inquiry might require its revision. Only a timeless conception of truth, not as a characteristic or feature of judgment, belief, or statement but as a fixed aspect of timeless propositions comprising something on the order of a transcendent realm of ideas or possible worlds, would be incapable of accounting for this Austinian point. But since the context has changed, there is nothing paradoxical in regarding a claim as true at one time and not true at another, inasmuch as the law of contradiction is time-relative and would not be violated.

57. For more on these matters along lines that are significant here, see Rand, op. cit., *Introduction*, p. 59: "For instance, one could observe that man is the only animal who speaks English, wears wristwatches, flies airplanes, manufactures lipstick, studies geometry, reads newspapers, writes poems, darns socks, etc. None of these is an essential characteristic: none of them explains the others; none of them applies to all men; omit any or all of them, assume a man who has never done any of these things, and he will still be a *man*. But observe that all these activities (and innumerble others) require a *conceptual grasp* of reality, that an animal would not be able to understand them, that they are the expressions and consequences of man's rational faculty, that an organism without that faculty would *not* be a man—and you will know why man's rational faculty is his *essential* distinguishing and defining characteristic." Also, it is important to realize that much of what is regarded as significant scientific evidence supporting the view that other animals are rational is not only sufficient to indicate only the most meager presence of conceptualization but, when closely scrutinized, falls to pieces. See Herbert S. Terrance, *Nim: A Chimpanzee Who Learned Sign Language* (New York: Alfred Knopf, 1979).

58. By 'test' I do not mean some pseudo-empiricist controlled experiment or observational evidence, but comparison and contrast involving a definition and its facility in rationally organizing what is known about the beings defined. In the case of the human sciences, ethics, politics, psychology, and so forth, this sort of testing is indispensable, sometimes all that is available. Indeed, given the truth of the definition here ad-

vanced, which implies that conditions of human behavior as such preclude control at crucial junctures, other sorts of testing could not be relied upon to yield dependable results.

59. For additional points, see my 'Essentialism *sans* Inner Natures', *Philosophy of the Social Sciences*, vol. 10 (1980), pp. 195–200.

60. Given the essential freedom of the human will — the fact that individual human beings must rely for the initiation of their own rational (integrative and differentiating) processes on themselves and may fail to carry on as they should — no such guarantee is possible. I discuss the free-will issue in ch. 1. But it is vital here because it serves as a basic factor in explaining problems of identification, the source of much error and misbehavior.

61. See Machan, op. cit., 'Kuhn's Impossibility Proof'.

62. Some of the considerations applying to this topic are handled very well in Stephen Toulmin, *The Uses of Argument* (Cambridge: Cambridge University Press, 1958) and there are valuable discussions of related topics in Stanley Cavell, *Must We Mean What We Say?* (New York: Charles Scribner's Sons, 1969).

Chapter 4. Rights as Norms of Political Life

1. See the mention of this in David Hume, *A Treatise of Human Nature* (Garden City, NY: Dolphin Books, 1961), p. 67.

2. Nielsen, op. cit., 'The Myth of Natural Law', p. 124.

3. Ibid.

4. Ibid.

5. David L. Norton, *Personal Destinies: A Philosophy of Ethical Individualism* (Princeton, NJ: Princeton University Press, 1976).

6. For a defense along such lines of the most extensive right to contract, see Eric Mack, 'In Defense of "Unbridled" Freedom of Contract', in Tibor R. Machan, (ed.), *The Main Debate* (New York: Random House, 1987), pp. 425–438.

7. Steven Kelman, 'Cost-Benefit Analysis, An Ethical Critique', *Regulation*, January/February 1981, pp. 33–40. For a view of John Stuart Mill's utilitarianism in which liberty is built into the concept of happiness, see Nicholas Capaldi, 'The Libertarian Philosophy of John Stuart Mill', *Reason Papers*, no. 9 (1983), pp. 3–19.

8. For the connection between body rights and property rights, see Samuel C. Wheeler, III, 'Natural Property Rights as Body Rights', in Machan, op. cit., pp. 272–289. Wheeler's view sheds light on the sense in which the Lockean idea that private property includes one's person may make the best sense. Cf., John R. Wilkse, *About Possession, the Self as Private Property* (University Park, PA: Pennsylvania State University Press, 1977), in which this idea is severely criticized in favor of a communitarian, interdependent idea of the self.

9. Ernest W. Pettifer, *Punishments of Former Days* (East Ardsley, England: EP Publishing, 1974), pp. 35–36.

10. Quoted in Harry V. Jaffa, *How to Think About the American Revolution* (Durham, NC: Carolina Academic Press, 1978), p. 41 (from *The Collected Works of Abraham Lincoln* [R. Basler (ed.), 1953], p. 108–115).

11. See, in particular, James Sterba, 'A Libertarian Justification for a Welfare State', *Social Theory and Practice*, vol. 11 (Fall 1985), 285–306. I will be referring to this essay as well as to a soon-to-be-published more developed version, titled 'The U.S. Constitution: A Fundamentally Flawed Document'.

12. H. L. A. Hart, 'Are There Any Natural Rights?' *Philosophical Review*, vol. 64 (1955), 175.

13. See, for my own discussions, Tibor R. Machan, *Human Rights and Human Liberties* (Chicago: Nelson-Hall, 1975), pp. 213–222; 'Prima Facie versus Natural (Human) Rights', *Journal of Value Inquiry*, vol. 10 (1976), 119–131; 'Human Rights: Some Points of Clarification', *Journal of Critical Analysis*, vol. 5 (1973), 30–39.

14. Sterba, op. cit, 'A Libertarian Justification', p. 295.

15. Ibid.

16. Ayn Rand, 'Value and Rights', in J. Hospers, (ed.), *Readings in Introductory Philosophical Analysis* (Englewood Cliffs, NJ: Prentice-Hall, 1968), p. 382.

17. Sterba, 'The U.S. Constitution: A Fundamentally Flawed Document'.

18. John Rawls, *A Theory of Justice* (Cambridge, MA: Harvard University Press, 1971), pp. 101–02. For a discussion of the complexities in the differential attainments of members of various ethnic groups—often invoked as evidence for the injustice of a capitalist system, see Thomas Sowell, *Ethnic America: A History* (New York: Basic Books, 1981). There is pervasive prejudice in welfare-state proponents' writings against crediting people with the ability to extricate themselves from poverty without special political assistance. The idea behind the right to negative liberty is to set people free from others so as to pursue their progressive goals. This is the ultimate teleological justification of Lockean libertarian natural rights. See Tibor R. Machan, *Human Rights and Human Liberties: A Radical Reconsideration of the American Political Tradition* (Chicago: Nelson-Hall, 1975). Consider also this thought from Herbert Spencer:

> The feeling which vents itself in "poor fellow!" on seeing one in agony, excludes the thought of "bad fellow," which might at another time arise. Naturally, then, if the wretched are unknown or but vaguely known, all the demerits they may have are ignored: and thus it happens that when the miseries of the poor are dilated upon, they are thought of as the miseries of

the deserving poor, instead of being thought of as the miseries of undeserving poor, which in large measure they should be. Those whose hardships are set forth in pamphlets and proclaimed in sermons and speeches which echo throughout society, are assumed to be all worthy souls, grievously wronged; and none of them are thought of as bearing the penalties of their own misdeeds. (*Man versus the State* [Caldwell, ID: Caxton Printers, 1940], p. 22)

19. Tibor R. Machan, 'Ethics vs. Coercion: Morality or Just Values?' in L. H. Rockwell, Jr. et al., (ed.), *Man, Economy and Liberty: Essays in Honor of Murray N. Rothbard* (Auburn, AL: Ludwig von Mises Institute, 1988), pp. 236–246.

20. John Kekes, ' "Ought Implies Can" and Two Kinds of Morality', *The Philosophical Quarterly*, vol. 34 (1984), 459–467.

21. Tibor R. Machan, 'Ethics vs. Coercion'. In a vegetable garden or even in a forest, there can be good things and bad, but no morally good things and morally evil things (apart from people who might be there).

22. Sterba, 'The U.S. Constitution: A Fundamentally Flawed Document'.

23. Sterba, 'A Libertarian Justification', pp. 295–296.

24. Sterba, 'The U.S. Constitution: A Fundamentally Flawed Document'.

25. For a more elaborate rendition of this kind of defense of paternalism and welfare statism, see Steven Kelman, 'Regulation and Paternalism', in T. R. Machan and M. B. Johnson (eds.), *Rights and Regulations, Ethical, Political and Economics Issues* (Cambridge, MA: Ballinger Publishing Co., 1983), pp. 217–248.

26. Robert Nozick, *Anarchy, State, and Utopia* (New York: Basic Books, 1974), p. 57. See, also, Tibor R. Machan, 'Conditions for Rights, Sphere of Authority', *Journal of Human Relations*, vol. 19 (1971), 184–187, where I argue that "within the context of a legal system where the *sphere of authority* of individuals and groups of individuals cannot be delineated independently of the sphere of authority of the public as a whole, there is an inescapable conflict of rights specified by the same legal system." (186) See, also, Tibor R. Machan, 'The Virtue of Freedom in Capitalism', *Journal of Applied Philosophy*, vol. 3 (1986), pp. 49–58, and Douglas J. Den Uyl, 'Freedom and Virtue', in Tibor R. Machan (ed.), *The Main Debate: Communism versus Capitalism* (New York: Random House, 1987), pp. 200–216. This last essay is especially pertinent to the understanding of the ethical or moral merits of coercion and coerced conduct. Thus it is argued here that 'coercive charity' amounts to an oxymoron.

27. See, Machan, op. cit., 'The Virtue of Freedom in Capitalism' and 'Private Property and the Decent Society', in J. K. Roth and R. C. Whittemore (eds.), *Ideology and American Experience* (Washington, DC: Washington Institute Press, 1986).

28 E.g. James Fishkin, *Tyranny and Legitimacy* (Baltimore, MD: Johns Hopkins University Press, 1979). Cf., Tibor R. Machan, 'Fishkin on Nozick's Absolute Rights', *Journal of Libertarian Studies*, vol. 6 (1982), 317–320.

29. Tibor R. Machan, 'Human Dignity and the Law', *DePaul Law Review*, vol. 26 (1977), 807–832. I discuss this issue in connection with the hard cases involving "unconscionability", a concept that has usually meant "an absence of meaningful choice on the part of the parties together with contract terms which are unreasonably favorable to the other party" (Williams v. Walker-Thomas Furniture Co., 350 F 2nd 445 [D.C. Cir. 1965]).

30. James Buchanan and Gordon Tullock, *The Calculus of Consent* (Ann Arbor, MI: University of Michigan Press, 1962).

31. Douglas J. Den Uyl and Tibor R. Machan, 'Gewirth and the Supportive State', in E. Regis, Jr. (ed.), *Gewirth's Ethical Rationalism* (Chicago: University of Chicago Press, 1984), pp. 167–179.

32. Ibid., p. 173.

33. Alan Gewirth, 'Replies to My Critics', in Regis, ibid., p. 244.

34. Alan Gewirth, *Reason and Morality* (Chicago: University of Chicago Press, 1978), p. 22 passim. Another defender of the view that rights can conflict, so that sometimes right R will override right S, other times vice versa, is Gregory Vlastos, 'Justice and Equality', in R. B. Brandt, ed., *Social Justice* (Englewood-Cliffs, NJ: Prentice-Hall, 1962). I have responded to Vlastos in Tibor R. Machan, 'Prima Facie versus Natural (Human) Rights'.

35. Gewirth, in Regis, op cit., p. 244.

36. See ch. 4. See, also, Machan, op. cit., 'The Virtue of Freedom in Capitalism', 49–58.

37. H. L. A. Hart, 'Between Utility and Rights', in Alan Ryan (ed.), *The Idea of Freedom, Essays in Honour of Isaiah Berlin* (Oxford: Oxford University Press, 1979), p. 84.

38. Ronald Dworkin, *Taking Rights Seriously* (Cambridge, MA: Harvard University Press, 1977), p. 269.

39. Ibid.

40. See Walter Block, 'A Free Market in Roads', *The Journal of Libertarian Studies*, vol. 3 (Summer 1979).

41. F. A. Hayek, *Law, Legislation, and Liberty* (vol. 2) 'The Mirage of Social Justice' (Chicago: University of Chicago Press, 1973). From the law one may expect general guidance, not particular statements of what is important in some individual's life. End-states are what persons can designate, with their individual human lives as the optimal standard. This is not possible for a legal system, meant to guide many generations.

42. Gewirth, in Regis, op. cit., p. 248.

43. Henry Shue, *Basic Rights* (Princeton, NJ: Princeton University Press, 1980).

44. Ibid., p. 37

45. Ibid.

46. Ibid., p. 39.

47. Ibid.

48. Ronald Dworkin, *Taking Rights Seriously* (Cambridge, MA: Harvard University Press, 1977), pp. 267ff, and James W. Nickel, 'Is There a Human Right to Employment?' *The Philosophical Forum*, vol. 10 (Winter-Summer 1978-79), 149-170. For a scrutiny of these views see Tibor R. Machan, 'Wronging Rights', *Policy Review*, vol. 17 (1981), 37-58.

49. Robert Nozick, *Anarchy, State, and Utopia* (New York: Basic Books, 1974), p. 57.

50. The concept 'government' is of course used often enough for institutions different from how they are conceived of within the negative-rights tradition. I would argue, however, that a consistent, coherent definition and characterization of government would exclude those features that conflict with the tenets of this tradition.

It is important to note, also, that in many other perspectives the term 'state' is preferred. Originally by 'government' was meant "the instrument, the helm, whereby the ship to which the state was compared, was guided on its course by the 'gubernator' or helmsman . . . ." (*Black's Law Dictionary*, p. 824). In general, the characterization of government is theory-laden and the best characterization belongs to the best theory. Shue and others who take government morally for granted are committing a conceptual error by placing the cart before the horse; the institution of government is tied to a political theory which is itself tied to a prior moral theory. In unearthing the nature of moral principles, including rights and duties, it is entirely question-begging to refer, then, to governments.

51. By "due process" I mean, literally, a process that must be invoked lest the result be invalid and thus unenforceable: "they refer to certain fundamental rights [of a] system of jurisprudence" (*Black's Law Dictionary*, p. 590).

52. J. Roger Lee, 'Reflections on Punishment', Tibor R. Machan (ed.), *The Libertarian Alternative* (Chicago: Nelson-Hall, 1974), p. 63.

53. For a discussion of the issues here, see ch. 7 and 'Dissolving the Public Goods Problem: Financing Government Without Coercive Measures', Tibor R. Machan (ed.), *The Libertarian Reader* (Totowa, NJ: Rowman and Littlefield, 1982), pp. 201-08. The view of funding government I advocate does not necessarily imply that government prohibit alternative means to itself for coping with crime. All it implies is that

none may violate due process of law and all are accountable to government if good reason can be given for suspecting such violation. Private agreements, though very insecure in some cases, are not prohibited at all. The value of government for dealing with crime would have to be shown to citizens, of course. There may be more stability with a just than an unjust government, but it cannot be guaranteed without the vigilance of the people.

54. James Fishkin, *Tyranny and Legitimacy* (Baltimore, MD: Johns Hopkins University Press, 1979).

55. See Tibor R. Machan, 'Fishkin on Nozick's Absolute Rights', *Journal of Libertarian Studies*, vol. 6 (Summer/Fall 1982), 317–320.

56. A. D. Lindsay, *The Modern Democratic State* (New York: Oxford University Press, 1947), pp. 103–04 (quoted in Hardin, op. cit., p. 71). Hardin remarks that Lindsay merely finds the relationship peculiar because it has this characteristic, whereas Amartya Sen, 'Liberty, Unanimity and Rights', *Economica*, vol. 43 (1976), 217–245, regards it as actually (morally) wrong. But in Sen's example, too, the morally questionable trade involves exchange of inalienable rights. Why inalienable rights can be exchangeable in the first place, given that 'inalienable' means 'not capable of being without', is something not addressed. (For more, see ch. 5.) At this point it might also be helpful to consider a somewhat different objection to natural rights advanced by Sen in his 'A Positive Concept of Negative Rights', *Proceedings of the Fifth International Wittgenstein Symposium* (Kirchberg-am-Wechsel, Austria, 1980). Sen, in criticizing Nozick's view of individual rights, suggests that in some cases violation of one right so as to protect another might have to be justified. This, he thinks, would make for a conception of rights as "consequence sensitive" or, ultimately, utilitarian. Suppose, for example, that A knows that B will rape C unless someone violates D's rights. A cannot convince the police that B will rape C but knows it, nevertheless, and violating D's property rights will hardly upset D, whereas B's raping C will have severe consequences for C. What should A do if not violate D's rights?

Sen thinks A should violate D's rights. But this only shows that there can on occasion be moral tragedies. Normally if A knows that B will rape C, A can demonstrate this to the police with sufficient force to create probable cause for surveillance of B and special protection for C. Or the police could gain a warrant to enter D's house to obtain what is needed to protect C.

Of course, stubbornness could obstruct justice here, and then we face a tragedy, in which case A ought to disregard D's rights. Yet here, as in connection with Sterba's occasional tragedies, there is no justification for altering the general character of the system of justice. I discuss this in Tibor R. Machan, 'Prima Facie versus Natural (Human) Rights'.

57. For a recent discussion of the varieties of doctrines of freedom, see William A. Parent, 'Recent Work on the Concept of Liberty', K. G. Lucey and T. R. Machan (eds.), *Recent Work in Philosophy* (Totowa,

NJ: Rowman and Allanheld, 1983), pp. 247-275. An interesting group of discussions on the topic may be found in John A. Howard (ed.), *On Freedom* (Greenwich, CT: Devin-Adair, 1984). The most recent 'classic' on this topic is Isaiah Berlin, *Two Concepts of Liberty* (London: Oxford University Press, 1958).

58. Larry M. Preston, 'Freedom, Markets, and Voluntary Exchange', *The American Political Science Review*, vol. 78 (December 1984), 961. See, also, Andrew McLaughlin, 'Capitalism versus Freedom', in Machan, op. cit., *The Main Debate*, pp. 217-232. Cf., Ernest van den Haag, 'Liberty: Negative or Positive?' *Harvard Journal of Law and Public Policy*, vol. 1 (1978), 63-87. A somewhat oblique answer to Preston's analysis may be found in Paul Craig Roberts and Matthew A. Stephenson, *Marx's Theory of Exchange, Alienation, and Crisis* (Stanford, CA: Hoover Institution Press, 1973). Roberts and Stephenson show that substituting rational planning for the exchange system introduces tyranny. The choice, then, may be between market exchange, which can involve some 'exploitation', meaning the opportunity of some to take advantage of the circumstances of others, and totalitarian rule, which *guarantees* that exploitation will occur, as a permanent and unalterable feature of the system. This general point can be inferred from such recent discussions of public-choice topics as the calculation problem—the impossibility of rational economic allocation under socialism; the impossibility of rational collective choice—the inherently conflicting public policies which arise if full democracy is in force; and the tragedy of the commons—how commonly-owned resources are overused.

59. Ibid.

60. Ibid., p. 964.

61. F. A. Hayek, *The Constitution of Liberty* (Chicago: University of Chicago Press, 1960), p. 12.

62. Karl Marx, *Selected Writings*, D. McLellan (ed.) (Oxford: Oxford University Press, 1977), p. 496. A curious claim can be found in G. A. Cohen, 'Are Disadvantaged Workers Who Take Hazardous Jobs Forced to Take Hazardous Jobs?' in G. Ezorsky (ed.), *Moral Rights and the Workplace* (Albany, NY: SUNY Press, 1987), pp. 61-80. Cohen states that "If you are forced to do A, you do A. But, if you do A, you are free to do A; you cannot do what you are not free to do. So, if you are forced to do A, you are free to do A." (ibid., p. 64) In other words, if you've got to do A, and no one stops you, you are both forced to do it and free to do it. But 'you've got to do A' isn't the same as "you're forced [by someone] to do A." If Cohen already has the conception of 'forced' in mind that means that one is being faced with an undesirable alternative if one refuses to act, then he begs the question. His use of "force" and "free" obfuscates the concept of political freedom.

There is a distinction between 'doing A' and 'manifesting behavior that would be doing A if one had chosen it'. When someone, say a victim of rape, is forced to have intercourse with the rapist, it is mistaken, to say the least, to construe the intercourse from the victim's part as the doing of anything. Rather the victim is made to behave in a way that would constitute doing a deed were it her choice to engage in the behavior. If by "forced" Cohen means more than 'is not having a better alternative', then he is equivocating between 'doing A' and 'behaving as one would when doing A'.

From his either question-begging or equivocal use of "force" and/or "doing", Cohen concludes that critics of capitalism who claim that workers are forced to do various acts are not contradicting defenders of the system who say that workers are free to do those same acts. In fact there is a contradiction, first, because being forced to do something is not the same as not having a more appealing alternative to it. In order to get well I need to take some vile-tasting medicine. I am not forced to take this medicine, granted that ideally I would rather avoid taking it. As to whether one is forced to work for capitalists, in the sense that one may not have other alternatives for staying solvent, such 'force' is no different from being forced to eat or breathe or stay away from poisons, provided it is true that the persons who employ the workers may offer work to the workers. Since, as I have argued, they may — they are justified in doing so — there is no coercion involved. This is true despite the linguistic fact that we can say and be clearly enough understood when we do, that the worker is forced, in some sense, to work for the employer — that this is his only viable option for remaining solvent. Cohen, along with other Marxists, is also fond of citing need as the candidate for just distribution. Yet what one may properly need — for a bank-robber improperly needs a reliable weapon — depends on what one ought to do, so justified need cannot function as the basis for justice but, in political contexts especially, presupposes some idea of justice. For more on this, see John Ahrens, 'Exploitation', *Reason Papers*, no. 12 (1987), 42–46.

63. Preston, p. 965.

64. Ibid.

65. Ibid.

66. Leonard Choptiany, 'A Critique of John Rawls' Principle of Justice', *Ethics*, vol. 84 (1973), 147.

67. William Pitt, Earl of Chatham, Speech, House of Commons, date unknown. Brougham's *Statesmen in the Time of George III*, First Series.

68. C. J. Harris, 'Charles E. Harris, Jr., Replies', *The Intercollegiate Review*, vol. 20 (Winter 1984), pp 66–68.

Chapter 5. Property Rights and the Good Society

1. Alasdair MacIntyre, *After Virtue* (Notre Dame, IN: University of

Notre Dame Press, 1981). See, also, John O. Lyons, *The Invention of the Self* (Carbondale, IL: Southern Illinois University Press, 1978), and some of the essays in Thomas C. Heller, et al., (eds.), *Reconstructing Individualism: Autonomy, Individuality, and the Self in Western Thought* (Stanford, CA: Stanford University Press, 1986). Cf. J. D. P. Bolton, *Glory, Jest and Riddle: A Study of the Growth of Individualism from Homer to Christianity* (New York: Barnes and Noble, 1973). See also Nathaniel Branden, *Honoring the Self* (New York: Bantam, 1985).

The 'invention of the individual' theme is, of course, heavily influenced by numerous philosophical reflections, including especially the historicism of Marx. Any way of understanding the world is seen largely as a product of socio-economic circumstances, with some ways useful in certain epochs, others in different epochs. In most cases it is implied that the only correct one is that proposed by the author of the analysis, which is supposed somehow to be trans-historical. See also John R. Wilkse, *About Possessions: The Self as Private Property* (University Park, PA: Pennsylvania State University Press, 1977), in which we are told that for most of its history in Western thought the self or ego of a person has been "a social artifact, an ideology: the self as private property" (p. x).

2. Marx, *Selected Writings* (Oxford: Oxford University Press, 1977), p. 53.

3. Heinrich A. Rommen, 'The Genealogy of Natural Rights', *Thought* 29 (1954), p. 419.

4. Ibid. Thomas Hobbes, too, spelled out his conception of natural rights along these lines, but for him 'right reason' had a purely materialistic, physicalist meaning, so that by Hobbes's theory, that is naturally right which accords with the innate drives which motivate some living being. For Hobbes's influence on the U.S. polity, see Frank M. Coleman, *Hobbes and America* (Toronto: University of Toronto Press, 1977). I believe Coleman's thesis is important — shared, to some extent, by such students of Leo Strauss as Walter Berns — but fails (and in the case of Berns refuses) to take into consideration the debt the Founding Fathers owed to the classical thinkers. See, in contrast, Harry V. Jaffa, *How to Think About the American Revolution* (Durham, NC: Carolina Academic Press, 1978).

5. As Locke observed, it is by the use of reason that we apprehend the natural law. See, also, Tibor R. Machan, 'A Reconsideration of Natural Rights Theory', *American Philosophical Quarterly* 19 (1982), 61–72, 'Human Rights: Some Points of Clarification', *Journal of Critical Analysis* 5 (1973), 30–39, and 'A Rationale for Human Rights', *Personalist* 52 (1971), 216–235.

6. Aristotle, *Politics*, Bk. II, ch. 3. 1261b34–1261b38.

7. For a discussion of how to determine the nature of public affairs,

see Tibor R. Machan, 'Rational Choice and Public Affairs', *Theory and Decision* 12 (September 1980), 229–258.

Chapter 6. Capitalism, Free Trade, and Economics

1. Karl Marx, *Selected Writings* (Oxford: Oxford University Press, 1977), p. 54.

2. For some of the evidence, see Michael Harrington, 'Corporate Collectivism: A System of Social Injustice', in *Ethics, Free Enterprise, and Public Policy* ed. R. T. De George and J. A. Pichler (New York: Oxford University Press, 1978), p. 44. For the conservative attitude toward commerce, see George Will, *Statecraft as Soulcraft* (New York: Simon and Schuster, 1982), and Russell Kirk, *The Conservative Mind* (Chicago: Henry Regnery Co., 1953, 1985). Consider, also, Charles Baudelaire, who wrote, in *Intimate Journals*, "Commerce is satanic, because it is the basest and vilest form of egoism." Quoted in Robert Beum, "Middle-Class Power and Its Critics', *University Bookman* 18 (1978), 6.

Harrington regards corporations as a kind of collectivity and then asks whether that kind or the democratic socialist kind ought to be championed. We may suppose that what Harrington calls "collectivist" about corporations is that much of the business they do involves the (voluntary) mutual efforts and investments of large numbers of people. But no individualist has even objected to such voluntary 'collectivism'. One complaint about corporations that has precipitated distrust of them as free institutions is that owners do not directly control management. But this is like complaining about dental care because the patient is not performing the dentist's work. Of course managers are hired to make the best use of one's wealth. This makes it possible for stockholders to carry on with what they know best, while retaining ultimate control.

The sort of collectivism which individualists regard as morally objectionable is probably best called 'natural collectivism', whereby, following Marx and others, human beings are seen to be *species-beings*, tied through and through to everyone else and independent in no meaningful way whatsoever. Collectivism is distinctive in regarding individuals as parts of a larger, *more important* whole. For a conservative view of individualism, see Will.

3. Bhikhu Parekh, 'Introduction', in *The Concept of Socialism* B. Parekh (ed.) (New York: Holmes and Meier, 1975), p. 6.

4. F. A. Hayek, *Studies in Philosophy, Politics and Economics* (New York: Simon and Schuster, 1967), p. 85.

5. See chs. 2, 3, and 4 above.

6. John Locke, *Essays on the Law of Nature*, W. von Leyden (ed.) (Oxford: The Clarendon Press, 1954), p. 111. Locke is obviously on the side of the moderns in the ancient/modern division. In this particular instance, however, his statement of the nature of reason is closer to what

was embraced by Aristotle than by Hobbes.

7. Hayek, *Studies*, p. 84.

8. Ibid., p. 85.

9. I discuss some problems I see with Hayek's own philosophical underpinnings in my 'Reason, Morality and the Free Society', in *Liberty and the Rule of Law* R. L. Cunningham (ed.) (College Station, TX: Texas A & M University Press, 1979), pp. 268–293.

10. Robert Nozick, *Anarchy, State, and Utopia* (New York: Basic Books, 1974), p. 000.

11. F. A. Hayek, *Individualism and Economic Order* (Chicago: University of Chicago Press, 1948), pp. 86–87.

Chapter 7. Individualism and Political Authority

1. Both 'good human community' and 'public interest' could possibly refer to the same state of affairs.

2. A recent treatment of this topic reaches rather pessimistic conclusions. See Richard Taylor, 'The Basis of Political Authority', *The Monist*, vol. 66 (1983), 457–471.

3. Robert Nozick, *Anarchy, State, and Utopia* (New York: Basic Books, 1974), p. ix.

4. A good example is Ronald Dworkin, *Taking Rights Seriously* (Cambridge, MA: Harvard University Press, 1977). Dworkin never establishes government's authority to govern but merely specifies some checks on its rule.

5. Some may hold that this conclusion presupposes very strong premisses. But the argument actually rests on considerations involving the value to most individuals of the economic practice of the division of labor, besides the ethical egoist premisses given here. Marx denied the former, except for certain periods of human history, and many critics of capitalism would agree, for independent but similar reasons.

6. State-of-nature arguments assume persons are *driven* into community life, with no moral choice present as to whether to do so, and contract theories tend to leave open the issue of whether it is morally right to enter the pertinent contract in the first place. See my 'Contract as the Basis of Norm', *Journal of Libertarian Studies*, vol. 7 (1983), 141–45.

7. The familiar slogan, 'Ought implies can', may not be taken for granted, of course, but we have already argued that ethics is best conceived as requiring it. Any other rendition of ethics would not differ sufficiently from mere value theory. See Tibor R. Machan, 'Ethics vs. Coercion: Morality or Just Values?' in L. H. Rockwell, Jr. et. al. (eds.), *Man, Economy and Liberty: Essays in Honor of Murray N. Rothbard* (Auburn, AL: Ludwig von Mises Institute, 1988).

8. See Tibor R. Machan, 'Rational Choice and Public Affairs', *Theory and Decision*, 12 (September 1980), 220–258.

9. I say "appears" because I haven't yet argued that self-defense is morally justified and even required for everyone.

10. For more, see Ayn Rand, *The Virtue of Selfishness* (New York: Signet Books, 1964).

11. See Douglas Rasmussen, 'Essentialism, Values, and Rights', in Tibor R. Machan (ed.), *The Libertarian Reader* (Totowa, NJ: Rowman and Littlefield, 1982), pp. 37–52.

12. For varieties of ethical egoism see Tibor R. Machan, 'Recent Work in Ethical Egoism', *American Philosophical Quarterly*, 16 (January 1979), 1–15.

13. Sometimes self-sacrifice, as commonly understood, could be called for on ethical-egoist grounds, for instance, when some rationally, egoistically chosen commitment implies its necessity. An egoist might join the military where such sacrifice would be appropriate.

14. The manner in which this kind of reasoning should be understood as a species of egoism which does not result in the sort of problems usually found in egoistic accounts of social life may be gleaned from Jesse Kalin, 'Two Kinds of Moral Reasoning', *Canadian Journal of Philosophy*, 5 (March 1975), and David L. Norton, *Personal Destinies: A Philosophy of Ethical Individualism* (Princeton, NJ: Princeton University Press, 1976). I am especially appreciative of Norton's idea of "consequent sociality" for purposes of a full development of this point.

15. It is at this point that the concern for private-property rights expressed by individualists and neglected by collectivists might be best appreciated. How can a person act morally if there is no sphere, territory, or domain of individual authority or if none is acknowledged in the legal system of a good human community? See Tibor R. Machan, 'The Virtue of Freedom in Capitalism', *Journal of Applied Philosophy*, vol. 3 (1986), 49–58.

16. Ayn Rand, 'Man's Rights', in *Capitalism: The Unknown Ideal* (New York: Signet Books, 1967), p. 320.

17. Ibid.

18. Karl Marx, *Selected Writings* (Oxford: Oxford University Press, 1977), p. 53.

19. Ibid.

20. This is what underlies the view that persons are neither guilty nor innocent collectively, but only individually.

21. I mean by "being at liberty morally" that no basic prohibition exists against this kind of conduct, although on some occasions one could be doing the morally wrong thing to engage in it.

22. Murray N. Rothbard, 'Society Without a State', in *The Libertarian Reader*, p. 60.

23. Eric Mack, 'Egoism and Rights', *The Personalist*, vol. 54 (1973), 30.

24. See Tibor R. Machan, 'Dissolving the Problem of Public Goods', in *The Libertarian Reader* (cited in n12, above), 201–208.

25. See Tibor R. Machan, *Human Rights and Human Liberties* (Chicago: Nelson-Hall, 1975).

26. The concept of consent appears to permit a usage in common discourse that contradicts the point being made here. One would seem to be able to consent to something – a policy, a law, a legal measure – that one had no moral authority to support. In referring to "consent" I have in mind a process of morally legitimate authorization, not merely agreement. It is in this sense that one cannot – morally may not – consent to something that violates another's rights. For a more detailed discussion of this point see J. Roger Lee, 'The Arrest and Punishment of Criminals', in *The Libertarian Reader* (cited in n11, above), pp. 88–89.

Postscript 1. The Unavoidability of Natural Law and Natural Rights

1. Ernest van den Haag, 'Against Natural Rights', *Policy Review*, no. 23 (Winter 1983), 143–175. For additional, less direct, attacks on Lockean natural rights from the political right, see essays by John N. Gray, Gary Herbert, Donald Livingston, and Roger Scruton in the March 1989 issue of *The World and I*.

2. David Hume, *A Treatise of Human Nature* (Garden City, NY: Dolphin Books, 1961), p. 423. The emotivist inferences from accepting Hume's argument on its face may be found in C. L. Stevenson, 'The Emotive Meaning of Ethical Terms', in A. J. Ayer (ed.), *Logical Positivism* (New York: The Free Press, 1959), pp. 264–281.

3. For a good objection to this line of criticism, see Renford Bambrough, *Moral Skepticism and Moral Knowledge* (Atlantic Highlands, NJ: Humanities Press, 1979). From 'I know that doing D is right for A' it does not follow that 'Someone ought to (or is authorized to) make A do D.'

4. See John Rawls, *A Theory of Justice* (Cambridge, MA: Harvard University Press 1971); Robert Nozick, *Anarchy, State, and Utopia* (New York: Basic Books, 1974); Ronald Dworkin, *Taking Rights Seriously* (Cambridge, MA: Harvard University Press, 1977).

5. See my 'Epistemology and Moral Knowledge', *Review of Metaphysics*, vol. 36 (September 1982), 23–49, and 'Another Look at Naturalist Ethics and Politics', *Cogito*, vol. 3 (December 1985), 75–114. This point, as we saw in ch. 1, applies also to John Gray's recent dismissal of natural law and rights theories. See his *Liberalism* (Minneapolis: University of Minnesota Press, 1987).

6. See, e.g., Rom Harré, *The Philosophies of Science* (New York: Oxford University Press, 1972). See also Tibor R. Machan, *The Pseudo-Science of B. F. Skinner* (New Rochelle, NY: Arlington House, 1974).

7. Aristotle, *Nicomachean Ethics*, Bk. II: ch. 5 1106a2, 1113b13.

8. See also Douglas J. Den Uyl, 'Freedom and Virtue', in Machan, *The Libertarian Reader*, pp. 211–225.

9. Even in Locke, although we find mixed signals, we also find reference to the Law of Nature, which is Reason, which governs the state of nature and that will guide one if one will but consult it. This suggests Aristotle's doctrine that the fundamental moral law is right reason. See Tibor R. Machan, 'An Aristotelian Foundation for Natural Rights?' *This World*, no. 10 (Summer, 1985), 83–86. (Many of the points in this work have been developed in some unpublished but more thorough work by Fred D. Miller, Jr.)

10. See Eric Mack, 'Individualism, Rights, and the Open Society', in Tibor R. Machan, *The Libertarian Reader* (Totowa, NJ: Rowman and Littlefield, 1982), pp. 3–15, 'How to Derive Ethical Egoism', *The Personalist*, vol. 52 (1971), 735–743, 'Egoism and Rights', *The Personalist*, vol. 53 (Winter 1973), 5–33, and 'Campbell's Refutation of Egoism', *Canadian Journal of Philosophy*, vol. 3 (1977), 659–663. Mack's essays on egoism are the best in print and have paved the way for others, including myself, to get clear on many problems. Several of the notions invoked by later libertarians — such as Lomasky's discussion of the relational character of moral prescriptions — were developed by Mack (as well as by Douglas Rasmussen and Douglas J. Den Uyl somewhat later) and turned out to be extremely helpful in showing why individualism does not get entangled in various paradoxes its critics often used to impute to it. I discuss some of these issues in my *Human Rights and Human Liberties* (Chicago: Nelson-Hall, 1975).

11. W. F. R. Hardie, 'The Final Good in Aristotle's *Ethics*', *Philosophy*, vol. 40 (1965).

12. Op. cit., Van den Haag, p. 49.

13. Ibid., p. 48.

14. For instance Leo Strauss, Walter Berns, George Will.

15. See Gregory Vlastos, 'Justice and Equality', in R. Brandt (ed.), *Social Justice* (Englewood Cliffs, NJ: Prentice-Hall, 1962), pp. 31–72.

16. See Tibor R. Machan, 'Prima Facie versus Natural (Human) Rights', *The Journal of Value Inquiry*, vol. 10 (Summer 1976), 119–131. Van den Haag gives us a good clue here when he tells us that "The legal never exhausts the moral." (Op. cit., van den Haag, p. 50). What we could learn from this is that the law is of narrower scope than ethics and might very well be aimed, as I suggested above, at less stressful circumstances, in principle, than morality.

17. See ch. 1.

18. Gilbert Harman, *Thought* (Princeton, NJ: Princeton University Press, 1973), p. 145.

Postscript 2. More Challenges from Welfare State Philosophers

1. For just how strong the case is for the protection of the rights to private property in the U.S. Constitution, see Bernard Siegan, *Economic Liberties and the Constitution* (Chicago: University of Chicago Press, 1980) and Richard Epstein, *Takings, Private Property and the Power of Eminent Domain* (Cambridge, MA: Harvard University Press, 1985). The classic work by John Locke, from which current natural-rights theories emerge, is *Second Treatise on Government* edited by J. Gough (London: Basil Blackwell, 1966). There is a controversy as to just how philosphically well-founded this theory is for purposes of actually establishing the existence of individual natural human rights. (Many current efforts, perhaps my own included, would probably be superfluous if the case had been made fully.)

For a detailed discussion of the relationship between the Declaration of Independence and the Constitution, see Harry V. Jaffa, *How to Think About the American Revolution* (Durham, NC: Carolina Academic Press, 1978). See, also, the exchange between Jeffrey Rogers Hummel and William Marina, 'Did the Constitution Betray the Revolution?' *Reason*, vol. 18 (1987), 28-35.

2. John Maynard Keynes, *The End of Laissez-Faire* (London: Hogarth Press, 1927), p. 40.

3. Recent works on the philosophical underpinnings of the welfare state include Nicholas Rescher, *Welfare* (Pittsburgh, PA: University of Pittsburgh Press, 1972); D. Marsh, *The Welfare State* (London: Longmans, 1970); Noel Timms and David Watson (eds.), *Talking About Welfare* (London: Routledge and Kegan Paul, 1976).

4. Henry Campbell Black, *Black's Law Dictionary* (St. Paul, MN: West Publishing Co., 1968), p. 281. "Let the buyer beware (or take care). Kellog Bridge Co., v. Hamilton, 110 U.S. 108, 116, 3 S.Ct. 537, 28 L.Ed. 86." One jurist observed recently that the rule of *caveat emptor* has now "given way to *caveat venditor* under pressure of growing complexity of products and hence increasing costs of inspection to buyers relative to sellers." Richard Posner, *The Economics of Justice* (Cambridge, MA: Harvard University Press, 1981), p. 184. Posner is too quick to assert that the cost of inspection to buyers is greater with the increasing complexity of products than it is to the seller. Product advisory firms, such as Consumers' Union, the familiar 'action reporter' (NBC's David Horowitz), and consumer-advice columns in magazines and newspapers—indeed the entire market of consumer guides—testify to the fact that *caveat emptor* could be continued in an era of product complexity, provided the task is not pre-empted by government regulation. The welfare state undercuts the prospect of the development of private, voluntary 'self-help' agencies.

(Consider that we do not expect guides to the arts from the government, but leave this difficult task to reviewers and critics.)

5. See, for example, Murray N. Rothbard, *Man, Economy and State* (Los Angeles: Nash Publishing Co., 1970); Robert Nozick, *Anarchy, State and Utopia* (New York: Basic Books, 1974), and Ayn Rand, *Capitalism: The Unknown Ideal* (New York: New American Library, 1967). The thrust of this view is that (adult) market agents are sovereigns, with their own responsibilities to pursue their own happiness — consistent with the rights of everyone to do the same.

6. Gregory Vlastos, 'Justice and Equality,' A. I. Melden (ed.), *Human Rights* (Belmont, CA: Wadsworth Publishing Co., 1970).

7. For a survey of contemporary rights theories, see Tibor R. Machan, 'Some Recent Work in Human Rights Theory,' in K. G. Lucey & T. R. Machan (eds.), *Recent Work in Philosophy* (Totowa, NJ: Rowman & Allanheld, 1983), pp. 227-246. The present work is an attempt to develop a updated, contemporary defense of natural individual rights theory.

8. Vlastos, p. 82.

9. Ibid., p. 82. As another philosopher notes, those who "declare that [a] human right is only *a prima facie* right . . . certainly do not mean a right that is merely apparent or presumptive . . . ." A. I. Melden, 'Introduction', in Melden, *Human Rights*, pp. 8-9.

10. Locke, op. cit., p. 82.

11. Gregory Vlastos, 'Justice and Equality', R. Brandt (ed.), *Social Justice* (Englewood Cliffs, NJ: Prentice-Hall, 1962), p. 56.

12. Alan Gewirth, *Reason and Morality* (Chicago: University of Chicago Press, 1979), pp. 209, 198.

13. Ibid.

14. John Rawls, *A Theory of Justice* (Cambridge, MA: Harvard University Press, 1971), pp. 101-02.

15. Ibid., p. 104.

16. Ibid.

17. Ibid.

18. That is *the* central political thesis of Rawls's theory of justice, namely, that justice *is* fairness.

19. See n7, above.

20. For a detailed elaboration of such a view, see Ronald Dworkin, *Taking Rights Seriously* (Cambridge, MA: Harvard University Press, 1977). See, also, Henry Shue, *Basic Rights* (Princeton, NJ: Princeton University Press, 1980). Of course, the three philosophers we have discussed are the most widely known proponents of doctrines which give

rise to special workers'-rights positions, based on the fact that workers are regarded by most advocates of welfare rights as in the greatest need of having their welfare or wellbeing looked after. For a discussion of some of these views see my 'Should Business Be Regulated?' in Tom Regan, ed., *Just Business* (New York: Random House, 1983).

21. Tibor R. Machan, 'Human Rights, Workers' Rights, and the "Right" to Occupational Safety', in G. Ezorsky (ed.), *Moral Rights in the Workplace* (Albany, NY: SUNY Press, 1987). See also 'Corporate Commerce vs. Government Regulation: The State and Occupational Safety and Health', *Notre Dame Journal of Law and Public Policy*, vol. 2 (1987), pp. 791-823.

INDEX

53, 61, 103, 130, 131, 140, 153, 172, 184
Marxism, 70, 130, 135, 139, 155, 163
  class interest, xx
  labor theory of value, xxi
Materialism, 10
  mechanical, 45
Matson, Wallace, I., 79
Mechanistic materialism, xiv, 45
Mens rea, xxvi
Mentalism, 15, 32
Meta-ethics, xv, xxvii, 36, 39, 84, 91
  naturalist, xiv, 38
Metaphysics, xv, xxvi, xxviii, 7, 9, 29, 47, 82
  anti-, xxviii
  dialectical, xxi
  Kantian objection to, 70
  neo-Aristotelian, 186, 187
  reductive materialist, 34
  teleological, xxi
Milton, John, 41
Monarchy, 167
Monism, xxx, 39
Moore, G. E., 94, 186
Moral
  autonomy, 164
  excellence, 96
  goodness, 45, 91
  nature, 58–59
  relativism, 43
  responsibility, 2, 12, 141, 161, 201, 202, 203
  space, 58–60, 99, 105, 125, 169
  statements, 94
  theory, xxvi, xxix
  value, 17, 22
Morality, 11–13, 18, 20, 28–57, 135, 154, 186
  basic principles of, 43–44
  bona fide, 42
  need for, 56
Morals, 1, 23
Morawetz, Thomas, xvii
Murder, 99, 100

Nagel, Thomas, xiii
Natural selection, 12
Natural rights, xvi, xxiii, 1–3, 7, 9, 23, 25, 50, 58, 61, 84, 97, 123, 138, 183, 188, 194, 203
  criticism of, 25–62, 183–205
  egoistically based, 30
  Lockean, xxiv, 25, 53, 106–07, 170, 183, 187
  moral foundation for, 170
  objectivistic foundations of, 80
  theory of, xxiv–xxviii, 26, 56, 95, 97, 172
Naturalism, xiv, 69–72, 81, 89, 186, 190–91
  ethical, xiii
  meta-ethical, xiv, xvi, xxiii
  metaphysical, 64
  pluralistic, 45
Nature of things, 88
  fixed, 68
Nelson, John O., xvii
Neo-Hobbesian, xv, xxii
Neo-Kantianism, 6, 7, 73, 75, 112
Neo-Marxism, xxii
Newtonianism, 13
Nickel, James, 124
Nielsen, Kai, 66, 71, 93–94, 186
Nietzsche, Friedrich, 71
Nominalism, 70, 78
Non-intrusion, 150
Norton, David L., xvii, xxviii, 95
Nozick, Robert, xii, xv, xx, xxiv, 23, 37, 60, 63, 79, 125, 160, 165–66, 172, 180, 184
Nuremburg Trials, 29

Objective principles
  moral, 72
  political, 72
Objectivism. *See* Epistemology; Rand
Objectivity, 75, 76, 81
Olin Foundation, John M., xvii
Ontology, 39, 40
Opportunity
  economics, 100

7241   7690